DATE DUE

*Power and Leadership
in Pluralist Systems*

Power and Leadership
in Pluralist Systems

ANDREW S. McFARLAND

Stanford University Press, Stanford, California, 1969

Stanford University Press
Stanford, California
© 1969 by the Board of Trustees of the
Leland Stanford Junior University
Printed in the United States of America
L.C. 68-26781

Dedicated to my mother, Lois Symons McFarland,
and to the memory of my father, John Harrison McFarland

Acknowledgments

The teaching, criticism, and advice of Professor Aaron Wildavsky have been invaluable in developing my ideas, especially since we frequently disagree. Suggestions and criticism from Kenneth Jowitt, Ernst Haas, Robert Dahl, and Fred DuBow were of great assistance. I am also grateful to several others who read all or part of this manuscript and who gave me useful advice: Eugene Bardach, Polly McAboy, William Bicker, Jack Nagel, Robert Blauner, Eric Levine, and Jeanne Nienaber.

This book especially reflects the teaching of David Apter, Ernst Haas, Kiyoshi Ikeda, Norman Jacobson, Michael Rogin, Dwight Waldo, and Sheldon Wolin. Several student friends have also been my teachers: Robert Jervis, Jill Henneman, James Payne, David Sturtevant, Frederick Blattner, and John A. Tyson. I would like to thank the following friends for essential good cheer: Thomas Bruneau, Everett Chard, Nannette Cochran, Stuart Fagan, Robert Jervis, and Kenneth Jowitt.

I wish to thank the Institute of International Studies, University of California, Berkeley, for generous grants for research assistance that greatly aided in writing this book. A Rockefeller Fund grant from the Department of Political Science, University of California, Berkeley, paid for the costs of preparing an earlier draft of this work.

Anne Firth Murray has been an extremely helpful editor. Mr. J. G. Bell of Stanford University Press has given me valuable assistance in preparing the manuscript.

Claire Gilchrist, Mrs. Vern McCroskey, and Shirley and Harold Raffill labored assiduously in typing various drafts of this book.

A. S. McF.

Contents

Introduction

Presumably as political scientists we are trying to contribute to new political theory. To do this, we need to criticize and synthesize existing research and theory, producing what is sometimes termed "empirical political theory," which in the words of David Easton "seek[s] to explore the theoretical assumptions of existing empirical research and to systematize and assess . . . findings in the hope of bringing added clarity to a subfield [and] enhancing its theoretical relevance."[1] The study of politics implies the study of political power. It can be shown that the study of power implies a concern for the salience of issues and necessitates an answer to the question "power over what?" Finally, power and salience may be combined in the study of leaders—men who exercise power.

In this book I conceptualize, criticize, and synthesize these topics. I seek clear meanings for the central concepts—power, critical decisions (issue salience), and leadership. After all, we cannot have theory if we do not know what we are talking about. To an extent I criticize existing "pluralist" studies of power in American politics, for these studies are valuable but quite insufficient. (I use "pluralism" in the sense of power-structure analysis, referring to the dispersal of power among many elites, as opposed to its exercise by a single elite.)[2] Most of all I attempt to synthesize rather than criticize, for there is an almost overwhelming amount of excellent and interesting empirical research now being reported. We must strive to link together this multitude of ideas, being sensitive to relationships among the various theories of the subfields of our discipline. To this end I have tried to show certain relationships among ideas in the study of American politics, comparative politics, public administration, sociological theory, and role theory.

The main conclusion of this book is that the existence of democracy cannot be proved just by demonstrating a dispersal of power. Studies of power structure must also deal with the difficult question—power over what?

In the first part of this book, I discuss power and power structure from the standpoint of pluralist theories of American politics. The first chapter, "Power As Causation," is concerned with power as it is commonly defined in terms of social causation. This line of thought, and its implications for the study of American politics, is furthered in the second chapter, "Pluralism As Complex Causation." However, since a complex explanation may be offered for anything, we must somehow distinguish between actual and spurious complexity; this I contend in the third chapter, "Pluralism as an Explanation," posing the question "power over what?" and looking to administrative theory and comparative politics for an answer.

In the second part of the book, "The Structure of Power," I deal with the question of issue salience, the discrimination of degrees of importance, though I do not claim to have solved this fundamental theoretical problem. The fourth and fifth chapters further demonstrate the need to evaluate the salience of issues for the development of a theory of political power. At this point, my argument concerning the insufficiency of the contemporary pluralist treatment of power is concluded. Chapter 6, "The Generality of Decisions," takes up the question of critical decisions in terms of the logic of generality, conceived in terms of game and set theory and related to the theory of public administration. "Structure and Behavior," Chapter 7, reviews the subject of power and critical decisions in terms of the structure-behavior distinction for the analysis of political and sociological theories. This distinction is relevant because it seems that a structural theory deals with general (or critical) decisions.

The last section of the book concerns leadership, for if a leader is defined as a person who exercises considerable power, then the theory of leadership is a theory of power, causation, and critical decisions; this idea is developed in the chapter entitled "The Concept of Leadership." Chapter 9, "Multilateral Conflict and Leaders' Response," treats leadership as an independent variable in a pluralist political system, a system in which the scope of individual action is ordinarily severely limited.

PART ONE

Power and Pluralism

1. Power as Causation

Although the concept "power" is used in a variety of ways, there is considerable agreement among empirical political theorists that the power relation is a type of causality relation.[1] Thus Herbert Simon has noted, "For the assertion, '*C* has power over *R*,' we can substitute the assertion, '*C*'s behavior causes *R*'s behavior.' If we can define the causal relation, we can define influence, power, or authority, and vice versa."[*]

In this chapter, I summarize various viewpoints linking power to causation. The relationships between power as causation and causation in general,[2] social causation in particular,[3] intended social causation, and intended social causation involving the use of sanctions are discussed briefly.

POWER AND SOCIAL CAUSATION

I accept the frequently expressed view that power best refers to a causal relationship among human beings. This implies that power does *not* refer to the world of nature and is thus a specific type or subcategory of causation; that power is *not* an attribute of a single actor in isolation from others; and that power is *not* freedom. Dahl has concisely expressed the first two of these ideas: "First, let us agree that power is a relation, and that it is a relation among people. Although

---

[*] Simon, *Models of Man*, p. 5. Throughout this book, I follow Robert Dahl's new usage, in which "*R* will always symbolize the responsive or dependent unit, *C* the controlling unit. These symbols . . . will be substituted even in direct quotations where the authors themselves have used different letters." See Dahl, "Power," p. 407. However, I use other symbols (*A* and *B*) when control shifts from one unit to another according to time or issue, or when the location of control is ambiguous.

in common speech the term encompasses relations among
people and other animate or inanimate objects, we shall have
our hands full if we confine the relationship to human beings."[4]

Power does not refer to the world of nature. According to
Dahl's formulation, when we view power as causation we
should restrict our definition of power to a specific type of
causation in which both the causal agent and the affected object are human beings. I shall term such causation *social causation*. As we shall see, some writers broadly define power to
mean *all* social causation, but I shall adopt a narrower definition.

Power is an attribute of social relationships. Dahl's statement "that power is a relation, and that it is a relation among
people" says that power is not an attribute of a single actor,
viewed in isolation from other actors.[5] Instead, power is an
attribute of relationships among actors, and thus is not an individual's or a group's "value position" or resource base. In
other words, a reputation for power, or a base of power,
should not be confused with the actual exercise of power;[6]
the bases of national power (military resources, economic resources, etc.) should not be confused with the actual exercise of power;[7] although wealth is obviously a power resource,
it is not the actual exercise of power.[8] Power is *not* a substance, possessed by an actor in isolation from others.[9]

Simon unmistakably opposes defining power in terms of individual attributes, value position, political resources, and so
forth:

I think that definitions which equate influence or power with the
values an individual possesses are unsuitable for political science.
The difficulty is revealed when we try to state what we mean by a
"value." If we list specific values—wealth, wisdom, or what not—
then the statement that "A possesses certain of these values" is not
what we *mean* when we say "A has power." For if these two statements are regarded as identical by definition, then a proposition
like "The wealthy are powerful"—dear to Marxists and anti-Marx-
ists alike—ceases to be an empirical proposition in political science, and becomes true simply by definition.[10]

He goes on to state that "we can then use value position as an
index of power" and that "*in equilibrium situations*, we can

use the value distribution as an index of the power distribution when the latter is difficult to ascertain directly."[11] (Italics in original.) However, defining social equilibrium is difficult, and assessing the relative significance of various resources is also difficult in most cases. (For example, does dispersion of the vote, a political resource, offset concentration of wealth in equilibrium situations?)

Viewing power as causation does not exclude the recognition of power as a trait, capacity, resource, etc. The crucial difference between the two conceptions is that causation theorists do not *define* power as a resource, although they may recognize that power can *become* a resource. For example, Simon states: "That power is a value, i.e., something desired and valued, is generally admitted; but if so, to define power as value position renders meaningless propositions like: 'We can measure a person's power by his ability to acquire power.' "[12] Thus one can observe that in the past a person has caused changes in the behavior of others, perhaps in the direction of realizing his will, and that this observed ability is something widely valued. Furthermore, this ability is a resource, both in the person's subjective experience and in the attitudes of others toward him, for his present and future exercise of power. However, a person's past exercise of power does not necessitate a similar exercise of power in the present,[13] just as past cause-effect sequences do not necessitate their repetition in the present. The matter is an empirical question, as Hume pointed out.[14] (Once more we see the identity of some definitions of power and common notions of causation.) For instance, a person in an institutionalized authority role, which regularizes the production of intended effects on subordinates, may not exercise the same amount of power in the present as others in the role exercised in the past.[15] Hence, whereas an authority role is a power resource, its correlation to the successful production of intended effects varies according to numerous circumstances. Community-power studies, for example, have demonstrated that successful exercise of power in the past should not be confused with power in the present.[16]

Even though reputation for power is an important resource, as Neustadt has argued cogently in reference to the Presidency,[17] community-power studies have also demonstrated that a reputation for power correlates only indifferently with the actual successful exercise of power.[18] A reputation for power may be based on past success that is not relevant to the present—owing perhaps to changes in a powerful person's motivation[19] or to changes in the general environment of political action. Moreover, a reputation for power may be incorrectly generalized from observation of activity in a single issue area to all issue areas.[20]

Power is not freedom. Power as causation is different from power as a state of human freedom, a usage common in conversational and literary discourse. A typical interpretation of power as freedom is Bertrand Russell's statement "Power may be defined as the production of intended effects."[21] Such a realization of human will, or freedom, clearly includes power over nature, for as Russell subsequently remarks: "There are various ways of classifying the forms of power, each of which has its utility. In the first place, there is power over human beings and power over dead matter or non-human forms of life. I shall be concerned mainly with power over human beings, but it will be necessary to remember that the chief *cause of change* in the modern world is the increased power over matter that we owe to science."[22] (Emphasis added.) We notice that power as freedom is closely tied to power as causation, for Russell refers to causing changes in his discussion of power. Indeed, "the production of intended effects" might be restated as "the causing of intended effects." Russell's definition of power as freedom refers to the causation of manifest (intended) effects in both the human and the nonhuman spheres, and thereby, as far as human action is concerned, rules out only the causation (production) of latent (unintended) effects.[23]

Influence is social causation. I define influence as social causation in general.[24] *C's behavior influences R's behavior if and only if C's behavior causes changes in R's behavior.* * It will become clear that I prefer to use "power" to denote

---

* Ambiguities lie in the use of "behavior" and "change." Suppose that when C asks R to do something, R refuses yet has an increased tendency (either conscious or unconscious) to comply. Did C change R's behavior? Analyti-

intended social causation; as we shall see, however, Simon, Dahl, and others have sometimes used "power" in the sense in which I use "influence." My definition of influence differs somewhat from Simon's statement that "For the assertion, '*C* has power [or influence] over *R*,' we can substitute the assertion, '*C*'s behavior causes *R*'s behavior,'" because I focus on causing *changes* in behavior. However, my definition of influence is certainly congruent with Simon's general perspective on power/influence and causation. He writes: "Presumably, we observe the influence of *C* over *R* by noting the differences between the way *R* actually behaves and the way he *would* behave if *C* were not present (or if *C*'s desires changed)."[25] In other words, we observe the influence of *C* over *R* by noting the extent to which *C*'s behavior causes changes (differences) in *R*'s behavior.

James March has clearly stated that influence is social causation, "a proper subset of the set of all causal relations":

> In general, it appears to be true of any statement of influence that it can just as easily be formulated in terms of causality. Since in common parlance (and the present framework) it is not true that all statements of causality can be treated as statements of influence (i.e., influence and causality are not equivalent), the set of all influence relations can be understood to be a proper subset of the set of all causal relations. Specifically, the set of all influence relations is here defined to be that subset of all causal relations such that the behavior of an individual appears as the terminal point in the causal linkage. Alternatively, we can say that two individuals are in an influence relation if their behaviors are linked causally.[26]

March also expresses the more specific idea of *C*'s behavior causing changes in *R*'s behavior: "It is in harmony with the

---

cally, we may say that *C* did so if we regard all of *R*'s subjective tendencies as behavior. Moreover, usually *R*'s increased ambivalence is expressed as some appreciable, if small, change in behavior, such as increased uncertainty, guilt, irritability, or tiredness (dysfunctions of conflict), or perhaps as rebellious energy, humor, creative activity, or emotional surgency (functions of conflict). However, such subjective ambivalence and consequent minor changes in behavior are usually difficult to observe, especially when we study the relatively gross incidences of control in a political process. On the other hand, if we have the opportunity to observe a few individual personalities quite extensively, we may be able to observe relatively subtle effects of control.

more frequent uses of the term 'influence' and with the present sense of that term to say that if the individual deviates from the predicted path of behavior [assuming observed regularities of behavior], influence has occurred, and, specifically, that it is influence which has induced the change."[27] For "induced" we can substitute "caused": it is influence that has caused the change. Or, in my terms, C's behavior influences R's behavior when C's behavior causes changes in R's behavior.

Dahl's well-known definition of power in "The Concept of Power" is equivalent to my definition of influence as social causation: "My intuitive idea of power, then, is something like this: C has power over R to the extent that he can get R to do something that R would not otherwise do."[28] Clearly, if C gets R to do something that R would not otherwise do, then C's behavior has caused a change (an effect) in R's behavior. Because "get" may refer to the production of both intended effects and unintended effects,[29] this definition refers to *all social causation*, both intended and unintended.[30] Hence Dahl's statement identifies power with all social causation, and it is thus equivalent to Simon's statement "For the assertion, 'C has power over R,' we can substitute the assertion, 'C's behavior causes R's behavior.'" But Dahl evidently became aware of the generality of this definition of power, for he later referred to the same idea as the "influence relation": "Our common sense notion, then, goes something like this: C influences R to the extent that he gets R to do something that R would not otherwise do."[31] This statement is, of course, equivalent to my definition of influence.

In "The Concept of Power," Dahl suggests "the possible identity of 'power' with 'cause.'" He contrasts two situations to illuminate what he means by power. In the first, a man stands at a street corner and, speaking inaudibly, commands automobile drivers to proceed on the right side of the road. In the second, a policeman publicly directs the traffic.[32] Dahl concludes that the policeman is exercising power and the other man is not. After stating his "intuitive idea of power," he writes:

If Hume and his intellectual successors had never existed, the distinction between the two events above might be firmer than it is. But anyone who sees in the two cases the need to distinguish mere "association" from "cause" could push us into some messy epistemological problems that do not seem to have any generally accepted solutions at the moment. I shall therefore quite deliberately steer clear of the possible identity of "power" with "cause," and the host of problems this identity might give rise to.[33]

Immediately after this passage, Dahl declares: "Let us proceed in a different way."[34] However, because his definition of power is equivalent to all social causation, Dahl could not proceed in a different way from a discussion of causation. (Dahl himself recognized this by 1965.)[35] Thus, in the next section of his article, Dahl specifies three "properties of the power relation" that are identical to three properties of the causality relation as commonly understood.

The first of Dahl's properties of the power relation is described as follows: "A necessary condition for the power relation is that there exists a time lag, however small, from the actions of the actor who is said to exert power to the responses of the respondent. This requirement merely accords with one's intuitive belief that C can hardly be said to have power over R unless C's power attempts precede R's responses."[36] Let us reword this statement. "A necessary condition for the causality (power) relation is that there exists a time lag, however small, from the first event (actions of the actor), which is said to be the cause (who is said to exert power), to the event said to be the effect (the responses of the respondent). This requirement merely accords with one's intuitive belief that an event can hardly be said to have caused another event unless the cause precedes the effect (C can hardly be said to have power over R unless C's power attempts precede R's responses)." This property of the causality relation is also a property of the power relation, and vice versa. Dahl's second property of the power relation is stated thus: "A second necessary condition is, like the first, obvious and nonetheless important in research: there is no 'action at a distance.' Unless there is some 'connection' between C and R, then no power relation can be said to exist."[37] Similarly, common conceptions of causality presuppose a connection between cause and effect and no action at a distance. I let go of the ball (I cause the effect of the ball's falling); the tidal wave destroys the village by smashing it; the sun warms the earth by sending radiation across outer space. A major part of Hume's argument is that there is no necessary connection between cause and effect, and that there is only an observed probability linking the two events.

Dahl's third property of the power relation involves the *amount* of power C has over R, which he calculates in terms of the difference in probability between R's doing something in C's presence and R's doing the same thing in C's absence.[38] Similarly, if an event occurs in the absence of the supposed causal agent C, we would say that C is not a cause of the event. However, if the addition of the supposed causal agent C precedes a new event E in time, and if there seems to be some connection between C and E, then we say that C caused an event that otherwise would not have happened, unless other functionally equivalent causal agents had been present.[39] Dahl's probability calculus concerning the amount of power is similar to discussions of causation. If event C always precedes E, then one usually says that C causes E, especially if there is some observable connection between the two events. If event C precedes event E less than 100 percent of the time, then the term cause is usually dropped in favor of probability and correlation. Thus, Dahl's statement concerning the amount of power is equivalent to one concerning the extent of causal relationship.[40]

In summary, Dahl's discussion of the "properties of the power relation" clearly demonstrates that his concept of power is identical to the concept of social causation. Thus, in "The Concept of Power," when Dahl says "power," he says "cause" (within a social framework).[41] Consequently, Dahl's other characteristics of power (scope, domain, comparability) are also characteristics of social causation.*

---

* Linguistic analysis helps to show the close relationship between concepts of power and cause. For example, Walter notes that the ancient Greek verb *archein* means both "to rule" and "to start," that the noun *arché* means both "sovereignty" and "beginning," and that one of the six meanings of "begin-

Definitions of power or influence based on such concepts as force,[42] incentives or utilities,[43] and minimal winning co-alitions[44] are also reducible to causal terms. The idea of force essentially refers to a cause that pushes; definitions of power based on force differentials refer to what happens when a first causal agent pushes one way (force) and a second causal agent pushes another way (resistance). The stronger push or stronger force is the "stronger" cause, i.e., the more powerful agent. Utilities and incentives are inward forces that start people moving, make them go, i.e., *cause* people to do things. Incentives and utilities are inward subjective causes that push or pull; in other words, they are subjectively experienced forces. Hence, definitions of power or influence that refer to *C*'s manipulation of *R*'s utility function or incentive system merely add a set of intermediary variables to the idea of power as causation: *C causes a change* in *R*'s utilities or incentives (the intermediary variables), which, in turn, *cause a change* in *R*'s behavior. Definitions of power that emphasize the last added member of a minimal winning coalition essentially refer to the idea of necessary and sufficient cause. Whereas all members of the minimal winning coalition are *necessary* causes for the changing of behavior of others, the last to join is the *sufficient* cause for the change in the others' actions. The last to join provides the final amount of needed force or causal push. However, it is usually impossible to determine empirically who provided the sufficient cause for the achievement of a winning coalition. For example, after the 1960 presidential election, numerous groups could have argued that they provided the winning increment (sufficient cause) for the attainment of Kennedy's tiny margin of 119,000 votes.[45]

So far, we have followed several strands of thought leading to the conclusion that *social causation is "the bedrock idea of power"*[46] *and influence*. In the next section we shall explore the usefulness of "power" as an analytical concept.

---

ning," according to Aristotle, is the group or individual "at whose will that which is moved is moved and *that which changes changes*, e.g., the magistracies in cities, and oligarchies and monarchies and tyrannies, are called *archai*." See E. V. Walter, "Power and Violence," p. 350. (Emphasis added.)

THE POWER OF POWER

James March has recently questioned "the power of power" for the development of empirical political theory, except as a concept to deal with certain highly restricted situations.[47] William H. Riker has even tentatively suggested banishing the concept of power: "The final question, once the full complications of the ambiguities [in the notion of power] are revealed, concerns the appropriate scientific attitude toward the conception of power itself. Ought we to redefine it in a clear way or ought we banish it altogether? My initial emotion, I confess, is that we ought to banish it. But this suggestion will, I am sure, find little sympathy among my colleagues."[48]

My analysis also suggests that the concept of power (or influence) has limited utility for the construction of empirical political theory if power (or influence) is defined to include all social causation, for *if power is all social causation, power refers to all social science.* (Hence if political power is all political causation, political power refers to all political science.) If we completely explain how the behavior of all individual actors causes changes in the behavior of all other actors, then we have explained all social behavior in a situation, which presupposes the development of a complete theory of social science. The complete answer to the question "Who has power in this situation?" is the complete theoretical explanation of the situation. The complete answer to the question "Who has political power?" is a completed empirical political theory. Therefore the concept of power as social causation has limited usefulness except as a means of asking the most introductory questions about a given situation (i.e., expressing the basic intention of asking causal questions about some situation), as a linguistic shorthand to represent more cumbersome phrases, or as adherence to usage that has become an established convention.

Thus one must define power in a more specific sense than as social causation if one wants to use the concept other than superficially. This line of reasoning is substantially equivalent to David Easton's in a passage that unfortunately has not gained the widespread currency it deserves. In 1953, Easton wrote: "Power, it has long been recognized, is a relational

phenomenon, not a thing someone possesses. It is based on
the ability to influence the actions of others. But not all influence needs to be considered power. Any reciprocal contact
between human beings leads to the modification of the actions
of each of the participants. *If power is so broadly conceived,
then every relation is an illustration of a power situation and
all social science must be considered the study of power."*[49]
(Emphasis added.) In this statement, Easton explicitly distinguishes between influence and power: "But not all influence needs to be considered power." Following his lead, let
us use "influence" to refer to social causation in general, and
"power" to denote *intended* social causation in particular. As
stated above, by influence I mean the "bedrock idea" of social
causation: *C*'s behavior influences *R*'s behavior if and only if
C's behavior causes changes in *R*'s behavior. Power, then,
may be taken to mean intended influence (i.e., intended social causation): *C*'s behavior exercises *power* over *R*'s behavior if and only if *C*'s behavior causes changes in *R*'s behavior *that C intends.*[50]

Discussions of intended influence (power) often postulate
the use of sanctions. For example, Easton continues his discussion of power by stating that a more specific, hence more
useful, view of power would add the two dimensions of intentionality and coercion to the general view of power as social causation, which he also terms "influence."

To give power any differentiated meaning we must view it as a
relationship in which one person or group is able to determine the
actions of another in the direction of the former's own ends. Furthermore, and this is the aspect that distinguishes power from
broad influence, this person or group must also be able to impose
some sanctions for the failure of the influenced person to act in the
desired way. Power, therefore, is present to the extent to which
one person controls by sanction the decisions and actions of another.[51]

Another statement of power as social causation that includes
intentionality and coercion is Max Weber's, which also lacks
the widespread currency it deserves in political science:
" 'Power' [*Macht*] is the probability that one actor within a
social relationship will be in a position to carry out his own
will despite resistance, regardless of the basis upon which the

probability rests." The reference to resistance clearly implies overcoming resistance through the use of sanctions.[52]

Analytically, power as suggestion must be separated from power as coercion. Power as suggestion is intended influence that is not resisted: C's behavior exercises *suggestive power* over R's behavior if and only if C's behavior causes changes in R's behavior that C intends and *that R himself then wishes*. Power as coercion, on the other hand, is intended influence which, although initially resisted, succeeds through the manipulation of sanctions (rewards and punishments): C's behavior exercises *coercive power* over R's behavior if and only if C's behavior causes changes in R's behavior that C intends *and accomplishes through the manipulation of sanctions, overcoming R's initial resistance*.[53]

Weber's and Easton's definitions of power include the dimensions of social causation, intentionality, and coercion that are parts of my statement of coercive power. Probably social scientists will ultimately agree that identifying power with all social causation (influence) is too general to be useful. A more specific and perhaps a preferable definition of power is that of coercive power as defined by Weber. But even among political scientists it is doubtful that one definition will be agreed upon. Perhaps, then, our aim must be to identify and define clearly the related concepts that are commonly associated with the term "power." Then, as Jack Nagel has suggested to me, we might dispense with the connotative confusions of everyday language, and communicate concepts according to a shared symbolic logic.[54]

To summarize, the set of human relationships termed coercive power—intended social causation involving the use of sanctions—is entirely included within the set of intended social causation, termed power. In turn, power relationships are entirely included within the set of social causation, termed influence, which is seen as "a proper subset of the set of all causal relations."[55] However, we should not overlook the main idea in our discussion: *power is a type of causation*. Accordingly sometimes "cause" may be substituted for "power" in a theoretical discussion, as in the next chapter, where we explore the idea that *a system of power is a system of causation*.

2. Pluralism as Complex Causation

COMPLEXITY

Analytic, subjective systems (existing in the mind) and natural, objective systems (existing in the "real world") have in common certain logical characteristics such as the dimension of simplicity-complexity. Propositions, hypotheses, and theories are types of subjective systems, and they accordingly share certain logical characteristics with the objective systems that they purportedly describe. Furthermore, because the concepts "power" and "influence" refer to certain subsets of causal events, then systems of power or influence are also systems of causation. Since power structures (i.e., systems of power) are a type of objective system, they may share logical characteristics with subjective systems (e.g., hypotheses and theories). Consequently, hypotheses, objective systems, causal systems, and power structures all may share certain logical characteristics. This reasoning may be summarized:

Subjective systems	purport to	objective systems
(e.g., propositions,	describe	which are a superset of
hypotheses, theories)		causal systems
		which are a superset of
		influence systems
		which are a superset of
		power systems
		(i.e., power structures)

Both subjective systems and objective systems share common logical characteristics, including the dimension of simplicity-complexity. Indeed, the subjective (analytic) and objective (natural) systems dichotomy usually lacks heuristic value, as Easton has pointed out:

From a methodological point of view, it would appear to be possible, profitable, and, therefore, sensible to abandon the notion that political systems are given in nature. We can simplify problems of analysis enormously, without violating the empirical data in any way, by postulating that any set of variables selected for description and explanation may be considered a system of behavior. At the outset, whether it is a system given in nature or simply an arbitrary construct of the human mind is *operationally* a pointless and needless dichotomy.[1]

This reasoning may seem strange, but such a mode of thought is in line with twentieth-century rejection of a major strand in the tradition of classical philosophy. Thus: "The major philosophical tradition stemming from Plato assumes a universal, static reality which is out-there, outside and independent of the particular thinker, a reality which may be grasped and expressed by the rational intellect."[2] An identification of natural and analytic systems becomes more familiar if we consider the case of a systems theorist *hypothetically postulating* a system in his subjectivity for the analysis of "objective reality out-there." In such a case, objective and subjective reality blur together, and it becomes pointless to separate them.

The dimension simplicity-complexity is an important characteristic of hypotheses, systems, causal systems, and power structures (systems of power). Here I ask the reader to shut his eyes and, within ten seconds, define "simplicity." Evidently a working definition of simplicity-complexity is not current in political science, perhaps because this is a difficult logical philosophical problem.[3] However, for the purposes of this discussion, I shall adopt the following working definition of simplicity-complexity:

The COMPLEXITY *of a system varies directly, but non-additively, with (1) the number and variety of its components; (2) the extent and incidence of relational interdependence among the components; (3) the variability of the components and their relationships through time. The* SIMPLICITY *of a system varies inversely with these factors.*[4]

The phrase "extent of relational interdependence" refers to

this dimension: at one pole is the extreme of every variable functionally related to all other variables at all times; at the opposite pole is the extreme of one variable determining all systemic activity (i.e., the activity of all other variables) at all times. In *Design for a Brain,* cybernetic psychologist W. Ross Ashby provides a good example of this dimension of complexity:

A third . . . example of a richly connected environment (now, thank goodness, no more) faced the experimenter in the early days of the cathode-ray oscilloscope. Adjusting the first experimental models was a matter of considerable *complexity.* An attempt to improve the brightness of the spot might make the spot also move off the screen. The attempt to bring it back might alter its rate of sweep and start it oscillating vertically. An attempt to correct this might make its line of sweep leave the horizontal, and so on. This system's variables (brightness of spot, rate of sweep, etc.) were dynamically linked in a rich and *complex* manner. Attempts to control it through the available parameters were difficult precisely because the variables were richly joined.[5]

The three dimensions of complexity are non-additive; that is, one cannot translate number of components, interdependence, and variability onto one dimension for easy comparison. Consequently, if one system has fewer components but greater interdependence and variability than another, it would be difficult or impossible to determine which system is the more complex, unless the system with fewer variables is identical to a subsystem of the second system. In other words, one system must exhibit a greater magnitude than another on all three dimensions of complexity if one is to order the systems. Nevertheless, my definition may be useful, especially since no treatment of this topic has gained widespread attention among political scientists.

My definition of simplicity-complexity is much the same as cybernetician Stafford Beer's definition of systemic simplicity-complexity: "A simple deterministic system is one having few components and interrelations, and which reveals completely predictable dynamic behavior."[6] "Completely predictable dynamic behavior" would refer to the same type of data as is indicated by my phrase "the variability of the components and their relationships through time." Evidently, complexity is related to such cybernetic concepts as indeterminacy, informational ambiguity, and negative entropy, but the delineation of such relationships is beyond the scope of this discussion.[7]

We can combine and summarize the preceding discussions of systems and simplicity-complexity in this statement: Complex (simple) systems are a superset of complex (simple) causal systems, which are, in turn, a superset of complex (simple) influence systems, which are a superset of complex (simple) power systems (i.e., power structures). Next I argue that we may equate the concepts of complex power structure, pluralist power structure, and decentralized system. Conversely, we may equate the concepts of simple power structure, elitist power structure, and centralized system.

A pluralist political system is a complex political system having complex causation. This may be shown by comparing pluralist findings with the three dimensions of simplicity-complexity. First, a pluralist political system has a great number and variety of components (individuals, groups, roles, etc.); Nelson Polsby has expressed this idea in a summary statement:

Pluralists, who see American society as fractured into a congeries of hundreds of small special interest groups, with incompletely overlapping memberships, widely differing power bases, and a multitude of techniques for exercising influence on decisions salient to them, are not surprised at the low priority Americans give to their class memberships as bases of social action. In the decision-making of fragmented government—and American national, state, and local governments are nothing if not fragmented—the claims of small, intense minorities are usually attended to.[8]

Second, a large number of component units in the pluralist political system exercise *power*, and therefore cause changes in the behavior of other component units. That is to say, many component variables are affecting many other component variables much of the time. Hence, there is a relatively high amount of relational interdependence among the components—the second dimension of complexity. Third, pluralist findings generally state the variability of systemic components and their relationships through time. Again Nelson Polsby has put this very well: "Another presumption of the pluralist approach runs directly counter to stratification theory's presumption that power distributions are a more or less permanent aspect of social structure. Pluralists hold that power may be tied to issues, and issues can be fleeting or persistent, provoking coalitions among interested groups and citizens ranging in their duration from momentary to semipermanent."[9] Thus, within the pluralist political system, power and coalitional relationships among systemic components vary considerably through time relative to specific situations. In summary, because pluralist findings reflect the three dimensions of complexity in political form, a *pluralist political system is a complex political system.*

If one studies power rather than the resource base of legality,[10] one may equate a decentralized power structure with a pluralist power structure.* By definition, a decentralized political system has a greater number of component actors causing intended changes in the behavior of other actors than does a centralized political system. Moreover, one finds that relationships of dominance and reciprocity between component actors fluctuate much more in a decentralized system than in a centralized power structure.[11] Therefore, a decentralized power structure, like a pluralist power structure, embodies the three dimensions of complexity in political form. Moreover, decentralized power means a dispersion of power, hence a dispersion of causation, which must be described with the aid of complex hypotheses and complex systems. Consequently, we can equate decentralized power structure with pluralist power structure, because they refer to the same concept—the complex system of intended social causation.

RECIPROCITY

One extremely important analytical characteristic differentiating complex and simple systems is the incidence of asymmetrical relationships among components. In the following

---

* Of course a formally centralized system may be decentralized in terms of actual power relationships, whereas a formally decentralized system may be centralized in these terms.

quotation, Herbert Simon explains asymmetry and discerns important links between this idea and concepts of power, independent-dependent variables, and causation:

I returned in about 1950 to the task of defining political power, only to find myself as unable as ever to arrive at a satisfactory solution. The difficulty appeared to reside in a very specific technical point; influence, power, and authority are all intended as *asymmetrical* relations. When we say that *C* has power over *R*, we do not mean to imply that *R* has power over *C*. The mathematical counterpart to this asymmetrical relation appeared to be the distinction between independent and dependent variable—the independent variable determines the dependent, and not the converse.... When I had stated the question in this form—as a problem of giving operational meaning to the asymmetry of the relation between independent and dependent variable—it became clear that it was identical with the general problem of defining a *causal relation* between two variables.[12]

Briefly, asymmetrical relationships can be described as involving dominance and one-way action, whereas symmetrical relationships involve reciprocity and mutual interaction among components.

In an asymmetrical relationship, one component is the causal agent, and another component is the affected object; the first component is the *independent variable*, and the other is the *dependent variable*; the first dominates or controls the action of the second. Within the sphere of social causation, the first systemic component (individual, role, group, etc.) *influences* the second and possibly exercises power over the second.[13]

In a symmetrical, reciprocal relationship, however, both components may be causal agents at the same time over different activity areas (e.g., issue areas) of their relationship, and accordingly both may be affected objects at the same time. Or the direction of causation may change with time in one or more activity areas. Thus, we may say that both components influence one another, perhaps over different matters at the same time, or perhaps over the same matter at different times.

In other words, we can view reciprocity in terms of one

activity area at one time; two or more activity areas at one time; or one or more activity areas at various times. Consequently, a polar model of two-party relational reciprocity exists when each party acts as the independent variable half the time, if we aggregate all interactions in all activity areas* over time.[14] And, in general, the polar model of n-party reciprocity exists when each party acts as the independent variable over $1/n$ of all aggregated interactions through time. (This is a state of complete equality.) On the other hand, the archetype of relational dominance in an n-party system exists when one party acts as the independent variable over all activity areas all of the time. (This is a state of absolute inequality.)

An increase in systemic reciprocity implies an increase in systemic complexity. Thus, as systemic reciprocity increases, more components cause changes in the activities of other components more of the time. In other words, as reciprocity increases, the incidence of relational interdependence increases, as many component variables begin to affect many other component variables much of the time. Accordingly, the second dimension of complexity—the extent and incidence of relational interdependence—varies with the amount of systemic reciprocity. Furthermore, as reciprocity increases, so does the variability of relationships among components through time. For example, certain components will act as independent variables at an earlier time, only to act as dependent variables at a later time. Consequently, the third dimension of complexity—the variability of systemic components and their relationships through time—increases as the extent and incidence of systemic reciprocity increases.

As noted in the quotation from Simon above, the language of asymmetry and symmetry, of independent and dependent variables, is the language of power, conceived as a type of social causation. Hence the language of reciprocity is the language of power. Furthermore, we have seen that as reciproc-

---

* Of course, such activity areas are almost never of equal importance in the judgment of all participants and observers at all times. Thus we eventually confront the awesome difficulty of ranking the activity areas according to significance. See Chs. 4–6.

ity increases, systemic complexity increases, and inversely, systemic simplicity decreases. Thus, the greater the extent of reciprocal power relationships, the greater the extent of systemic complexity, and hence the greater the extent of systemic pluralism, the embodiment of complexity in political form. Conversely, systemic simplicity and elitism vary inversely with the extent of reciprocity in power relationships. For example, a very simple power structure is characterized by one-way relationships at any particular time: leaders change the behavior of followers in significant areas of activity, but followers do not change the behavior of leaders in such areas.[15] Similarly, reciprocity does not develop over time in a very simple power structure: the power elite *always* determines the behavior of the other components in significant areas of behavior, at least insofar as any group possesses detectable power.* On the other hand, a complex power structure is characterized by reciprocal relationships at any particular time: A changes the behavior of B in respect to one activity, but B changes the behavior of A in respect to another, different activity. Moreover, reciprocity increases through time in the complex power structure: A changes the behavior of B at an earlier time, but B changes the behavior of A at a later time.

We have seen that reciprocity can be expressed in terms of independent and dependent variables. Thus, in a very simple system, the power elite may be viewed as the independent variable that determines the behavior of other components in all activity areas at all times. But in a complex, plural system, the components are seen as mutually interdependent. For example, in the American national governmental budgeting process, executive agencies, congressional subcommittees, and Budget Bureau executives all change one another's behavior in an interdependent process.[16]

---

* In this respect, as well as in the discussion that follows, the influence/power distinction makes little or no difference. Thus, to an extent greater than any other comparable group, a power elite realizes its intentions through changing the behavior of others. Analogously, the power elite might be styled an "influence" elite, for it probably causes more changes in the behavior of others, regardless of its intentions, than any other comparable group.

We may contrast pluralist and elitist power structures in terms of the foregoing discussion. A pluralist system, by definition, has fragmented power and causation, and is described by complex hypotheses. *A pluralist power structure is a complex power structure*: many components have causal impact on the system; the actors are mutually interdependent; and relationships among actors vary considerably with time, in a shifting flux of ad hoc coalitions, limited to particular issues. A pluralist system has a high degree of reciprocity and is a decentralized system, in power-analysis terms.

In contrast, an elitist system has concentrated power and causation, and is described by simple hypotheses. *An elitist power structure is a simple power structure*: few components have causal impact on the system; power relationships are not interdependent, but spring from the action of one or few components that act as independent variables; and relationships among actors remain relatively constant through time, since the power elite determines policy at all times in all important issue areas. An elitist system is asymmetrical, being dominated by one-way action. Such systems are centralized structures, in power-analysis terms.

Because description of simple systems entails the use of simple hypotheses, the operations of an elitist, centralized system are easier to understand, since there are fewer variables to be considered and fewer shifting relationships among the variables.[17] Intuitively, it seems easier to understand the operations of a centralized political system; for example, one may "simply" state that political policy is caused by the preferences of the dictator, of the politburo, or of the power elite. This does not imply, however, that *the origins and development* of an elitist power structure *must* be explained with simple hypotheses, and the growth of a complex power structure *must* be explained with complex hypotheses.[18] The reverse could apply in both cases.

COMPLEX CAUSATION IN AMERICAN POLITICS

In a given situation, a scholar may observe a complex or a simple system of variables. If the scholar chooses to make normative statements, he may prescribe a simple or a complex system as preferable. These four categories—complex description, simple description, complex prescription, simple prescription—are very useful for organizing and comparing the work of students of American politics. For example, those advocating a more responsible party system recognize the existence of a complex system (i.e., fragmentation of power), but prescribe as preferable the development of a less complex system* involving greater centralization of power within the parties, hence involving greater centralization of causation within the parties, thus implying the development of a simpler political subsystem (that of political parties).[19] Others recognize the existence of a complex system of fragmentation of power within the American party system, and prescribe the retention of the presently complex system with its widely dispersed causation and power.[20]

On many occasions, observers may prescribe the development of a simpler system to replace an existing complicated system, so that anarchy (widely dispersed power), chaos (widely dispersed causation), etc., may be eliminated. On all such occasions, remembering that power is a type of causality, one may properly inquire whether the workings of the existing complex system are sufficiently understood, for observers may reject a complex system because they do not understand its operations, and they may call for the substitution of a simpler system whose operations are easier to understand. However, comprehensibility of operation is only one of many important factors that should be considered in evaluating a political structure.

In almost every substantive area of the descriptive study of American politics, there is a polarization between those who assert complex hypotheses, see complex systems, and find pluralism (widely dispersed power and causation) and those who assert simple hypotheses, see simple systems, and find concentrated power and causation, and power elites.† Pluralists

---

* However, to the extent that a simplified party subsystem would increase democracy (followers controlling leaders) within the total political system, then the simplified party subsystem would *complicate* the total political system by increasing the number of actors with significant power, if one took actors rather than roles as the components of the system.

† Such disagreements also occur in the field of normative prescription.

usually generalize that power in the American system is dispersed, widely shared, and fragmented into kaleidoscopic bits and pieces.[21] C. Wright Mills and others (often political radicals of the left and the right) see power as concentrated, shared by few, and consolidated into large lumps.[22] For instance, there is Mills' "power elite," and the detached, unrepresentative governmental elite of Senator Goldwater's *The Conscience of a Conservative*.[23]

In studying the American national government, political scientists have tried to demonstrate that reality is characterized by more complex systems, greater dispersal of power (causation), and more pluralism than the prescriptive theory of Constitutional separation of powers or certain observers would imply. In studying the Senate, for example, the "inner club" thesis (an elitist, simple hypothesis and system, having centralized causation) of William White is discredited by Nelson Polsby, Ralph Huitt, and other writers who describe a more complex senatorial reality.[24] Matthews' more sophisticated thesis of the controlling power of senatorial folkways is countered by Huitt's demonstration that even systemic deviants retain considerable power because a countervailing set of folkways, the Senate rules, provides for an extraordinary decentralization of power and causation.[25] Rossiter and Neustadt show that the President is not a great white god or demon, controlling national policy by acting as a single, independent variable, as polemical writers (especially on the issue of the war in Vietnam) have implied.[26] On the contrary, such political scientists portray the President as merely one variable acting within a complex system. Moreover, they demonstrate that the President cannot even be viewed as the single independent variable controlling events within the executive branch. Indeed, Neustadt prescribes simplification of our national government's politics by concentrating more power (causation) in the President.[27] Normatively speaking, even Rossiter prefers Tory conceptions of leadership (relatively more central causation) to Whig conceptions of leadership (relatively less central causation).[28]

In studying the executive branch, many political scientists have broken down the naive, legal-formalist view of a concen-

tration of power and causation in the President, who delegates authority (legitimated causal impact) to cabinet heads
and other executives. Instead, the dominant view is one of
complex hypotheses and systems, pluralism and dispersed
causation involving complex, shifting coalition formation
across congressional, agency, and departmental lines, and
even across the formally constituted lines of the government
itself.[29] From the simple systemic point of view, on the contrary, Mills and a few others see a power elite of cabinet and
sub-cabinet officials linked to business and military leaders in
a stable, controlling coalition, with the President being an irrelevant factor, as in the case of Eisenhower, or an especially
appropriate elitist leader, as in the case of Lyndon Johnson.[30]

Interesting arguments have appeared concerning various
proposals to simplify public administration by reducing the
number of relevant variables acting within the executive
branch. For example, some have proposed coordination of
executive action through more centralized budget formation,
although such simplification (centralization of power) is expressed in terms of rationally relating means to ends.[31] (As
Lindblom has shown, centralized political systems may possess a seemingly rational structure that dissolves under further analysis.)[32] Aaron Wildavsky, however, has tentatively
suggested a "radical incrementalist" approach to governmental budgeting, which would decentralize causation and lessen
comprehensive planning still further at the national policy-
making level.[33] Other discussion, ad hoc in nature, concerns
various reorganization proposals intended to make specific
agencies more dependent on central control, thereby additionally centralizing power and causation. In contrast, however, advocates of an agency's policies may propose reorganization schemes that would render their favorite agency less
amenable to central control, thereby additionally decentral-
izing and complicating causation.[34]

American political parties clearly are exceedingly complex
systems, characterized by extraordinary dispersal of power
among shifting, decentralized factions of politicians and activists. Hence, American political scientists have argued for
party "responsibility" by simplifying the party subsystem,

thereby concentrating power and causation.[35] One readily sees that the very term "responsibility" implies simplification, especially in terms of the low level of political information among the general public. Proponents of party responsibility wish to simplify a complicated party system by centralizing power, hence centralizing causation, hence making the system easier to understand. Presumably, if the system's operations are easier to understand (less complex), the average citizen could have greater knowledge of which politician caused what to happen. Then, the citizen would be more able to use sanctions to affect politicians. However, problems could develop in the process of centralizing causation (power) within political parties: political conflict could be expected to increase, for example.[36] Perhaps the next step toward the scholarly understanding of the American party system is the development and testing of a theory of decentralization of power, such as Lindblom's theory of partisan mutual adjustment and incremental policy making.[37]

The Supreme Court may be described in terms of the opposition of simple and complex systems. Here the political scientist must deal with the troubling question: How can the power of the Supreme Court be reconciled with the theory (or theories) of representative government? Once again we find a widespread polemical view of the existence of a power elite, which could become an unchecked tyrannical body of "nine old men." New Deal supporters in the 30's were disturbed by the Court's vetoing and modifying the decisions of the other components of government, thereby exercising considerable power in Dahl's terms. Conservatives in the 50's and 60's were concerned by the Court's dramatic initiations in the fields of civil rights and redistricting, as well as the Court's vetoes and initiatives in the fields of subversion control and police procedure. Both in the 30's and in recent years, there has been much unsophisticated speculation about the Court arrogating powers to itself to the point of becoming an unrepresentative power elite. However, analysis of the overall judicial process shows that there are numerous checks on the Court's power (causal impact).[38] Thus, the Court may be viewed as a single variable in a complex system having many

components, mutually interdependent action, and great variation of relationships over time. Accordingly, one may show
that the court is not a single independent variable operating
on many dependent variables in the one-way action characteristic of a simple system, and that there are many checks
on the Court's power. (The idea of a check is the idea of
relational reciprocity. If a first variable's activity is checked
by the activity of a second variable, then the two are mutually interdependent variables within a system. "Check" implies
that a component's activity cannot be conceived as an independent variable, always causing changes in the activity of
other systemic components.)

The Court usually makes major decisions in slow stages and
may be viewed as an incremental decision-making body.[39]
Thus public reaction—both criticism and support—may
modify subsequent behavior in the Court's decision-making
process. However, the Court is not pursuing maximum political popularity. Instead, it is comparable to an agency with
a public interest purpose, which is modified to suit the demands of its political environment.

The discovery and analysis of interest groups complicated
early analyses of the political system. After the pioneer specu-
lative theory of Bentley, and the case studies of Odegard,
Schattschneider, Herring, and others, a large set of new variables entered the picture.[40] Certainly, the interest-group system is complex in terms of the number of its components, the
amount of interdependent relationships among the components, and the variability of the components and their relationships through time. Evaluation of interest-group activity
may be viewed in terms of simplicity versus complexity. Some
would prefer to reduce the power (causal impact) of interest
groups, thereby simplifying the American political system,
and supposedly rendering the total system more responsive to
the public interest.[41] Others would prefer the retention of a
powerful interest-group system, having considerable causal
impact within the total system, thereby increasing the complexity of the overall political system.[42] Exemplifying prescriptive simplification, Schattschneider saw interest-group
activity as thwarting the public will and making government

unresponsive to the public interest.[43] Thus, the projected systemic simplification (centralization of power, concentration of causation) of the party system by such theorists implied the reduction of direct interest-group access to governmental decision-making bodies, which would be placed under the control of the governing political party's leadership. But a careful reading of certain theorists who stress the functions of decentralization (e.g., Lindblom, Truman, Ranney, Wildavsky) suggests that they prefer retaining the present complexities of the American interest-group system, because of the groups' interest representation and information-processing functions. Furthermore, according to the theory of cross-pressures (which needs further analysis), elite and mass sociopolitical demands are moderated by individual membership in multiple groups, if the interests of these groups are not mutually reinforcing.[44] Such moderation of demands contributes to the maintenance of stable democracy, according to most such hypotheses. Thus, once more, we find a polarization between those advocating systemic simplification and those preferring systemic complexity.

Few would deny the descriptive findings that American metropolitan area government, conceived as a single political system, is extraordinarily complex. Nevertheless, again disagreement arises concerning prescriptive simplification. Most scholars have advocated some kind of centralization of power (system simplification) within the metropolitan region, a view exemplified by the various governmental consolidation plans. However, Banfield, Long, and a few others have restrained their enthusiasm for such systemic simplification, although they have not necessarily opposed reorganization proposals.[45] They point to the political effects of consolidation of local governmental units; like almost all reorganization plans, such a proposal aids the interests of some and hurts the interests of others.

In the field of community-power studies, a division between simple, elitist findings and complex, pluralist findings is again apparent. Pluralists see numerous actors as having power (causal impact) within the system, which thus contains numerous significant components. Leader-follower relationships are characterized by mutual interdependence and a high degree of reciprocity, complicating the system in comparison with elitist power structure. Further, pluralists see power relations as varying with time and issue area, in patterns of shifting coalition formation. However, specific issue areas may have self-contained power structures, thus limiting the complexity of the whole system in an interesting way.[46]

The picture of community power as drawn by the pluralists contrasts sharply with the findings of other observers, who describe communities as controlled by power elites, cliques, or "crowds" that dominate many issue areas.[47] This "stratificationist" image is a simple system, characterized by simple causation, concentrated power, and simple hypotheses. As always, the power elite is viewed as the single important independent variable, whereas all other actors are viewed as dependent variables.

Nelson Polsby has excellently delineated the differences between the stratificationists (simple systems) and the pluralists (complex systems) in his book *Community Power and Political Theory*. Under the category "stratification studies," Polsby has consolidated the findings of numerous community-power studies, as follows: (1) the upper class rules in community life; (2) political and civic leaders are subordinate to the upper class; (3) a single power elite rules in the community; (4) the upper-class power elite rules in its own interests; (5) social conflict takes place between the upper and lower classes.[48] The first three of Polsby's criteria posit a simple system. The upper class, or part of the upper class, constitutes a power elite, which is often construed as a single, independent variable. Political and civic leaders, and other actors whom many think to have significant power (causal impact), are viewed as dependent variables. Relationships between actors are not complex; instead, such relationships may be likened to strings, held by the power elite, who make their subordinates (everyone else in the community) jump and dance like marionettes for the fun and profit of the elite. (Compare the usage of the metaphor "puppet.") The fourth and fifth of Polsby's criteria express the idea that the power elite always gets what it wants, no matter what other actors

desire, and these criteria also express, in their way, the definition of power that contained the dimensions of causation, intentionality, and coercion. In other words, Polsby's five characteristics of stratificationist theory describe a simple, elitist
power structure (causal structure), involving a useful, specific definition of power.

In this section a theoretical contrast between simple and
complex systems in several substantive areas in the study of
American politics has been described. This polarity exists in
hypotheses, causation, power structures, and descriptive and
prescriptive systems. Generally speaking, theorizing about
power structures in the various areas of study has proceeded
in a dialectical fashion, as political scientists have posited
complex theories in reaction to simpler theories presented by
unsophisticated observers, social critics, and reform-oriented
activists and scholars.

SUMMARY

Five ideas represent the core of my argument to this point:
(1) social causation is the bedrock idea of influence and
power; (2) a system of power is a system of causation; (3)
simplicity-complexity may be defined in terms of three non-
additive dimensions—the number and variety of components,
the extent and incidence of relational interdependence
among components, and the variability of components and
their relationships through time; (4) a pluralist political system is a system of complex causation, embodying the three
dimensions of complexity in political forms; (5) a theoretical
contrast between simple, elitist systems, and complex, pluralist systems can be discerned in several substantive areas in
the study of American politics.

3. Pluralism as an Explanation

Two major chains of reasoning characterize pluralist findings (decentralized power structures, fragmented causation, complex systems) in the study of American politics. One such analytical mode is a direct attack on ruling elite or stratification models of power within some political arena (e.g., local communities, Congress) as exemplified by the community-power studies of Robert Dahl, Nelson Polsby, and Aaron Wildavsky.[1] A second mode of analysis leading to pluralist findings is group-process theory, as exemplified by the studies of A. F. Bentley and David Truman. Both types of pluralist theory find complex systems of causation.

The ruling-elite models of Hunter and Mills,[2] the stratification models of the Lynds, W. Lloyd Warner, and others,[3] and the mass-society theses of Mills, Vidich and Bensman, and Warner and Lowe[4] are targets for attack by pluralist community-power analysts. The following quotation from Dahl's "A Critique of the Ruling Elite Model" exhibits the empiricism and the complexity of such analysis: "Now it is a remarkable and indeed astounding fact that neither Professor Mills nor Professor Hunter has seriously attempted to examine an array of specific cases to test his major hypothesis. Yet I suppose these two works more than any others in the social sciences of the last few years [up to 1957] have sought to interpret *complex political systems* essentially as instances of a ruling elite."[5] (Emphasis added.) This empiricism and complexity typifies the analytical mode of numerous political scientists who have replaced ruling-elite models with complex, pluralist models. Such analysts have very skillfully destroyed simple

ruling-elite images such as that of the President being in absolute control of the executive branch,[6] an inner club controlling the Senate,[7] national party leaders controlling local
party leaders,[8] business controlling political policy at the national and local levels,[9] the federal government controlling
the state governments,[10] pressure-group leaders controlling
pressure-group followers,[11] a military-industrial complex controlling defense and foreign policy,[12] and local ruling elites
controlling local communities.[13] Everywhere in the study of
American politics, ruling-elite images are smashed into kalei-
doscope fragments of power and causation.

Dahl's method of ascertaining political power by studying
decisions supports my general argument about the meaning
of power, causation, pluralism, and complexity. Thus, Dahl
sought to discover who initiated and vetoed policies within a
particular issue area; those initiating or vetoing actions he
designated as having political power.[14] Obviously, the initiation of a new social activity necessarily implies causing
changes in others' behavior by *starting* certain behaviors that
would not occur otherwise. Similarly, the vetoing of a social
activity causes changes in others' behavior by *stopping* certain behaviors that would otherwise occur. Thus, in *Who
Governs?*, Dahl finds numerous actors having significant
power (causal impact) within the political system of New
Haven. Further, he finds a fair amount of interdependence
among the system's actor components, although this interdependence is limited by a certain degree of self-containment of
activity within specific issue areas. Finally, the influential actors and their relationships vary considerably with time.[15]
Thus, the political system of New Haven is relatively complex, and we may conclude that the system is pluralist, having
a complex structure of power and causation.

The group-process theorists have also found complex systems of power and causation. Thus, in Part One of *The Process
of Government*, Bentley scathingly criticizes many of the
leading social theorists of his day for oversimplification and
insufficient empiricism.[16] Bentley's viewpoint, like Dahl's, is
one of empiricism and complexity. This pioneering observer's
rejection of clear-cut, simple models of society and preference

for ambiguous, complex models is evident in the following quotation:

Perhaps I may be permitted to offer a geometrical picture of this mixture of the groups, under the assurance, however, that no proof depends on it, and that it pretends to be nothing more than a crude attempt at illustration. If we take all the men of our society, say all the citizens of the United States, and look upon them as a spherical mass, we can pass an unlimited number of planes through the center of the sphere, each plane representing some principle of classification, say, race, various economic interests, religion, or language (though in practice we shall have to do mainly with much more specialized groupings than these) .... Assuming perhaps hundreds, perhaps thousands, of planes passed through the sphere, we get a great confusion of the groups. No one set of groups, that is, no set distinguished on the basis of any one plane, will be an adequate grouping of the whole mass.[17]

Bentley's complex picture of social groups is similar to Polsby's statement that pluralists "see American society as fractured into a congeries of hundreds of small special interest groups, with incompletely overlapping memberships."[18]

Emphasizing concepts of group, interest, and activity, Bentley's viewpoint has much in common with that of attitudinal social psychology, a field that is a basis for Truman's viewpoint.[19] Thus, the concepts of interest and activity have much in common with the social psychological idea of attitude. Interest is nearly synonymous with such terms as desire, or goal, unless the concept is restricted, in Marxist fashion, to economic, material goals. On the other hand, "an individual's attitude toward something is his predisposition to be motivated in relation to it";[20] i.e., an attitude is a tendency to exhibit some sort of *activity* toward some kind of goal (interest). The social psychological approach is usually highly complex, in the sense of my definition, as a multiplicity of components, a high degree of relational interdependence, and much variation with time are often discovered.[21]

In *The Governmental Process*, Truman shares Bentley's view of *politics as a complex system in process*—group, goal (interest), and attitudinal components interacting in variable fashion over time. This may be seen not only in Truman's explicit citations from Bentley, but also in his frequent description of institutional power structures in terms of the three elements of a complex system, which he contrasts to the models of formal constitutional theory. The following quotations (with my added emphasis) are representative of Truman's thought and illustrate his findings of pluralism or complexity:

[In modern society there is] a vast multiplicity of groups.[22]

The moving pattern of a complex society such as the one in which we live *is one of changes and disturbances in the habitual subpatterns* of interaction [variation in relationships between numerous components], followed by a return to the previous state of equilibrium or, if the disturbances are intense or prolonged, by the emergence of new groups whose specialized function it is to facilitate the establishment of a new balance, a new adjustment in the habitual interactions of individuals.[23]

Alterations in response to technological or other changes are more rapid and more noticeable in a *complex society* in which a larger number of *institutionalized groups are closely interdependent.* Changes in one institution produce compensatory changes in tangent institutions and thus, inevitably, in government [a complex group system, with a high degree of interdependence between the components]. *A complex civilization necessarily develops complex political arrangements.* Where the patterns of interaction in the society are intricate [i.e., complex], the patterns of political behavior must be also. These may take several forms, depending upon the circumstances. In a society like ours, whose traditions sanction the almost unregulated development of a wide variety of associations, the new patterns are likely to involve the emergence of a wide variety of groups peripheral to the formal institutions of government, *supplementing and complicating their operations.*[24]

Truman concludes his chapter on "Techniques of Interest Groups in the Legislative Process" by noting the "diversity of relationships" among the participants.[25] (Thus, we have diverse relationships among numerous systemic components.) Truman also sees variability of such relationships over time: "Each completed legislative act represents a unique amalgam of these elements."[26]

The techniques utilized by interest groups and their "members" in the legislature to enhance and exploit the degree of access that a group has been able to achieve *are enormously complicated and*

varied. The *diversity of relationships* that culminate in the successful assertion of group claims upon and through the legislature is
impressive, including not only those within groups, but also arrangements between groups and relationships with legislators,
committees, and committee staffs as well as with elements in the
executive branch. *Each completed legislative act represents a
unique amalgam of these elements.*[27]

A prime reason for the complexity of the legislative process in the
Congress and various of the State legislatures is the absence of an
integrated and continuing leadership [a system of a few independent variables in a constant state over time]. *The diffusion of
power* within the legislature, the multiple lines of access, and the
diverse means of leverage make an inherently *complex process still
more complicated.*[28]

Truman entitles a chapter on the executive branch "The
Web of Relationships in the Administrative Process,"[29] the
apt image of a web indicating a high degree of interdependence among components, as a web has many lines (relationships) connecting many points (components). Truman notes
at the very beginning that the complex systems of Congress
and the executive are interdependent, thereby forming an
overarching complex system with two subsystems reinforcing
each other's complexity:

The executive branch of government in the United States normally
exhibits a diffusion of leadership and a multitude of points of access comparable to that in the legislature. The preceding chapter
has demonstrated this point; it has also indicated that these characteristics of the legislature and the executive are not so much
parallel as they are interdependent. Dispersed leadership and multiple points of control within one branch reflect and reinforce similar patterns in the other.[30]

Thus, in general, Truman in *The Governmental Process*
sees pluralist, complex systems, characterized by numerous
varied components, great interdependence, and variability
of components and their relationships.

In "The Group Basis of Politics: Notes for a Theory,"[31]
Latham's perspective on simplicity and complexity has much
in common with the ideas of Dahl, Bentley, and Truman.

Thus, the world of group politics is a complex world, with numerous mutually interdependent relationships, which vary over time "in a flux of restless alterations":

Official groups are simply inhabitants of one pluralistic world which is an aggregation, a collection, an assemblage, a throng, a moving multitude of human clusters, a consociation of groups, a plurality of collectivities, an intersecting series of social organisms, adhering, interpenetrating, overlapping—a single universe of groups which combine, break, federate, and form constellations and coalitions of power in a *flux of restless alterations*. . . . To some, this view of the political process may seem formless, inchoate, ambiguous, and disordered.[32]

Latham observes that, lost in the flux of the complex group-process system, many people will miss the simple causal systems, with centralized power (either descriptive or prescriptive) exercised by single independent variables: "Some may miss in the concept under discussion the mystique of the law, with its authoritarian constructs, its assumption that there *must* be a supreme power, like father in the household or the Absolute, some authority which arranges disorder and judges our transgressions and supplies us in an infinite universe with a finite demesne of which we can see the walls."[33]

We have seen that Dahl's power-structure analysis (and critiques of ruling-elite models in general) and group-process theory present American politics as a complex system. In the next section, I shall examine the meaning of such findings of complexity (pluralism) for the development of empirical political theory.

THE VALUE OF A PLURALIST EXPLANATION

All theories both include and exclude a range of events in stating an explanation or prediction. Thus, when an explanation states that something has happened, it implies that other events have *not* happened. For example, explaining a system in terms of a complex power structure (pluralism) implies that a simple power structure explanation for the same system cannot apply. Accordingly, one's judgment about the utility of a theory depends on one's evaluation of the theoretical import of the range of events included within the theory's ex-

planatory or predictive statements. For instance, one observer
might consider pluralist explanations of great theoretical importance because he has hitherto believed in a power-elite
explanation. A second observer, however, could regard the
pluralist explanation as excessively general and vague because he has considered power-elite explanations grossly inaccurate and unworthy of serious consideration. In other
words, the importance of events included in a study can only
be measured in terms of the significance of events that are
left out. Likewise, the theoretical value of pluralist explanations is relative to the subjective significance of elitist explanations. Finally, there is no a priori answer concerning the significance of either elitist or pluralist theories of American
politics. Therefore, there is no a priori method of assessing
the significance of pluralist (complex systemic) findings.

My own view is that pluralist explanations are of considerable theoretical importance in understanding most aspects of
American political behavior. Evidently, simple systemic, single independent variable, elitist theories (both descriptive
and prescriptive) have a tenacious, continuing appeal for
many highly intelligent observers. However, as far as theory
building is concerned, there is a need to advance beyond *Who
Governs?, The Governmental Process,* and other similar complex-systemic interpretations and to distinguish types of
pluralist (complex) systems.

After a dialectical rejection of an elitist theory, an undifferentiated pluralist theory can easily degenerate into par-
ticularistic, atheoretical description. Thus, when one describes political *power* as widely shared, dispersed, fragmented into bits and pieces, and so forth, one is asserting that political *causation* is widely shared, dispersed, fragmented,
and so forth. Hence, it is relatively easy to explain why certain initiated political policies failed to be adopted: one may
readily locate a particular piece of political power that was
missing (e.g., a congressional committee chairman wouldn't
go along). However, it is much more difficult to explain why
a given political initiative becomes governmental policy, if
one wishes to go beyond the descriptive, case-study method
of enumerating how bits and pieces of political power co-

alesced in the particular case. In meeting this problem, after
examining the power exercised by political parties, interest
groups, governmental agencies, and politicians acting as individuals, pluralist writers sometimes assert that policy is
made by ad hoc coalitions, which aggregate the particular
power fragments relevant to the issue at hand.[34] In other
words, elite bargainers form ad hoc coalitions, which cause
policy outcomes. This is an important generalization, but its
value is limited. Thus, a theory of ad hoc coalition formation
could easily become no theory at all, since it implies that
coalitions tend to be unique. In Truman's words, cited above:
"Each completed legislative act represents a unique amalgam
of these elements [i.e., groups, legislators, committees, committee staffs, elements in the executive branch]."[35] And if each
coalition is unique, policy making can be understood only by
specific, unique case studies concerning the adoption of each
specific measure. That is to say, if we content ourselves with
an undifferentiated pluralist theory, we may content ourselves
with the finding that power structure is complex, hence causation is complex, strongly implying that the system's operations are unique in each specific case. (However, theories of
bargaining may provide generalizations about the dynamics
of complex political processes.)[36]

We gain some understanding of how to differentiate types
of pluralism by noting Dahl's five "patterns of leadership."
Clearly, a political leader is one who has political power, i.e.,
one having significant causal impact on the system. In other
words, *a pattern of leadership is a pattern of power and causation.* Dahl's five patterns of leadership are:

1. Covert integration by Economic Notables [a type of power
   elite].
2. An executive-centered "grand coalition of coalitions."
3. A coalition of chieftains.
4. Independent sovereignties with spheres of influence.
5. Rival sovereignties fighting it out.[37]

Let us examine the implicit differences among these five models of power. Using Dahl's mode of analysis (initiation, vetoing)[38] and overlooking the problem of weighting power
among issue areas,[39] one can assign to each actor (individual

or group) a number of power-points according to the number
of times the actor successfully initiates and vetoes policy.
Thus a power elite is represented by a (10, 0, 0, 0, . . .) configuration; the grand coalition is represented by something
like (6, 2, 1, 1, 1, . . .); the last three patterns are represented
by (2, 2, 2, 2, 2, . . .). The last three models differ according
to the dual criteria of goal conflict and goal interdependence.
In other words:

Pattern	Goal conflict	Goal interdependence
Coalition of chieftains	low	high
Independent sovereignties	low	low
Rival sovereignties	high	medium or high

Hence Dahl differentiates pluralist political systems by distinguishing patterns of power, conflict, and interdependence.

Dahl's analysis responds to certain basic questions in the
study of politics: (1) Who are the actors? (2) What are the
actors' goals? (3) Are these goals interdependent; if so, which
ones; which goals conflict? (4) When actors' goals conflict,
who wins and who loses?[40] Probably any empirical political
theory must answer these basic questions. For example, sociological theory categorizes the actors (question 1) under
concepts of class. Similarly, goals (2) are categorized into
ideological, value, and interest classifications and related to
previous generalizations concerning classes of individuals.
Ideological, value, and interest conflicts are analyzed (3);
such considerations are then related to the specific events
manifesting sociopolitical conflict. In summary, Dahl's analysis of patterns of pluralism points to individualistic, specific
concepts that are analogous to classificatory, general concepts
of sociology.

Most of these ideas also apply to theories of bargaining.
First, let us ask: What is "bargaining"? Dahl and Lindblom's
consideration of this topic in *Politics, Economics, and Welfare*
ably sets forth what many would regard as bargaining. They
open a chapter entitled "Bargaining: Control Among Leaders" with the following statement, which provokes further
analysis:

Bargaining is a form of reciprocal control among leaders. It takes place among leaders when all of certain conditions are met; what these conditions are will be seen shortly [social pluralism, goal interdependence, and a mixture of goal agreement and conflict]. . . . Bargaining exists in all societies. In general, the extent to which it takes place is inversely related to the amount of hierarchy and the extent of initial agreement. Even in modern totalitarian societies, however, some bargaining takes place.[41]

In other words, a system of bargaining has a high degree of mutual interdependence among the components, usually conceived as individual leaders. Thus, the presence of reciprocal control indicates reciprocity of power and causation within the system—none of the components acts as a single, independent variable, as in a hierarchy.

The necessary conditions[42] for the existence of a bargaining system are social pluralism, a mixture of goal agreement and goal conflict, and goal interdependence, according to Dahl and Lindblom. The authors define social pluralism as "a diversity of social organizations with a large measure of autonomy with respect to one another."[43] Consequently, the pluralist social system is relatively complex, because of the diversity of social organizations (number and diversity of components) and the relatively fragmented structure of power and causation. (Here "autonomy" refers to the lack of central control, a fragmentation of power. "Autonomy" also refers to a certain degree of self-containment of groups, a limitation on the mutual interdependence dimension of complexity.)* Social pluralism is seen as a base for political pluralism (complex power structure): "Pluralism develops a *complex distribution of control.* . . . Ordinary citizens control their immediate leaders and are controlled by them. These leaders in turn control other leaders and are controlled by them. Hence a society of reciprocal relationships exists to control government policy."[44] (Emphasis added.) Thus, Dahl and

---

* Autonomy of social groups limits the interdependence dimension of systemic complexity in the same sense that autonomous issue areas limit the interdependence, and hence the complexity, of a political system. But, on the other hand, autonomy of social groups or of issue areas implies that an increased number of actors possess causal impact within subsystems and hence on the entire system.

Lindblom demonstrate complexity of power structure by indicating the large number of systemic components and a high degree of interdependence of relationships (reciprocal relationships). Hence, Dahl and Lindblom describe both social and political pluralism as complex systems.

A second condition for bargaining is the mixture of goal agreement and goal conflict among leaders: "Social pluralism makes bargaining necessary and basic agreement makes it possible. . . . If leaders agreed on everything they would have no need to bargain; if on nothing, they could not bargain."[45] A third condition for bargaining is interdependence among the components of the system,

for if autonomous groups were not interdependent, or if they were fully in agreement at the outset, they would scarcely need to bargain. . . . The more the actions of one group are thought to be capable of adversely or beneficially affecting another, the more the second group is likely to protect itself by attempting to control the first. In the United States, as in other polyarchies [democratic systems], social pluralism has been accompanied by increasing interdependence. Hence the interdependent groups must bargain with one another for protection and advantage.[46]

Thus, of the three necessary conditions for the existence of bargaining, one is pluralism itself, and the other two (goal conflict and agreement, goal interdependence) are the criteria used by Dahl to differentiate patterns of power and leadership.

In view of the numerous convergences between discussions of pluralism and bargaining, one may wonder what the difference is between the two concepts. I suggest that pluralism and bargaining indicate identical phenomena and that *bargaining denotes the activity of a pluralist system over time.* Hence, the strengths and weaknesses of pluralism as an analytical concept apply to bargaining as a concept. Thus, Dahl and Lindblom's observation that the extent of bargaining generally "is inversely related to the amount of hierarchy" parallels the idea that complex, pluralist systems and simple elitist systems are at opposite poles.[47] In other words, the extent of pluralism is inversely related to the extent of elitism, as the extent of bargaining "is inversely related to the amount of hierarchy." This is true because bargaining refers to the operations of a pluralist system over time. Yet this implies that if we regard pluralism as an overly general concept for many explanatory purposes, then we must also regard bargaining as excessively general for similar purposes.

Consequently, the need for differentiating types of pluralism implies a need for differentiating types of bargaining. Along these lines, ideas that apply to pluralism necessarily apply to bargaining. As in the case of pluralism, types of bargaining systems may be distinguished by patterns of power distribution, goal conflict, and goal interdependence. Moreover, as with Dahl's analysis of types of pluralism, distinguishing patterns of bargaining may suggest individualistic, specific concepts that are analogous to classificatory, general concepts of sociology. Such individualistic, bargaining-oriented, utilitarian analysis, concerned with extending rationality, was characteristic of the late-eighteenth and early-nineteenth-century British school of political economists, including Adam Smith, Jeremy Bentham, James Mill, and the earlier John Stuart Mill.[48] Similarly, such modern pluralist theorists as Dahl, Lindblom, and Wildavsky show particular affinity for the theoretical realm of political economy.[49] As the individualistic political economics of Smith contrasted with the class-conscious, social-structural economics of Marx, so the individualistic, political economics of Dahl and Lindblom contrasts with the class-conscious, social-structural theories of Lipset, or of C. Wright Mills.[50]

The need to differentiate types of complex systems of power and of bargaining implies a need to differentiate the types of contested rewards, a need to answer "power over what?" or "bargaining for what?" Clearly, a hypothetical "bullheaded pluralist" could find pluralism and complexity in places that would startle one's common sense. Let us briefly consider three examples of the hypothetical work of a bullheaded pluralist. First, he could find pluralism in a prison, for many scholars have observed that prisoners exercise a certain amount of control over their guardians. Second, he could find pluralism in a totalitarian country, for as Dahl and Lindblom have observed: "Even in modern totalitarian societies . . .

some bargaining takes place."[51] Thus, the bullheaded pluralist could regard Berliner's excellent *Factory and Manager in the U.S.S.R.*[52] as a case study of Soviet industrial politics, and he could observe local factory managers initiating policies and covertly vetoing decisions of their hierarchical superiors. Third, he could observe that the U.S. Forest Service is superficially an archetype of decentralization, i.e., an archetype of complex, pluralist power structure.[53] But scholars who have made such an observation agree that professional-ideological socialization controls the 792 (in 1956) local forest rangers to such an extent that the formal organizational decentralization is misleading. However, the bullheaded pluralist might continue to insist that the local ranger, seldom restrained by overt hierarchical controls, often successfully initiates policy within his local issue area. Therefore, as 792 local rangers all have considerable power, the bullheaded pluralist could regard the U.S. Forest Service as an incredibly complex, pluralist system, with decentralized power fragmented into at least 792 regional issue areas.

How may we counter the contentions of the bullheaded pluralist? Chiefly, we may ask "power over what?" or "bargaining for what?"[54] That is, we may seek to differentiate pluralism and bargaining by distinguishing among types of contested rewards. Thus, prisoners may successfully control some of the conditions of their recreation breaks, but they do not set the wage rates in the license-plate factory, or decide the timing of their release. Soviet managers may bargain over production quotas and initiate changes in the quality of goods produced, but they never refuse to follow the latest All-Union economic plan. Forest rangers may determine which areas of their district are to be used for recreation and which for lumbering, but they will not ban entirely the entry of lumberjacks and campers into their district to protect its wildlife and primeval beauty.

Unfortunately, differentiating types of power structure by examining contested rewards involves us immediately in questions of value relativity. For example, observers might disagree over the relatively easy questions of the significance of prisoners' vetoing mandatory gymnastics, the Soviet managers' usage of *blat*[55] (personal influence), or the rangers' allocation of lumbering permits as instances of power or social causation. But usually much more difficult are similar problems concerning political analysis. For instance, from his analysis of Floyd Hunter's *Community Power Structure,* Polsby observes that "members of the lower-class Negro minority apparently exercised a considerable influence over many community policies" in Atlanta during the late 1940's.[56] Indeed, from one perspective, this statement is quite correct, as thousands of Negroes were permitted to vote, and these voters sometimes exercised bloc voting tactics to swing close elections. But from another perspective, it seems meaningless to speak of Negroes' exercising "considerable influence over many community policies" in the 1940's, in a situation of segregated public facilities and schools. A Whitney Young might see considerable Black Power in this situation; a Stokely Carmichael would not. In other words, one's interpretation of the significance of the rewards contested in a political process is partially dependent upon one's political and social values. Moreover, one must take a position, either explicitly or implicitly, vis-à-vis the importance of such rewards when one decides whether an exercise of power is important or trivial, i.e., whether an instance of social causation is important or trivial.[57] Thus, because power analysis is equivalent to stating which *causes* are important or unimportant, it also implies stating which sociopolitical *effects* are important or unimportant. In other words, power analysis presupposes a judgment about the importance or unimportance of certain political events. This confluence of values and power analysis poses fundamental questions that will provide challenging problems for political philosophers and social scientific methodologists for a long time to come.

The theory of public administration and the theory of organizations provide a convenient starting point for analyzing power structures by examining contested rewards. For example, we usually picture such systems as Soviet industrial administration, the U.S. Forest Service, and a prison as hierarchical administrative organizations. A hierarchical model of behavior implies that the *critical decisions* are made at the top levels, while the *routine decisions* are made at the lower levels.[58] In other words, if we conceive of politics as involving decisions concerning the authoritative allocation of values (i.e., contested rewards),[59] the general limitations for the allocation processes are set at the top levels of a hierarchy, whereas the specifics are filled in at the bottom. Thus a designer of children's coloring books sets the outlines of the pictures and may even designate the correct colors, which the child applies with his crayons. My three examples of administrative hierarchy greatly simplify the analysis of power structure in terms of contested rewards, because the specification of power is represented by the specification of levels in a hierarchy.

Unfortunately, we soon realize that the hierarchical model of levels of activity may beg the question of who has power. The sociological literature in organization theory contains many observations about bureaucratic "dysfunctionality";[60] the literature of public administration contains many observations about political policy making at the lower levels of a hierarchy. In many cases, lower-level actors make more "important" decisions than top-level actors. Thus, a group of librarians, supposedly engaged in routine decision making, may decide to restrict as much as possible the circulation of books, in spite of a top-level decision to circulate the books as widely as possible. Or, for instance, a designer of children's coloring books may set only the outlines of the pictures without stipulating the correct color, and analysts might argue forever whether the outline or the coloration constituted the most important decision in the final construction of the picture. This question becomes even more difficult if the imaginative child adds an extra green trunk and two purple legs to the original outline of the elephant! Similarly, we may ask whether the aggregate decisions of the Soviet industrial manager, the Forest Ranger, or the prisoners add up to a top-level critical decision or remain within the sphere of routine decisions. And, in the analysis of political power, we may ask whether Negro bloc voting in segregated Atlanta constituted a significant or a trivial modification of the community's power structure. At this point, I will not explore further the idea of levels of power. I wish only to demonstrate the relevance of ideas in the fields of public administration and organization theory to the study of power in structures other than formally constituted hierarchies.

Another means of distinguishing systems of power and bargaining is to compare varying systemic responses to similar environmental inputs.[61] For example, the cities of Nashville, Tennessee, and Shreveport, Louisiana, which are roughly equivalent in population, both had segregated schools at the time of the historic Supreme Court integration decision of 1954; Nashville began integrating its schools in 1957, but Shreveport waited until 1965. In these cases, an identical stimulus (input) was presented to both political systems, yet the outputs were considerably different. Thus, we might hypothesize that Nashville and Shreveport had different structures of power and bargaining.

This method of differentiating systems of power and bargaining can be applied to various arenas of American politics. In the field of community power, for example, one might compare varying responses to the similar stimuli of industrialization, assimilation of European immigrants, assimilation of Negroes, or urban sprawl with its attendant traffic problems. (Of course the postulated similar inputs must be carefully judged to be actually similar in such cases.) One could differentiate systems of power and bargaining within legislatures, executive agencies, and judicial bodies by comparing varying responses to similar problems of decision making in a complex political and technical environment,[62] individual orientation toward principled behavior versus compromise, and so forth.[63] Using modern psychological research[64] or otherwise stipulating fundamental axioms, some observers might wish to postulate fundamental similarities in human nature, viewing such similarities as identical stimuli that may be handled differently by various political systems. Thus, observing varying systemic responses to similar stimuli may be an excellent way of distinguishing systems of power and bargaining.

CONCLUSION

We have seen that the value of pluralist findings depends on the significance of elitist views, and that such value judgments may vary with the observer. My own opinion is that pluralist findings in the study of American politics are quite valuable because of the continuing appeal of various types of elitist theories of power structure. Nevertheless, we may wish to further differentiate systems of power and bargaining (a term describing the activities of a pluralist power structure over time). We have seen that such an extension of the theory of power structure can profitably rely on theories that may seem somewhat removed from the theory of political power. These possible theoretical contributions may be summarized as follows: (1) Analyses like Dahl's of patterns of power and leadership yield individualistic, specific categories of power, conflict, and interdependence that are analogous to the classificatory, general categories of sociological theory. Perhaps, then, sociological theory has more to offer to the analysis of power structures than some political scientists would initially believe. (2) The question "power over what?"—the necessary response to the bullheaded pluralist—involves questions of value relativity that should interest both political philosophers and social scientific methodologists. (3) The study of public administration and of complex organizations is the study of power in a particular context. Distinguishing between policy and administration, or critical and routine decisions, is equivalent to differentiating important and unimportant sociopolitical events, which in turn implies differentiating important and unimportant (critical and routine) sociopolitical causation (power). (4) Comparing varying systemic responses to similar stimuli is useful for discriminating among systems of power and bargaining. This approach may make use of theories of general social processes (e.g., industrialization), social-psychological theory (types of cognition in a complex social environment, orientation toward compromise), or psychological theory (general similarities in human needs).

The pluralist theorists of American politics are limited by their excessive concern with demonstrating the insufficiencies of elitist models. The dialectical tie between elitism and pluralism eventually leads to a theoretical dead end. Nevertheless, as I outlined above, pluralist theory can gain impetus from attention to sociological theory, social psychology, organization theory, and political philosophy.*

By now it is clear that one must deal with the question "power over what?" before one can show the existence of democracy, defined as a high amount of control over leaders by followers. Democracy increases with a "real" increase in the dispersal of power, seen as followers causing intended changes in leaders' behavior. But somehow the salience of varying types of issues and decisions must be evaluated. Thus we must show that the people control many *important* decisions, and we must somehow derive criteria of importance. Demonstrating widespread dispersal of power, pluralist systems, and complexity cannot ipso facto prove the existence of democracy, unless we consider "power over what?" Consequently, to discriminate theoretically between important and unimportant political events is central to any theory of political democracy.

---

* Political philosophy is presumably concerned with what is important and unimportant, significant and insignificant, good and bad, in political life. These questions are necessarily related to a theory of power, for a theory of power presupposes a perspective on the relative importance of various issues and decisions, the relative importance of various causes and effects.

PART TWO

The Structure of Power

4. Spurious Pluralism

The reader will surely agree that one can find complexity and pluralism almost anywhere, if one is sufficiently obstinate. One need only adopt some perspective that results in conclusions embodying the three elements of complexity. To explore this problem of the erroneous observation of complexity, or "spurious complexity" as I shall term it, two specific cases will be examined: the Soviet firm and the U.S. Forest Service. Both these cases deal with the structure of organizations, which may be seen as analogous to political systems but more easily analyzed in terms of complexity-simplicity (or pluralist-elitist). Moreover, much of organization theory is political theory because it pertains also to political systems. (For example, the analysis of oligarchy may be relevant both to organizations and to governments.)

James W. Fesler, in his recent article "Approaches to the Understanding of Decentralization," used the cases of the Soviet administrative decentralization and the U.S. Forest Service as examples for his remarks on "illusory decentralization."[1] Much of my analysis in this chapter is an expansion of Fesler's argument concerning "illusory decentralization."

THE SOVIET FIRM

Berliner's *Factory and Manager in the U.S.S.R.*[2] and other studies of Soviet bureaucracy find pluralism within Soviet industrial administration, which is part of Soviet government and part of Soviet "politics" (if one accepts both the definition of "politics" as processes pertaining to "the authoritative allocation of values for a society"[3] and the standard interpretations of totalitarianism). Berliner notes that most observers have pictured Soviet industrial politics as a simple system, a logically organized pyramid, with the orders flowing from a power elite, an independent variable at the top, to the administrative dependent variables below. Berliner, however, finds such a formal model of Soviet industrial administration to be an oversimplification:

> More than most modern states, the Soviet state evokes among outsiders an image which stresses the formal, the logical, the homogeneous. Soviet society is often thought of as more "rational" than others, in the technical sense that larger segments of it have been consciously and deliberately legislated into existence. There is a stern neatness in the system of enterprises responsible to chief administrations and chief administrations to ministries; and in plans which flow smoothly from bottom to top and from top to bottom. This table-of-organization image is partly the consequence of our enforced reliance upon published sources, which dulls our sensitivity to the role of people in the system. It may seem like a rude intrusion to thrust such activities as *blat* [personal influence], and such persons as the *tolkach* [an influence peddler], into a system otherwise so thoroughly automatic and well integrated.[4]

Berliner proceeds to complicate this simple power-elite model of Soviet industrial administration. The following passage typifies many of Berliner's findings:

> Meanwhile *much continuous negotiation* goes on at various levels of management: a shop chief insists that a particular output target is absolutely impossible, another *demands* that a difficult assignment be transferred to some shop other than his own, a third *refuses* to be responsible for a proposed target unless he is provided with certain equipment which the purchasing department insists cannot be obtained. Eventually *such conflicts* are resolved by the director or chief engineer and the detailed draft plan is ready for submission to the chief administration. The submission of the draft plan is also often accompanied by *some hard bargaining*.[5] [Emphasis added.]

This passage does not present a picture of centralization, an administrative power elite, and a simple system. Instead, Berliner presents a picture of a multiplicity of actors (variables), each with a certain amount of power over policy making (drafting the plan). Indeed, the terms used by Berliner to describe Soviet administrative "pluralism" are used also by students of American administrative pluralism and of American politics in general. Thus we have references to "much continuous negotiation," "demands," "such conflicts," and "some hard bargaining" within the administrative hierarchy. Furthermore, Berliner describes a system of interaction that seems complex.

Indeed, Berliner's description of Soviet industrial administration becomes so complex, decentralized, and pluralist that at the end of the book it becomes necessary to remind the reader that the power of the local managerial field administrators is sharply limited: "For a proper perspective on the practices of managers, account must finally be taken of the limits within which they are confined. . . . What, in other words, are the 'stabilizers' in the system of industrial management, the counteracting forces which hold the practices of management within reasonable bounds?"[6]

The reader may be startled to note that Soviet industrial administration exhibits incrementalism and bargaining over margins, processes described by Charles Lindblom in American pluralist contexts. Such decentralized bargaining over marginal changes in policy has been observed in American politics by Charles Lindblom, Aaron Wildavsky, Richard Fenno, and Roger Hilsman, and apparently seems to many to be a distinguishing characteristic of pluralist politics.[7] The following passage from the concluding section of Berliner's book expresses ideas similar to those of Lindblom in "The Science of 'Muddling Through'" and subsequent works:

The bounds [on local managerial field administrators' power] are established, in the first place, by the system of planning. Each new set of plans is not drawn up *ab ovo* but takes as its point of departure the actual production results of the preceding period. This procedure immediately establishes a *benchmark* from which the state can gauge production possibilities for the next period. Rarely can a ministry persuade the State Economic Committee to give it a smaller production plan than its actual production in the preceding period. *The bargaining usually centers about the extent to which the new plan is to be increased.* . . . Similar considerations apply to the planning of procurement, finance, labor productivity, and other items. In fulfilling the current plan the manager shows his hand, as it were, and thus limits his own freedom of operation in the drafting of the next period's plan.[8] [Emphasis added.]

In Lindblom's terms, Soviet planning and policy making is not "synoptic," nor does it follow "root" calculations that comprehensively relate means to ends.[9] Instead, Soviet industrial policy making exhibits partisan mutual adjustment around marginal, incremental changes from the "benchmark" set by the preexisting policy base.

Furthermore, Soviet industrial policy making exhibits the "remedial" and "serial" characteristics described by Lindblom: "The practices [by which local managerial field administrators elude central control] are limited, in the second place, by the existence of the agencies of control. Those which have a stake in the success of the enterprise are willing to 'look the other way' only as long as the transgressions of managers are within what are considered to be reasonable limits."[10] Thus the central control agencies may be said to exercise control over the local field administrators (or industrial managers) *remedially*, that is, when the field administrators transgress the reasonable limits of eluding central authority. Central control is remedial in that it is *not* fully exercised as long as the local field administrators (industrial managers) stay within ordinary bounds of administrative behavior. However, this generalization does not hold in the event of a special campaign (usually not sustained for long) against some particular malpractice or some particular industrial sector. Central control may also be serial; i.e., problems will be remedied in order of occurrence or in order of importance, step by step in a sort of series.

Thus we see that serial, remedial use of cognitive capacity (the ability to comprehend) and other power resources is a practice of totalitarian administration as well as of our own. Indeed, Soviet administrative behavior would probably exhibit budgeting strategies similar to those found by Wildavsky in American national administration, since many such strategies are based on bargaining over marginal changes in policy and the exercise of serial, remedial control by congressional appropriations subcommittees and agency chiefs.[11] Hence, it seems useful to compare the central process of Soviet administrative policy making, the derivation of production plans, with the central process of American administrative policy making, the derivation of the budget. There is much in common between the Soviet planning process and the American national budgeting process, and sometimes "a budget may be called a plan":

In the most general definition, budgeting is concerned with the translation of financial resources into human purposes. A budget, therefore, may be characterized as a series of goals with price tags attached. Since funds are limited and have to be divided one way or another, the budget becomes a mechanism for making choices among alternative expenditures. When the choices are coordinated so as to achieve desired goals, a budget may be called a plan.[12]

Certainly, a Soviet plan exhibits all these characteristics of an American governmental budget. Superficial similarity between the politics of Soviet planning and American budgeting may be seen in passages such as the following, from Berliner: "It is clear from the interviews that the output plan [for the local industrial firm] depends in large measure upon what the enterprise has been able to bargain out of 'Moscow,' the supply of materials hinges upon how much can be haggled out of the functionary in the State Economic Committee. . . . The cultivation of good relations is a prime principle of plant management."[13] Similar propositions hold for American administrative hierarchy: bargaining and negotiation concerning criteria of satisfactory performance occur on all levels; money must be haggled out of congressional Appropriations Committee members, the Bureau of the Budget, and administrative superiors; the cultivation of "good relations" or "confidence" is of the highest importance.[14] The following extensive quotation from Merle Fainsod's *How Russia Is Ruled*, probably the most respected book on Soviet government, could be restated in propositional form and applied to American national administrative politics and to the national budgetary process:

The success of the bureaucracy is judged by its ability to meet the demands made on it. Since the demands are great and the resources available to meet them are ordinarily limited, each sector of the bureaucracy is driven to fight for a plan which it can carry out and for an allocation of resources which will enable it to discharge its obligations. This struggle is in essence political. Although it is broadly contained within the framework of the ruling priorities of the leadership, there is still considerable room for maneuver. . . . Indeed the planning bodies are [the budgeting process is] a focal point around which the battle for special treatment rages. The battle is waged by negotiation, by personal influence, and by invoking the assistance of the powerful. . . . Bureaucratic representation in the Soviet [American] context expresses itself in a struggle for preferential advantage. Because each part of the bureaucracy operates with an eye to the feasibility of the demands which are made on it, it becomes an unwitting spokesman for the claims of that sector of Soviet [American] life for which it is responsible.[15]

Because a pluralist power structure is a complex power structure, one may easily show that Soviet industrial administration is pluralist. First, there are obviously many actors with significant power. (For some purposes, one might substitute the analytic category "roles" for the concrete category "actors.") Thus Fainsod stated, in the above quotation: "*each sector of the bureaucracy* is driven to fight for a plan which it can carry out and for an allocation of resources which will enable it to discharge its obligations."[16] (Emphasis added.) In other words, Fainsod finds that numerous, diverse actors have significant power over administrative policy. This is the first element of complexity-pluralism.

Certainly Berliner finds that numerous, diverse actors have "significant" power over Soviet industrial policies. For instance, he depicts the manager of the industrial firm (field administrator) as the builder and leader of a political-economic coalition. In addition to the local manager, other figures prominent in the politics of such field administration include: the local Party committee, middle-level ministry officials, the Party secretary in the plant, inspectors and auditors from the State Bank and from Gosplan, tax collectors from the Ministry of Finance, secret police officials, the management's *tolkachi*, local bankers, plant union leaders (who could report damaging information), and others.[17]

The second element of complexity-pluralism is the amount of interdependence among the variables (actors or roles). And again, Berliner's findings on Soviet industrial administration reflect this second element of pluralism. As I noted, the industrial manager may be viewed as the builder and leader of a political-economic coalition to protect the interests of the local firm (field office).[18] An important type of Soviet administrative political coalition is the "family circle," a concept becoming rather well-known to political scientists. The family circle is a coalition of local administrative interests seeking to conceal information from central control interests.[19] This coalition often includes many of the field men of the control agencies themselves—such as the plant Party secretary, regional ministry officials, and others who have a role conflict between controlling the local firm and at the same time helping it *appear* to be successful.[20]

The phenomenon of family circles brings up again the proper interpretation of differences between Soviet and American administration, for the family circle is a local administrative interest group of the type presumably flourishing in American "pluralist" administration. As Kenneth Jowitt has noted: "Such behavior is not limited to the Soviet Union. Any bureaucratic polity is characterized by such phenomena as 'families.' "[21] He then points out that family-circle and similar behavior is chronicled in Kautilya's *Arthasastra*, a work on an Indian empire of the fourth century B.C.: "One is able to read in Kautilya's *Arthasastra* how administrative personnel 'when in concert . . . eat up the revenue, when in disunion . . . mar the work.' . . . One finds mention of forty ways that agencies and personnel embezzle the state by falsifying accounts, juggling figures, etc. There is the same demand to circulate personnel, establish overlapping controls and check on the existence of 'families.' "[22] Thus, there seems to have been a certain amount of pluralism within the administration of an ancient Indian empire! (At least to the extent that widespread clique behavior checks the power of the administrative center.) In general, then, Berliner, Granick, Fainsod, and others find much more complexity in the relationships between Soviet administrative personnel than is described in formal organization tables. Instead of a neat, simple-systemic, centralized set of relationships, with lines flowing from superior to subordinate in one-way independent-to-dependent-variable fashion, we are left with a confusing, complex-systemic, decentralized set of relationships, with many more significant relationships than those denoted by the pyramidal pattern of the table of organization.

The reciprocal interaction between variables is an especially important element of complexity-pluralism. Certainly, one of the most important findings in the literature on Soviet administration is the demonstration of reciprocal interaction between superior and subordinate, in contrast to the one-way action of the independent and dependent variables pyramidally arranged in the formal organizational image. Berliner's findings of the local firms' counteractivity to central control (supposedly an independent variable) demonstrate such reciprocal interaction. In addition, Berliner's and Fainsod's references to bargaining between administrative levels are references to reciprocal interaction, in contrast to simple, one-way action.

Thus one can demonstrate a high degree of interdependence among the component variables (actors, roles) of Soviet industrial administration and hence a similar degree of complexity-pluralism.

The third element of my definition of complexity is the amount of variation of relationships over time. In this respect, Fainsod's and Berliner's descriptions of Soviet industrial administration depict an image of administrative coalitions, *blat* ("pull"),[23] and personal relationships far more unstable and fluctuating than the relatively permanent, pyramidal relationships suggested by the formal table of organization. Such informal coalitions and personal relationships are inherently unstable as personnel are shifted and as the organizational environment changes. Relationships vary with such factors as remedial clamp-downs by control agencies, All-Union campaigns concerning particular errors or directed against particular agencies, and the occasional appearance of conscientious industrial managers and factory Party chiefs who break up family circles and *blat* because of their rigorous adherence to Leninism. In addition, relationships vary with the fluctuating activities of the influence brokers, the *tolkachi*. Thus, from one perspective, the relationships between the component variables in Soviet industrial administration are seen to be constantly changing—thus the third element in my definition of complexity-pluralism is reflected in Soviet industrial administration. (From another perspective, however, these relationships could seem to be relatively stable. If one aggregated the activities of *tolkachi*, for example, and measured them with certain indices, such indices could show a stable pattern. Yet one could predict the activities of a single *tolkach* only on a probabilistic basis. In addition, from the perspective of a single point in the administrative system, the activities of *tolkachi* might seem to fluctuate greatly because of the circulation of managerial personnel, the announcement of All-Union campaigns, etc. Nevertheless, from the standpoint of the total administrative system, the indices measuring the aggregate activity of *tolkachi* might exhibit stability.)

In summary, we see that one can describe Soviet industrial administration as pluralistic, decentralized, characterized by fragmented causation—as a complex system, necessarily described by complex hypotheses. But an equation of American administrative pluralism and Soviet administrative pluralism would strike most observers as erroneous. Most would agree that an analysis of the Soviet system as pluralist is a case of spurious complexity, spurious pluralism, spurious decentralization. Presenting such a pluralist analysis of Soviet industrial administration, therefore, reinforces the idea that one can analyze any social system as pluralist (complex). The case of Soviet industrial administration also supports the contention that there is a need to differentiate forms of pluralism (i.e., differentiate types of complex political systems), since the term "pluralism" now covers a wide range of possible political systems. We would like to make additional distinctions beyond the tripartite categories: power elite, absolute equality, pluralism.[24] For example, it seems unreasonable to assert that Soviet administration is pluralistic, that it exhibits fragmented power, just because it does not resemble a power-elite system as closely as had formerly been assumed.

Instead of using Soviet industrial administration as a case of spurious pluralism, perhaps one could use Soviet politics as a whole. Especially in the post-Stalin era, one could identify a considerable number of competing groups and persons, each with significant power over policy, but the power of each potentially could be dwarfed by a dominant leader such as Khrushchev. No doubt one could find numerous relationships among the political actors, and considerable change of such relationships over time. A Dahl decision-making study might reveal considerable "pluralism" or "decentralization" in many issue areas, as in the formulation of overall military strategy (which might be as decentralized as in the United States), or in the specification of educational policies. (Since Khrushchev was a particularly dominant figure in most significant issue areas, such areas as defense and education are probably more "pluralist" and "decentralized" in the present Kosygin-Brezhnev era.)

Indeed, one can conceive of a pluralist analysis of the Communist Party itself, as is suggested by the following quotation from Fainsod: "The informal organization of the Party probably approximates a constellation of power centers, some of greater and some of lesser magnitude and each with its accompanying entourage of satellites with fields of influence extending through the Party, police, the administrative and military hierarchies."[25] This is equivalent to saying that the C.P.S.U. is a pluralist organization. Thus Fainsod is asserting that if one goes beyond formal description, "the informal organization" (i.e., informal power structure) of the Party probably approximates *a constellation of power centers*; in other words, he suggests that there are numerous centers of power, or that power is decentralized.[26] One could also say of the notoriously fragmented, decentralized American national political party that "the informal organization of the Party probably approximates a constellation of power centers, some of greater and some of lesser magnitude and each with its accompanying entourage of satellites with fields of influence." (The Soviet institutions listed are not appropriate, however.)

My contention that pluralism can be found in almost any system, depending on the perspective of the observer, should by now be clear. Soviet politics provides an excellent illustration of the problem of spurious pluralism, showing that there is a need to refine the empirical pluralist theory predominating among political scientists studying American politics.

THE U.S. FOREST SERVICE

Studies of Soviet industrial administration have shown that the formal organizational image of centralization is an over-simplification. Pluralism and complexity may be found, although the theoretical question of spurious pluralism remains. Study of the U.S. Forest Service, on the other hand, has shown that the formal organizational image of great *de*centralization is an exaggeration. Rather disparate students of public administration—Herbert Kaufman, Luther Gulick, James Fesler, and Ashley Schiff—have all agreed that the Forest Service is a case of "illusory decentralization" (in Fesler's terms), and hence, according to my analysis, illusory complexity and illusory pluralism.[27] In contrast to Soviet industrial administration, which turned out to be more decentralized than expected, the U.S. Forest Service turns out to be more centralized than a table of organization would imply.

The following quotations from Kaufman's *The Forest Ranger* illustrate the formal organizational complexity of the Forest Service.*

The Chief constitutes the apex of a traditional administrative pyramid—or, perhaps more accurately, what amounts to two pyramids. One is organized for the administration of the national forests and co-operation with the states, local governments, and private forest owners; it consists of ten regional foresters, 124 forest supervisors (who manage a total of 149 national forests, some of which are combined for administrative purposes), and 792 district rangers. The other is organized for research, and is made up of nine directors of experiment stations, 51 research centers under them, 102 experimental forests and 14 experimental ranges, and three special units.[28]

Each of the regional foresters is responsible for all the functions of the Forest Service, except research, within his own region. At

---

* It is of interest to note in passing that, according to Kaufman, the expenditures of the Service in 1956 were $128 million and receipts totaled a business-like $137 million. Kaufman, *The Forest Ranger*, Baltimore: Johns Hopkins Press, 1960, p. 30.

the regional level, these are defined in the agency as: timber management, fire control, range and wildlife management, recreation and lands uses (including land acquisition and watershed management), engineering (construction planning and execution), operation (administrative management), personnel management, information and education, state and private forestry, and fiscal control. Each of the functions is under an assistant regional forester.[29]

It takes some 11,000 full-time, permanent employees—almost half of whom are professionals, most of them foresters, many of them specialized technicians—as well as a temporary force of up to 16,000 seasonal and part-time employees to man this organization. Dispersed as they are, holding them on a common course of policy would be a managerial challenge even if they were all doing identical work. Functional and territorial specialization, as well as status differences, tend to heighten the challenge. . . . What makes it [management] even more of a trial, however, is that so much of the work by which the objectives of national forest administration are accomplished depends heavily on the Rangers.[30]

Thus the Forest Service, in 1956, had 792 branches, with a manager responsible for the activity at each branch, which in itself tended to encompass the entire scope of Service functions. Thus, in structure, the Forest Service resembles a large chain-store operation, except that the activities of the local managers are much more varied. (Instead of selling the same products to different customers, the Ranger must solve problems unique to his district, e.g., which trees to cut, which kinds of recreation to encourage.)

However, as Fesler notes: "In some circumstances even the substantial delegation of decision-making power may have some element of illusion."[31] Such is the case with the U.S. Forest Service, Fesler notes, which is "a more telling instance" of "the phenomenon of illusory decentralization" than federal grants-in-aid to the states, which are hemmed in by numerous detailed restrictions.[32] Fesler states that the U.S. Forest Service is "generally regarded as highly decentralized" but is "interpreted by Herbert Kaufman as a case of illusory decentralization. . . . The forest rangers in the field, goes his [Kaufman's] argument, have been so well-trained in the forestry schools of the country and in the Forest Service itself that their decisions, apparently freely made, are substantially pre-dictable, uniform, and nicely *conformable to the headquar-ters doctrine.*"[33] (Emphasis added.) Thus the Rangers seem to possess a wide latitude of decision-making authority, but they actually make similar decisions because they all believe the same doctrine, which tells them what to do.

Or, as Luther Gulick noted in 1951, "The degree of decen-tralization which has been achieved in the U.S. Forest Service has been greatly affected by the personnel employed in the Forest Service. Maintenance of uniformity in the field in spite of decentralization rests fully as much on the uniformity of professional training and doctrines as upon the administrative techniques and supervisory red tape. *This raises a point of great significance for administrative theory.*"[34] (Emphasis added.) Gulick also notes that "there are few major differ-ences of opinion as to what has to be done, or how to do it, among men who have been trained in the same schools, *brought up on the same philosophy,* and are working for the same great purposes."[35]

Gulick makes another interesting argument: "The perfor-mance standards, developed and used in the daily work of for-esters throughout the U.S. Forest Service, are more compre-hensive and specific than any set of administrative standards we have encountered in any other area of public administra-tion."[36] For example, Kaufman mentions that the Rangers have a "bible"—the *Forest Service Manual*—"which incorpo-rates, explicates, and interprets the relevant legal documents applicable to the agency, and which contains also additional provisions promulgated by the Washington office under the authorizations in those documents."[37]

Four of the seven volumes . . . are issued to Rangers. . . . They run to more than 3,000 pages, and *it is difficult to think of anything likely to happen on a Ranger district that will not fall fairly un-equivocally into one or another of the hundreds of categories* cata-logued in this *Manual*; indeed, only a fraction of the *Manual* covers most of the recurrent problems of the average district, the remain-ing provisions applying to events that are not ordinary occurrences anywhere, but which may conceivably come up, or may in fact have already developed here or there.[38] [Emphasis added.]

Perhaps Gulick is wrong in his impressionistic observation that the Service's performance standards are the most detailed of any observed public agency, but Kaufman also provides considerable evidence of such detail. Nevertheless, Gulick, Kaufman, Fesler, and Schiff continue to stress the importance of professional values (doctrine) in unifying the service. Gulick states: "While these procedures [performance standards] have had their supervisory and coordinating effect within the U.S. Forest Service, and to a lesser extent in the forestry work of the states, their total impact is secondary to the coordinative effect of the ideas and standards developed and maintained through the profession."[39] This passage is cited by Schiff with approval; he proceeds to cite Kaufman's unpublished dissertation concerning the surveying activities in a George Washington National Forest ranger district.

Though one type of organization may manipulate the thinking and values of its members while the other directly controls their behavior by orders, both types succeed in obtaining the kind of administrative decisions and behavior they desire; one just as certainly as the other molds the actions of its members. The Forest Service has succeeded ... in putting inside the Ranger a predisposition to act in an organizationally prescribed pattern under certain circumstances. ... With respect to purpose and action, the Forest Service is, to all intents, a centralized organization.[40]

Schiff maintains: "Although foresters have always regarded grass-roots management as the touchstone of democratic administration, the Service was, in actuality, a centralized organization by virtue of the 'unified philosophy' which guided a decentralized decision-making process." He comments that this " 'unity of education and doctrine' constituting the 'dominant central idea' of Service administration made decentralization possible."[41]

Thus, Kaufman, Gulick, Fesler, and Schiff agree that: (1) even though the Forest Service (in 1956) is divided into 792 separate units, which undertake the organization's substantive tasks, the Service cannot be described as "decentralized"; (2) even though the Washington office issues an extraordinary number of procedural standards, these rules are less im-

portant than Service doctrine and professional values;* (3)
an important theoretical issue is introduced when the distribution of power within the Service is described. On this third
point, we have already noted that Gulick regarded the importance of doctrines vis-à-vis explicit regulation "a point of
great significance for administrative theory."[42] Kaufman
wrote that: "This ambiguity [internalized doctrine versus explicit regulation] beclouds one of the great issues of administration: the nature of centralization and decentralization."[43]
Schiff cites both these writers on this point; Fesler expands
Kaufman's observation in his article "Approaches to the Understanding of Decentralization," in which he discusses the
Forest Service under the category of "illusory decentralization."

It is clear that if we analyzed Soviet industrial administration further, we could observe a pattern similar to that
described by analysts of the Forest Service. We could observe illusory decentralization (hence illusory complexity and
illusory pluralism), a huge amount of detailed formal-legal
regulation from the administrative center, and finally, a different type of centralization achieved through "unity of education and doctrine" and the "unified philosophy" (in Schiff's
terms) imposed by the Communist Party. (Yet one could
analyze even the Party as pluralist, Fainsod implies.)

If we had used Dahl's empirical decision-making analysis,
we might have found considerable pluralism, complexity, and
decentralization within both organizations.[44] Thus we might
have observed the manager of the Soviet firm successfully
concluding certain policy initiatives (e.g., on disagreements
concerning quotas), or local family-circle coalitions modifying the policies of the central administration by strategically
concealing information, as is done in the U.S. budgeting process. Strangely, perhaps, the U.S. Forest Service could easily
seem more centralized than Soviet industrial management if

---

* Kaufman does not definitely state that doctrine is more important than
explicit regulation, but he seems to favor this position, and he urges in the
concluding chapter of *The Forest Ranger* that an empirical study be made to
test the relative importance of explicit regulation and internalized doctrines
in the Rangers' decision making.

we used Dahl's mode of analysis, for presumably we would observe the Rangers carrying out many decisions in the manner stipulated by their centrally issued rulebook. Nevertheless, presumably the numerous rules sometimes conflict; Kaufman gives the impression that in such cases the local Ranger would usually successfully conclude his policy initiative without significant modification or vetoing from the center. Moreover, in the writings on the Forest Service there seems to be a contradiction between the role of the numerous procedural regulations and the overt decentralization of the organization. Thus, even though Gulick states that the Service's performance standards "are more comprehensive and specific than any set of administrative standards we have encountered in any other area of public administration,"[45] he also states in another passage:

The U.S. Forest Service has gone a considerable distance in placing administrative responsibility for the management of the national forests in the hands of its own regional and local foresters. ... There is, however, considerably more decentralized authority within the U.S. Forest Service than there is in the localized administrations of the Department of the Army, the Postal Service, the Bureau of Internal Revenue, or the Veterans' Administration, to cite a few examples. The only localized federal services which actually assign a comparable measure of authority out of Washington and to their decentralized offices would seem to be military activities abroad in time of war [united by doctrinal unity?] and some parts of the National Park and Soil Conservation Services.[46]

Kaufman makes similar points. For instance, he writes:

[Leaders] must accept their heavy dependence on their field officers. The substantive content of the agency program is shaped by what the men in the woods do from day to day. Not only does the conduct of each function reflect the field men's interpretations of their jobs, but the balance among functions grows out of their activities and decisions. By emphasizing one function over others, by aggressiveness or passivity, by inventiveness or adherence to the status quo, by risking the displeasure of superiors or colleagues or neighbors or by following the path of least resistance, by enthusiastic or indifferent or reluctant performance, *the Rangers in effect*

modify and even make policy—sometimes without knowing it. . . .
These factors provide strong thrusts toward disunity [i.e., extreme
decentralization].[47] [Emphasis added.]

Neither Kaufman nor Gulick clearly specifies the actual role of
the detailed, explicit procedural regulations vis-à-vis the evidently wide range of discretion of the local Ranger. In addition, Kaufman states that local Rangers modify and make policy, and hence could be viewed as having significant power in
Dahl's terms. As a matter of fact, the Service would be more
decentralized than New Haven if each of the local Rangers
had significant power over policy.

Hence, using either my complexity-pluralist analysis or
Dahl's decision-making analysis (which reduce to the same
thing), both Soviet industrial administration and the U.S.
Forest Service would be pluralist, decentralized, complex systemic organizations. Indeed, the Forest Service would be a
paragon of pluralism, with 792 actors having significant
power, in addition to the central administration and regional
officials. But if Soviet administration is pluralist, then our conception of "pluralism" is too general to be useful, unless our
ideas concerning "unity of education and doctrine" imposed
by the Communist Party are totally incorrect. Moreover, either Kaufman, Fesler, Schiff, and Gulick are wrong in their
description of the U.S. Forest Service, a paragon of pluralism
according to decision-making analysis, or there are flaws in
the theory. I contend that there are flaws in the theory, a point
that I shall expand in the next chapter, following the guide-
lines established by James Fesler and by the Bachrach and
Baratz critique of *Who Governs?* and other pluralist community-power studies.

5. *Critical and Routine Decisions*

In this chapter I continue my analysis of spurious pluralism by referring to the arguments advanced by James Fesler and by Bachrach and Baratz in their article "Two Faces of Power."* Both arguments stress the importance of values as limitations on the emergence of possible political issues. The question of the proper selection of issues and decisions for the study of political power is also considered; this leads to an emphasis on a critical-versus-routine-decisions distinction, which especially pertains to the importance of boundary issues, issues that involve changes in values and beliefs that determine the issue scope of politics.

THE TWO FACES OF POWER

As noted above, Fesler regards the U.S. Forest Service as a "telling instance" of "illusory decentralization," citing the findings of Kaufman: "The forest rangers in the field, goes his [Kaufman's] argument, have been so well trained in the forestry schools of the country and in the Forest Service itself that their decisions, apparently freely made, are substantially predictable, uniform, and nicely conformable to the headquarters doctrine."[1] Fesler then comments that the example of the Forest Service "suggests a broader and a more perplexing range of considerations in appraising, and especially comparing, nations' patterns of formal decentralization."[2] I would add that such considerations would apply to the study of decentralization (hence pluralism) not only within and be-

---

* The first face of power is the formation of political issues; the second face of power is the action on issues after they have appeared.

tween nations, but also within and between communities and organizations. Next, Fesler equates this "more perplexing range of considerations" with social and psychological factors that "make even a political approach seem unduly restricted."[3] A reasonable implication of this statement is that empirical political decision-making studies "seem unduly restricted" in the analysis and comparison of decentralization and the distribution of political power in general. Fesler then states that knowledge of how people are taught values seems necessary for comparison of patterns of decentralization, which, in my view, are conceptually identical to patterns of the distribution of political power:

The "preconditioning" of citizens, including local and state officials and national field officers, occurs through children's experience, with family patterns of authority and with groups of childhood friends through the school system's *inculcation of values* and modes of acceptable behavior, and through the lessons inadvertently taught by the nation's communications media. Such preconditioning may build a sense of national or parochial identity, establish habits of conformity or rebellion, foster dependence on authority or harmonious accommodation of a variety of points of view, emphasize reliance on arbitrary use of power or concern for individual and minority interests.[4] [Emphasis added.]

Fesler adds that a national value consensus is conducive to political decentralization, an idea that also applies to organizations and communities.

The building of a national *culture in which certain kinds of action are "unthinkable," or at least would precipitate strong disapproval by one's peers,* helps create a situation in which formal authorization of autonomous behavior creates few risks. Decentralization, therefore, is more compatible with this kind of situation than where the range of autonomous behavior is very broad, including extremes that threaten the values of those responsible for deciding whether to decentralize or not.[5] [Emphasis added.]

This observation certainly applies to the organizational cultures of the Forest Service and Soviet industrial administration. Thus, the Forest Service thoroughly socializes the local ranger with respect to the professional values of forestry institutionalized within this organization. Successful socialization results in a "unity of education and doctrine" and a "unified philosophy," implying that "certain kinds of action are 'unthinkable,'" and creating "a situation in which formal authorization of autonomous behavior creates few risks" from the standpoint of the policy goals of the central administration in Washington. Similarly, the Soviet Communist Party has created "a national culture in which certain kinds of action are 'unthinkable,'" a situation that is conducive to some administrative decentralization; at the same time, however, the goals of a mobilizing society create great production strains, thus limiting the degree of decentralization compatible with the goals of the ruling elite.

Fesler's "illusory decentralization" argument has much in common with the argument about spurious pluralism advanced by Bachrach and Baratz in their article "Two Faces of Power."[6] A critique of illusory decentralization is identical to a critique of spurious pluralism. (More precisely, Bachrach and Baratz do not challenge the findings of the pluralists, but instead contend that the pluralists' findings have insufficient basis. "Let it be understood clearly that in making these points we are not attempting to refute Dahl's contention that the Notables lack power in New Haven. What we *are* saying, however, is that this conclusion is not adequately supported by his analysis of the 'issue areas' of public education and party nominations.")[7]

As noted above, Fesler comments that the example of the Forest Service "suggests a broader and a more perplexing range of considerations in appraising . . . patterns of formal decentralization." He then states: "Social and psychological factors make even a political approach seem unduly restricted [for the study of decentralization]."[8] He then calls for a study of socialization with respect to values and the relating of such considerations to the study of administrative decentralization. Then, Fesler notes that values and value consensus should be related to the question of restriction of issues through consensus (i.e., when "certain kinds of action are 'unthinkable'").[9]

Similarly, Bachrach and Baratz are suggesting that a broader and a more perplexing range of considerations be studied in appraising patterns of decentralization of power, i.e., pluralism. "We contend in this paper that the pluralists themselves have not grasped the whole truth of the matter. . . . Our argument is cast within the frame of our central thesis: that there are two faces of power, neither of which the sociologists see and only one of which the political scientists see."[10] Like Fesler, Bachrach and Baratz think that social and psychological factors must be studied in addition to political factors (such as the empirical analysis of political decisions in the mode of Dahl).

In effect, we contend, the pluralists have made each of these mistakes; that is to say, they have done just that for which Kaufman and Jones so severely taxed Floyd Hunter: they have begun "their structure at the mezzanine without showing us a lobby or foundation," i.e., *they have begun by studying the issues rather than the values and the biases that are built into the political system* and that, for the student of power, give real meaning to those issues which do enter the political arena.[11] [Emphasis added.]

Thus, like Fesler, Bachrach and Baratz point to a study of values as a way to address the problem of spurious pluralism. Similarly, Bachrach and Baratz stress that values and value consensus should be related to the question of the restriction of issues through consensus (i.e., when "certain kinds of action are 'unthinkable'"): "Of course power is exercised when *C* participates in the making of decisions that affect *R*. But power is also exercised when *C* devotes his energies to creating or reinforcing *social and political values and institutional practices that limit the scope of the political process.*"[12] (Emphasis added.) We have seen that there is a general similarity of argument in Fesler's "Approaches to the Understanding of Decentralization" and Bachrach and Baratz's "Two Faces of Power."[13] What does this similarity imply for the study of power?

In the concluding section of their article, Bachrach and Baratz outline five points that may be considered a basis, however sketchy, for a new method of studying political power.

[1] We have contended in this paper that a fresh approach to the study of power is called for, an approach based upon a recognition of the two faces of power [the structuring of issues, conflict over issues when they appear]. Under this approach the researcher

would begin ... by investigating the particular "mobilization of bias" in the institution under scrutiny. Then, having analyzed the dominant values, the myths and the established political procedures and rules of the game,

[2] he would make a careful inquiry into which persons or groups, if any, gain from the existing bias and which, if any, are handicapped by it.

[3] Next, he would investigate the dynamics of *nondecision-making*: that is, he would examine the extent to which and the manner in which the status quo oriented persons and groups influence those community values and those political institutions (as, e.g., the unanimity "rule" of New York City's Board of Estimate) which tend to limit the scope of actual decision-making to "safe" issues.

[4] Finally, using his knowledge of the restrictive face of power as a foundation for analysis and as a standard for distinguishing between "key" and "routine" political decisions, the researcher would, after the manner of the pluralists, analyze participation in decision-making of concrete issues.

[5] We reject in advance as unimpressive the possible criticism that this approach to the study of power is likely to prove fruitless because it goes beyond an investigation of what is objectively measurable. In reacting against the subjective aspects of the sociological model of power, the pluralists have, we believe, made the mistake of discarding "unmeasurable elements" as unreal.[14]

The first point is an injunction to study "mobilization of bias," a term borrowed from Schattschneider, indicating the means by which some "issues are organized into politics while others are organized out."[15] Bachrach and Baratz implicitly equate this concept with "the dominant values, the myths and the established political procedures and rules of the game" in a political system. I consider this point highly useful and will treat it more extensively in the section of this chapter entitled "Values and Issue Scope" and in subsequent portions of this book.

The authors' second point requires considerable discussion, and therefore I will treat it last. Their third point, concerning the investigation of "the dynamics of nondecision-making," asks the researcher to examine the way persons and groups influence values and institutions that restrict the scope of decision making to those issues considered "safe" by status quo oriented actors. This point presents the difficulty of deciding which non-issues might be considered "safe" by partisans of the status quo, when such issues may never appear overtly. Furthermore, "status quo oriented persons and groups," presuming that these can be defined satisfactorily, may not act overtly or consciously in restricting the scope of political issues to those considered "safe." Hence, this third point poses difficult problems for the study of power.

The fourth point concerns decision making in specific issue areas (Dahl's methods), bringing into consideration "key" and "routine" political decisions. The fifth point is an injunction against an overemphasis on empiricism at the expense of significance.

The second point in Bachrach and Baratz's proto-method clearly leads to serious problems. Here the observer is told to decide who gains and who loses from a particular set of values and institutions. Immediately we see that an observer could introduce his own opinions in deciding who gains or loses, since the losers themselves may not be aware of their losses and may rest content, and the winners may not be aware of their gains and may become extremely active in politics (e.g., many American conservatives feel that they are losers even while profits mount). How can we maintain that someone has won or lost in a system if that person himself disagrees? Carefully selected criteria are necessary to identify who wins and who loses in a political system. Such analysis of who benefits from a system is tied to the analysis of nonoccurrences, sometimes termed "non-issues," i.e., activities that do not happen, that are *not* seen as issues by the actors themselves. An oberver may identify a group as the loser in a particular situation, but perhaps the group itself is content and does not try to change the situation. The observer then feels there *should be* an issue involved in the situation, even though there is no activity that would indicate an issue.

We may also consider the term "nonoccurrence," or "non-issue," as a general concept that includes various types of nonactivity. For example, value consensus, definition of the scope of politics, and anticipated reaction are restrictions on events (sources of nonoccurrences) that are particularly important for the analysis of politics. Thus a person may never conceive of a particular desire that is outside the mode of thought of his culture; or having conceived of a desire, the person may not perceive it to be a political demand able to be articulated within the political system; or even seeing a demand as a political one, the person may not act upon it, because he anticipates his own defeat and possible accompanying punishments (the anticipated reaction). If an issue is to appear, it must get past these three limitations on political possibility. Otherwise it may be considered a non-issue.

Treating nonoccurrences poses a very difficult theoretical problem—how can we know which nonoccurrences are the important ones worthy of study? Clearly a huge number of nonoccurrences could be postulated as significant by various observers. A partial solution to this problem may be achieved if the observer (1) explicitly states assumptions concerning all human behavior, or (2) utilizes a comparative method. For example, let us suppose that one observes a polity in which one percent of the population owns 90 percent of the gross wealth, but the poor 99 percent are not trying to take wealth away from the rich stratum. In discussing this situation, one could, with some basis, consider redistribution of wealth a non-issue if one explicitly stated that one assumes that all people wish to increase their supply of economic goods, and will use political or violent means to do so in cases of extreme disparity of wealth. (Alternatively, one might consider this assumption a comparative generalization.) Extreme disparity could be defined according to some disparity in percentages of ownership (e.g., 10 percent owning 90 percent).

Alternatively, one might make direct comparative generalizations. For example, one might generalize that "strong" socialist movements have appeared in all "industrialized" nations since 1900. "Strength" could be defined in terms of voting percentages over some length of time, or some other rough measure of general support. "Industrialized" could be defined in terms of the usual production and consumption indices. Using these criteria, one might then say, with some reasonable basis, that a strong socialist movement is, in the U.S.A., an important nonoccurrence that presumably benefits capitalists, assuming that all men wish to maximize their economic goods. Finally, we should note that such comparative generalizations have this form: System A and system B have everything in common except political phenomenon P and associated factors P_1; therefore P and P_1 are related. Clearly numerous problems arise with this comparative framework. In practically all cases, numerous political phenomena will be different when two or more polities are compared. Consequently, it becomes much more difficult to isolate relationships between a phenomenon and its associated factors. For this reason (and others) the social scientist has difficulty establishing controlled experiments, or alternatively, controlled observations, in order to compare two systems in which everything is the same except for a given phenomenon and its associated phenomena. (Note that it is possible for human behavior to produce spontaneously this situation without any manipulation by an observer.)[16]

Thus we have seen that the second point in Bachrach and Baratz's proto-method, assessing who benefits from the existing bias of a political system, leads to the difficult question of analyzing nonoccurrences, which necessitates the statement of axioms or the use of comparative observations.*

Beyond its criticism of Dahl, Bachrach and Baratz's sketchy methodological outline does not clearly contribute to the theory of political power. However, many ideas may be gained from an analysis and criticism of various portions of the essay. The authors' views concerning the relationships of values, scope of issues, and "key" political decisions can be reworded in the following way:

1. Political values define the scope of issues appearing in the political process.

2. "Key" or important political decisions are those concerning changes of political values and issue scope. (I use the term

---

* At this point we again see a link between the interests of the empirical political scientist and the normative concerns of political philosophers and students of ethics. To discuss who benefits from a system and which are the important nonoccurrences, the criteria of importance can be normative as well as empirical, and thus might be derived from theories of political philosophy and of ethics, as well as from the theories of social scientists.

critical decision, rather than key decision, to refer to important political decisions. My idea of critical decision differs somewhat from Bachrach and Baratz's idea of key decision in that my concept of critical decision can refer to important decisions other than those concerning a change in an issue scope. I use the terms *boundary issues* and *boundary decisions* to refer to possible changes in an issue scope.)

3. In studying political power, emphasis should be placed on values, issue scope, and critical decisions.

These concepts are highly important for understanding the first face of power—the formation of political issues. The second face of power—action on issues after they have appeared —can be treated by Dahl's method.

VALUES AND ISSUE SCOPE

"Value" usually denotes either an appraisal or a prescription.[17] Thus the first meaning of value refers to the goodness or badness of some thing or state of affairs. The second meaning—value as prescription—is a statement of a "should" or an "ought" rather than a statement of an "is." It is this meaning that I am concerned with in this book. In this usage, a value statement is an imperative: "Thou shalt not kill." It is a *generalized,* not a *specific,* imperative—"thou shalt not kill" rather than "thou shalt not kill John Doe." Such a statement delimits boundaries for action, either by positive injunction ("Do this") or by negative prohibition ("Don't do that"). In other words, *a value may be a generalized imperative concerning scope of activity.**

In politics, value as appraisal concerns activities; appraising activities as good or bad amounts to stating an imperative for one's self or for others. Thus, in almost all cases, a value in political science can be stated as a generalized imperative. In other words, a *political* value is a general statement concerning the proper scope of *political* activity. Accordingly, one of Bachrach and Baratz's central points is true, almost by definition, and is also significant; most observers would consider significant those factors delimiting the scope of issues arising in a political process. However, the conceptual and the meth-

---

* *Specific* imperatives are often called "norms" in the sociological literature.

odological implications of relating values to issue scope remain unclear and will be treated subsequently.

Bachrach and Baratz recognize this relation between values and issue scope, although they never develop this point in theoretical terms. Thus we read (with my emphasis) in their article:

But power is also exercised when *C* devotes his energies to creating or reinforcing *social and political values and institutional practices that limit the scope of the political process* to public consideration of only those issues which are comparatively innocuous to *C*.[18]

As is perhaps self-evident, there are similarities in both faces of power. In each, *C* participates in decisions and thereby adversely affects *R*. But there is an important difference between the two; in the one case, *C* openly participates; in the other, he participates only in the sense that he works to sustain *those values and rules of procedure that help him keep certain issues out of the public domain.*[19]

Can the researcher overlook the chance that some person or *association could limit decision-making to relatively noncontroversial matters, by influencing community values and political procedures* and rituals, notwithstanding that there are in the community serious but latent power conflicts?[20]

[The researcher should] examine the extent to which and the manner in which the *status quo* oriented persons and groups influence those community *values and those political institutions . . . which tend to limit the scope of actual decision-making to "safe" issues.*[21]

The last three quotations suggest a state of affairs in which the political sectors consciously attempt to manipulate values for their own benefit. However, one must note that such conscious activity may have less effect than the existence of a value consensus, which no one planned and which is seen as "right," "natural," a "way of life." I think there is a need within current American political science to formulate more explicitly the relationship between value consensus and issue scope. Bachrach and Baratz, unfortunately, do not provide such an explicit treatment.

We should note that these authors place more emphasis on anticipated reactions as a factor limiting issue scope than they do on value consensus, perhaps because political scientists are generally more accustomed to thinking in terms of anticipated reactions. Their example of a professor who did not bring up an issue in a faculty meeting is a case of anticipated reactions—the professor was conscious of an issue but did not bring it up, because he calculated that he would lose.[22] Such an example may be contrasted with an instance of restriction of issues by consensus—a professor would perhaps like to institute an experimentally oriented college (something like the Meiklejohn system) within his multiversity, but the thought never occurred to him because the values of his academic community prohibited such experimentation.

The problems of studying anticipated reactions are well-known, but they are easier to manage than the problems of studying limitation of issue scope through value consensus. For example, the researcher may get some idea of anticipated reactions by careful interviewing or perhaps by immersing himself in political events to the extent that he can almost read the minds of the participants. In an interview, a question such as "Are there any problems in this locality that you feel are not being met?" might be asked. The respondent might mention some that he would not perceive as proper issues for politics; the interviewer could then ask why he thought so. If the respondent mentioned problems that he perceived as political, the interviewer could then ask why the respondent or his friends did not attempt to remedy the problem through politics. A similar technique can be used in questionnaires, as was done by Aaron Wildavsky to study of possibility of nonissues due to widespread lack of political skills.[23]

One step for analyzing the relationship between values and issue scope would be to combine the three-point scale of issue formation with guarded assumptions of what constitutes an "appropriate" nonoccurrence to study. Thus, after explicitly stating his assumptions concerning the nature of man (or human behavior under some particular set of conditions) or using comparative generalizations, the researcher could ask, either by interview or by questionnaire, why particular persons never desired something, or why they never perceived such a desire as subject to political action. Probably such a procedure would be more valuable in interviewing leaders than in interviewing followers, because responses would require considerable participatory experience, as well as imagination and analytical ability.

BOUNDARY ISSUES

To determine political power in the study of politics, one is faced with these alternatives: to study all political issues; to study a random sample of political issues; to study a sample of political issues selected according to some criteria. The first research strategy is a lot of work, although it has been attempted by Aaron Wildavsky and fifty students for the town of Oberlin from November 1957 to June 1961.[24] Such a strategy protects researchers from an obvious criticism of practically any power study: you studied the wrong thing! (This criticism can easily become very subjective: you studied the *wrong* thing.) The second research strategy, random selection, has an obvious flaw: how do you determine the sampling universe to begin with?[25] (All three strategies present the problem of how to decide what is an "issue.") But presuming this sampling universe problem can be solved, most researchers would have to restrain themselves from violating their sample and including political issues that seemed more interesting or significant. Whatever the merit of this research strategy, and it may have more than at first appears, it is subject to all the criticisms that have to do with nonoccurrences. The third research strategy for the study of power is the selection of issues by some criteria. But to decide which criteria necessitates theory.

Bachrach and Baratz criticize Dahl too harshly for his selection of issues, I think. Dahl's justifications for selecting the issues of political nominations, education (importance of children, amount of money expended), and urban renewal (the most famous such program of any in the small cities of the United States) are quite convincing.[26] One might wish he had included taxation and welfare, but even without discussion of these issues Dahl produced in *Who Governs?* one of the most useful works ever written by a political scientist. Furthermore, it is not difficult to formulate more rigorous criteria for issue selection from a perspective similar to Dahl's. For example, Nelson Polsby has written:

We can, I think, in principle rank decisions according to their importance by making use of one or another, or a combination, of at least four criteria:

1. How many *people* are affected by outcomes,
2. How many different *kinds of community resources* are distributed by outcomes,
3. How much in *amount of resources* are distributed by outcomes,
4. How drastically present community *resource distributions* are altered by outcomes.[27]

Switching the focus from "outcome" to "issue," we can use the four criteria of number of people affected, number of different types of resources affected, amount of resources distributed, and extent of redistribution of resources. (The last criterion suggests that a political issue involving $100 million would be more important in Honduras than in the U.S.A.)

Polsby's four criteria are observer oriented: they do not depend on the perceptions of the actors. At least four other criteria for selecting important issues, which do focus on the perceptions of the actors, are: (1) the number of people actually engaged in the political issue; (2) the amount of money, time, and other resources engaged in the issue; (3) other measures of the intensity of conflict, particularly violence or near violence;[28] (4) whether or not the issue involves possible changes in the procedural rules of the game. I shall refer to these four criteria as the "activity criteria" for the selection of issues. It should be noted that, to some extent, the sets of important issues indicated by Polsby's four criteria and by the activity criteria would not overlap. For example, Congress's grant of alternate sections of land along the projected roadways of the Union Pacific, Great Northern, and other railroads, would rank fairly high according to Polsby's criteria, but rather low according to the activity criteria. The disparity is especially pronounced in many foreign-policy decisions, such as the actions taken by President Kennedy and his advisers during the Cuban missile crisis, which would rank very high according to Polsby's criteria but very low according to the activity criteria if one measured only within American domestic politics. However, since the two sets of criteria are mutually compatible, they can be combined to yield eight criteria for differentiating important from unimportant issues.

The three issues selected by Dahl in *Who Governs?* would meet these criteria quite well. Political nominations would rank quite high according to Polsby's criteria, as there is much evidence that politicians have power in New Haven, but this issue would rank lower using the activity criteria, unless one extended its scope to cover elections. Education ranks quite high according to both lists. New Haven's urban renewal program would rank quite high on either list, except for being low on intensity of conflict (activity criterion 3) and not involving a change in the rules of the game (activity criterion 4).

It is apparent to me that Dahl, Polsby, Wildavsky, and other pluralists have used these eight criteria to determine important issues. But Bachrach and Baratz, who stress the importance of key decisions, would not be satisfied with these criteria. Some issues, linked to a possible change in issue scope, would rank extremely low according to the activity criteria, although they would be covered by Polsby's more general and (for this reason) probably less useful criteria. As an example, let us imagine a sequence of events that could have happened in numerous Deep Southern communities. Suppose that in 1950, in Smalltown, Alabama, a group of ten-year-old Negro boys chanced to play in the "white only" city park. They are chased out by a cursing town policeman. One of the children relates the incident to his father—Reverend Black, a graduate of Segregated University. Reverend Black is thoroughly incensed by the incident, and begins to wonder why his children cannot play in the park, when he pays taxes as high or higher than most of the whites in town. After all, he muses, the park is so large that children of both races could play there separately. The minister discusses the matter with his deacons, and together they make an appointment to see the mayor. The city official informs the Negroes that their suggestion is impossible, that it would be a threat to racial peace. When his comments are received rather coolly, he becomes vaguely threatening, intimating that "uppity niggers" could lose their jobs. The delegation sadly leaves and decides to give up the project, for the mayor had only grown more hostile when they pointed out that there was enough space for all children to play in the city park. The Negroes agree that they should not bring up such issues for a while. Perhaps the next mayor would be more lenient; perhaps the next sheriff would appoint more understanding deputies.

In this case, one might say that we are discussing one of the key issues in the city of Smalltown for a period of a couple of years. According to the four activity criteria, the importance of the conflict would seem to be low, for few people were directly involved, little time, money, or other resources were engaged in the issue, the actual intensity of conflict was low except for the mayor's anger (although a possibility of intense conflict, including violence, was present), and the issue did not involve changing any political procedures. The issue would rate higher according to Polsby's more general criteria, especially if one included racial pride and dignity as a resource, but this does not seem to help much theoretically. However, according to Bachrach and Baratz's idea of key decisions affecting values and therefore issues, such an incident would have greater importance than it would according to the activity criteria. The Smalltown Park incident directly affected values and beliefs that shaped an issue scope, for the generalized imperative of racism implied that "uppity niggers" must be knocked back into place.

The Smalltown Park incident is presumably the sort of situation that Bachrach and Baratz are referring to in "Two Faces of Power." The activity of Smalltown's mayor fits with such statements as: "any challenge to the predominant values or to the established 'rules of the game' would constitute an 'important' decision; all else, unimportant."[29] It is important to realize that the park incident would rank much lower on the activity criteria than, let us say, a fight over the construction of the local consolidated high school. We can imagine this high-school fight going on for five years, involving the stiff resistance of several local school boards, more tax money than had ever been spent by local government, disputes over the most appropriate location, etc. By the usual activity criteria, then, the local consolidated high-school issue would rank far higher than the park incident. But in a way, the high-school decision seems routine, for after the smoke clears, the style of life presumably will remain relatively unchanged. But the park incident perhaps was the beginning of a challenge to a style of life, as the mayor feared. This example suggests that Bachrach and Baratz make a useful point with their concept of a key decision (boundary decision), involving a change in issue scope.

Therefore, I add the concept of the boundary decision to the other criteria we have listed for determining important issues. However, we must recognize that it is difficult for the observer to determine whether some sequence of events is quietly altering the issue scope of a political system. A boundary decision involves a major change in the nature of politics; it involves the appearance of novel activities that are difficult to foresee. Thus it is much easier to recognize a boundary decision of the past than it is to recognize such events in the present. For instance, at one time I was critical of Dahl for neglecting to discuss de facto housing segregation in *Who Governs?* Even though there might have been little activity in this issue area in the late 1950's, I maintained that a study of housing segregation could have provided some understanding of changes in the nature of politics of New Haven. But after further reflection, I would not charge Dahl with neglect, since almost all political scientists in the late 1950's would have given insufficient treatment to the boundary issue of de facto housing segregation. The importance of such issues is more easily seen in retrospect. Similarly, it is difficult to ascertain the nature of boundary issues and decisions in political communities at the present time. Someone could argue, for example, that the use of force by the police (or by the populace against police) in 1968 is a boundary issue. Or perhaps one might argue that the behavior of militant Negro high-school students is much more important than other political issues. Such incidents might involve a small amount of activity relative to the total context of politics, yet perhaps such events are determining the future issue scope of politics and hence are more important than conventional political events, such as local elections.

There is no sure way to deal with the difficulty of identifying boundary issues and decisions, but the comparative method and general theories of society can be helpful. If some sequence of events unobtrusively altered the issue scope in one political system, we might theorize that similar events would have similar effects in comparable systems. A general theory of society might imply that political rebellion among high-school students indicates a decisive change in political socialization practices, suggesting a change in basic political values.

So far, I have indicated that observers should study boundary decisions and issues that affect possible changes in issue scope, even though such issues may rank below others on the activity criteria for importance. We should also realize that such boundary decisions are linked to the difficult problems of dealing with nonoccurrences. Accordingly, location and study of boundary decisions on certain issues gives some idea of mechanisms restraining similar issues that never appeared. Thus the park incident gives some idea of what would have happened if Negroes had decided to protest segregation of swimming pools, bus service, bus terminals, seating in lunch counters, and voting. (Issues of this sort may be picked through the use of comparative criteria or assumptions about human desires in similar situations.) Studying boundary decisions orients the observer to considering political values and issue scope to a greater extent than if he used standard decision-making methods. Such an approach might help rate reasonably based non-issues according to their challenge to prevailing values and beliefs. For instance, desegregation of a public swimming pool would probably challenge the values of the Smalltown whites more than the proposal to allow Negro children to play in a large park. Although one could not treat them extensively, such quasi-empirical factors would, I think, help give a better description of the distribution of power in a community or larger political system. Furthermore, consideration of quasi-empirical factors might paradoxically aid prediction, an important goal of the scientific method. For example, consideration of the park incident in Smalltown would give us some idea of what would happen ten years later, when Negroes might begin to press for the desegregation of all municipal facilities. In contrast, analysis of the issue of locating a consolidated high school would probably not help us predict events (e.g., desegregation issues) that were to become the center of attention.

This sort of boundary decision is probably what Bachrach and Baratz were referring to in this suggestion for studying political power: The researcher would next "investigate the dynamics of *non-decision-making*; that is, he would examine the extent to which and the manner in which the status quo oriented persons and groups influence those community values and those political institutions . . . which tend to limit the scope of actual decision-making to 'safe' issues."[30]

Thus I would reformulate these authors' method by greatly de-emphasizing the who-benefits factors, and placing more emphasis on values, "beliefs" (cognitive frameworks), and their relation to issue scope through boundary decisions. Such considerations would enrich the methods and theories of Dahl and other pluralists. Regarding the authors' injunction against an excess of empiricism at the expense of significance, I would add that some ideas, whose operational verification is murky, may yield better predictions. For example, the study of boundary decisions concerning desegregation (although sometimes inconsequential according to activity criteria in the late 1940's) and the relation of such decisions to nonoccurrences would have yielded more predictive insight than the study of educational reform (apart from race) or other routine issues. These points might contribute somewhat to the theory of values and their relation to the "two faces of power."

CRITICAL AND ROUTINE DECISIONS RECONSIDERED

We have noted that the catch-all critique of an empirical decision-making analysis of political power is the assertion: "You have studied the wrong issues." Such a criticism, we have also noted, implies criteria for selection of issues. We saw that Polsby provides four such criteria, although these objectively oriented criteria often need additional specificity. In addition, I have listed four activity criteria. From "Two Faces of Power," the concept of boundary decision has been derived; although possibly low on participant-activity criteria, such a decision is significant because it affects the issue scope. However, additional problems remain.

The wrong-issue critique may be restated as the question: Power over what? Critics may charge that a decision-making study errs in focusing on unimportant, routine issues, as Bachrach and Baratz continually emphasize. We must note that such ideas are relevant to the concept of spurious pluralism in general, and to Soviet industrial administration and the U.S. Forest Service in particular.

Why does Fesler view Soviet industrial administration as an instance of "illusory decentralization," hence of spurious pluralism? Fesler writes: The problem of illusory decentralization "is presented when formal powers or administrative arrangements are purportedly decentralist but politically controlled or influenced by the center. This underlies the often skeptical reactions in the West to Soviet and East European decentralization."[31] In other words, Fesler says that decentralization of power is "illusory" when someone else makes the important decisions, i.e., when the supposedly decentralized administrative apparatus is "politically controlled" or "influenced by the center." Or, one could say that the administrators make unimportant, routine decisions, whereas the Party makes the important, critical decisions.[32] Fesler continues: "Local elections in a one-party state, if accompanied by strong hierarchical controls within the party, appear not to afford that freedom of making choices that is the essential ingredient of decentralization."[33] In other words, voters do not possess political power under these circumstances, because the important, critical choices have already been made by the Party. To continue to quote from Fesler: "Similarly, a substantial decentralization of the bureaucratic apparatus, such as that effected by Khrushchev in 1957, may be offset by inclusion of all local-government and administratively decentralized activities in a national economic plan and comprehensive national budget, and by centralization of functions on which decentralized activities must depend (e.g., construction and equipment)."[34] That is to say, the important, critical decisions are made in constructing the national economic plan, the comprehensive national budget, and in allocating crucial resources such as production equipment. The functionaries of the spuriously decentralized bureaucracy, on the other hand, make only unimportant, routine decisions.

Fesler analyzes the problem of illusory decentralization of power with a critical-versus-routine, important-versus-unimportant distinction. He asserts that an actor must have power over an important issue to have significant power. (For example, the local bureaucrats do not have much power if all the critical, important decisions have already been made in the national plan and budget.) Fesler's reply to a pluralist analysis of Soviet industrial administration would be that the local actors make only unimportant, routine decisions. Accordingly, Fesler's critique of spurious pluralism in totalitarian administration is conceptually similar to Bachrach and Baratz's critique of pluralist community-power studies.*

We noted above that basic elements of Lindblom's theories of incrementalism and partisan mutual adjustment (derived from American data) seem to apply to Soviet governmental administration. Berliner's observations indicate that we cannot regard Lindblom's processes as distinctive to democratic government, unless we add further theoretical qualification. I suspect that such qualification must involve another distinction concerning important-versus-unimportant, critical-versus-routine decisions. There is more bargaining by more people over more important, more critical policy decisions in American politics than in Soviet politics. Lindblom's theories are, indeed, extraordinarily useful in counteracting impractically rationalistic ("synoptic") descriptions and prescriptions. Furthermore, he gives us highly important ideas about the operations of decentralized (pluralistic, complex) political and administrative systems. However, if Lindblom's theories are to be useful for comparative purposes, the type of decision must be analyzed, as well as the type of decision-making process.

Now let us return to the study of power in the U.S. Forest

* Bachrach and Baratz state, as I noted, that Dahl's pluralist conclusions could be correct; they do not intend the implication that American society is ruled by power elites or is totalitarian in nature.

Service. Scholars regard this organization as exhibiting spurious pluralism because the 792 local Rangers' decisions are affected by a "unified philosophy," a "unity of education and doctrine" resulting from professional training. In other words, scholars maintain that the important, critical decisions are implicit in the doctrines of the Forest Service, and the local Ranger makes unimportant, routine decisions. Once more we see a conceptual similarity—critiques of pluralism in the Forest Service, in Soviet industrial administration, and in American communities are very similar. All these assertions of spurious pluralism contend that a critical-versus-routine, important-versus-unimportant distinction must be made regarding decisions.

Here we see that Polsby's criteria for distinguishing important issues are more helpful. For example, we see that Soviet national planning and budgetary decisions affect more kinds of resources, distribute a greater amount of resources, and alter resource distributions more drastically than the sum total of the efforts of the local administrators. Furthermore, the Soviet national plan and budget may be said to constitute a critical decision, setting the issue scopes for each local administrator.

Similarly, the ideology of the Forest Service would seem to have greater importance, using Polsby's criteria, than the sum total of the activities of the 792 local Rangers. Or, more clearly, the Forest Service doctrine affects resource allocation within the local Ranger district more importantly than the decisions of the Rangers themselves. Furthermore, from "Two Faces of Power," we see that the professional values of forestry set the issue scopes for the local Rangers, or in Apter's terms, professional values set the *structure* for the local Rangers' *behavior* within that structure.[35] In addition, the Forest Service provides a good illustration of the usefulness of studying boundary decisions and issues. Here, it would seem especially significant to study boundary issues concerning changes in the professional values of forestry. Conventional administrative literature usually omits such discussion. However, Schiff's volume *Fire and Water* is partially concerned with a value conflict between scientific method and a generalized

imperative of the Forest Service: "Never burn over a forest."
The writer shows how the latter value interfered with the
planning and interpretation of certain kinds of research. This
controversy over the merits of burning over certain types of
forest was a boundary issue in the Service. While at one time
it might have ranked low according to activity criteria, this
burn-over issue eventually proved to be highly important in
terms of the Service's activity, for the rigidity of a Service
value led directly to huge forest fires in the Southeast in the
early 1940's.

In addition, we should note that the study of boundary decisions as an example of power is sometimes more productive
than a study using *only* Dahl's decision-making analysis. (A
study should use *both*.) Thus an observer using Dahl's technique, applied to the Forest Service's hierarchy, would find a
certain number of initiations, modifications, and vetoes by
the local Rangers vis-à-vis regional units and the center. He
would probably find numerous instances of local Rangers
initiating policies that met with the approval of their superiors, if they paid much attention at all. In a few cases, regional and central units would veto local Rangers' initiations.
Thus, it seems evident from Kaufman's and from Gulick's
studies that pluralism would be found, using Dahl's techniques. However, the pattern of decision making might be
very different when professional values are undergoing modification, and some understanding of such patterns is at least
as necessary as understanding the patterns of initiation, modification, and vetoing on routine issues.

In general, we see that questionable findings of pluralism
(decentralization, complexity) are met with criticisms involving an important-versus-unimportant, critical-versus-routine
distinction concerning decisions and issues. Specifically, Fesler implicitly uses such criteria in his treatment of illusory
decentralization in the totalitarian state. Analysts of the U.S.
Forest Service implicitly make such a distinction when they
find that the important, critical decisions have been made by
a professional doctrine. Bachrach and Baratz also stress this
critical-versus-routine-decisions distinction in their critique
of pluralist community-power studies.

Such ideas are intimately linked to democratic theory. If we define democracy as the existence of relatively great control over leaders by followers, then of course democracy increases with a "true" increase in the dispersal of power, seen as followers causing intended changes in leaders' behavior. But, as we have seen, discriminating between "true" and spurious dispersal of power implies a theory for determining the salience of issues and decisions. Consequently, democratic theory presupposes a theory of issue salience, a subject that will be discussed in the next chapter in terms of certain game- and set-theory models.

6. The Generality of Decisions

We have noted the need to distinguish between important and unimportant, critical and routine, decisions in the analysis of political power and for the development of democratic theory. Unfortunately, however, this distinction has not received sufficiently coherent treatment in pluralist theory. But there is a place to look for help—the literature of public administration and organization theory. Clearly, the distinction between politics and administration involves some distinction between important and unimportant issues, which is what we are searching for. (I have frequently added an appositional "critical-versus-routine decisions" in the foregoing discussion to suggest the relevance of administrative studies.)[1]

As is well known, Progressive reformers and early students of administration made a definite distinction between politics and administration. In the next generation, numerous students of administration and politics broke down this distinction. As Waldo wrote in 1955: "The rigid, even dogmatic, separation of politics and administration has been almost wholly abandoned during the past fifteen or twenty years [before 1955]. Indeed, it has become correct to regard administration as a process diffused or permeated with politics—meaning by the term both the contest for power (whether or not it is *party* contest) and the making of policy."[2] Nevertheless, if we wish to distinguish the functions of the Secretary of State and the Foreign Service's newest officer, of the president of the multiversity and the foreman of a grounds crew, we must derive some theory to explain these differences between policy (politics) and administration.

Intuitively, we may see that such a policy-administration distinction involves the relative generality or specificity of activities.[3] The Secretary of State makes general decisions; the Foreign Service recruit makes specific decisions; the president of the multiversity makes decisions that are more general than those of a grounds-crew foreman. Intuitively, we identify generality with importance and power. The Secretary of State makes more important decisions and has more power than the Foreign Service recruit; the multiversity president makes more important decisions and has more power than the grounds-crew foreman. Here we see a commonsense relationship between power and decision making on important issues. But this idea needs a better theoretical formulation.

The concept of a decision-making "tree" provides such a formulation, in my opinion. The importance of the concept of a decision-making "tree" has been stressed by Herbert Simon. Discussing his own administrative theory and its relationship to "current developments in formal decision theory" in the introduction to the second edition of *Administrative Behavior,* he notes:

There are at least five separate and distinct concepts, all of them important, built into the structure of the Von Neumann and Morgenstern game theory: (1) The idea of representing possible future behavior as a "tree," with a number of branches radiating from each choice point; so that the individual must select at each such point the appropriate branch to follow. . . . This concept is much older than the modern theory of games, being traceable in publications at least back to 1893. It is intuitively familiar to most chess players and to psychologists who have run rats through mazes.[4]

Simon continues:

If we are to find a "common conceptual roof" under which both economic man and administrative man can live, that roof can include only item (1) of the above list—the "tree" of possible future behaviors. Remarkably enough, this tree provides also the central concept for another theoretical development of the past decade that has attracted wide attention—the theory, owing to Shannon, Wiener and others, of selective information. The Bush-Mosteller learning theories, in turn, make use of this very same notion, probably derived by way of the Shannon theory. The fact that this concept has been seized upon independently in such a variety of contexts to provide a framework for a theory of behavior *suggests that it represents the real core of the new behavioral Zeitgeist.*[5] [Written in 1956. Emphasis added.]

Simon also notes that "this idea of a behavior tree . . . can be traced back convincingly to the early development of Boolean algebra, symbolic logic and set theory."[6] This may be seen in Von Neumann and Morgenstern's *Theory of Games and Economic Behavior,* in which the idea of the tree is presented as a restatement of simple set theory.[7]

Since the behavior tree is a concept from game theory, I refer to a simplified presentation of game theory, Rapoport's *Fights, Games, and Debates,* for an explanation. (See Figure 1.)[8]

In the terminology of decision making, the tree's node indicates a point of decision. (One might say that a decision is the choice of a move.) Furthermore, we see that the branches represent alternative activities, with payoffs associated with the outcomes of the various activities.

Another of Rapoport's tree diagrams indicates how somewhat more mundane human activity can be represented. Although the following example is from Shakespeare, we can easily imagine similar diagrammatic trees representing crises in international politics, the derivation of governmental budgets, simulation of production quotas, and practically any other form of human activity. (See Figure 2.) For example, the flow-chart models of business decisions in *A Behavioral Theory of the Firm* can be represented in the tree form. The flow charts for decision making in Figures 3 and 4 have the same basic form as the game tree, with the boxed decision premises taking the place of nodes.[9]

At this point, one can see that a decision (choice of move, node) is the selection of a set of possible future decisions, alternatives, and outcomes, and is the exclusion of other such possible future activities. Thus, if we designated the set of possible future activities at decision point D as S, then selection of an alternative at D implies the division of S into a

THE MEANING OF STRATEGY

LET US INVENT A GAME so simple that it can be analyzed in its entirety. Suppose there are just three moves. On the first move, the first player A has two choices: he may say "1" or "2." On the second move, the second player B has three choices: "1," "2," or "3." On the third move, A has again two choices, "1" or "2." It follows that the whole game can be played in just 12 different ways: $2 \times 3 \times 2 = 12$. To each of these 12 ways we will assign a payoff, a certain amount to be paid by B to A, which may also be negative, in which case A actually pays B, or zero.

Now we need a rule for the assignment of payoffs. We shall make this rule somewhat involved, so that it will not appear immediately obvious to either player how best to play. The rule will be the following: If the three numbers chosen by the players on their three moves were x, y, and z, the payoff to A shall be the quantity $[xyz - (x + y + z) + y^2]$, if this quantity is odd; but if it is even, then the payoff to A is the same quantity with its sign changed. Table 2 tells the whole story.

Figure 8 is another representation of the same game. The letters at the nodes of the "game tree" indicate whose move it is. The numbers on the branches are the choices available on that move. The numbers at the end points are the payoffs to A. The payoffs to B are, of course, the same numbers with the opposite sign.

Table 2

x y z	(xyz)	(x + y + z)	$[xyz - (x + y + z) + y^2]$	Payoff to A
1 1 1	1	3	-1	-1
1 2 1	2	4	2	-2
1 3 1	3	5	7	7
1 1 2	2	4	-1	-1
1 2 2	4	5	3	3
1 3 2	6	6	9	9
2 1 1	2	4	-1	-1
2 2 1	4	5	3	3
2 3 1	6	6	9	9
2 1 2	4	5	0	0
2 2 2	8	6	-6	-6
2 3 2	12	7	14	-14

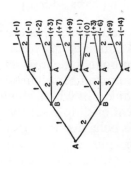

Figure 8. The three-move game in extensive form, showing the game tree. The letters at the nodes indicate whose move it is. The numbers on the branches indicate the choice of move. The numbers in parentheses indicate payoffs to A.

Figure 1

chosen subset S_1 and a complementary unselected subset $(S - S_1)$. In Rapoport's game diagram (Figure 1), if A selects alternative 1, then the top six outcomes are elements of the set of possible outcomes, while the bottom six outcomes are elements of the set of excluded outcomes. (In this case, the values -1 and $+3$ represent an intersection of these two sets. Neither of these outcomes is excluded by A's first choice.) Similar operations may be performed for the flow diagrams of Figures 3 and 4, in which we have a sale price in dollars and cents rather than a payoff expressed in cardinal numbers. Thus, we may conceive of an article of merchandise being "run through" a flow chart as a rat might be run through a maze, or as a token may be run through the game in Figure 1, showing the decision rules of the players. As decision rules are activated at various points of the flow diagram, the set of possible prices for the article running through the decision network is progressively narrowed. (One could imagine short-term fluctuations in the set of possible sale-price outcomes, however.)

Thus we are not surprised to learn that the game tree and set theory are closely linked in *Theory of Games and Economic Behavior*, for indeed the game tree is a graphical representation of a set, its partitions, and subpartitions. In the following reproductions from Von Neumann and Morgenstern's *Theory of Games and Economic Behavior,* we see that set theory (hence the game tree) can be represented also by a certain type of dot diagram. (See Figure 5.)[10]

Now let us return to the previous discussion of politics and administration, important and unimportant decisions. We noted that the politics-administration distinction seems to imply a distinction concerning generality and specificity of activities. But how can we define "generality" and "specificity"? If the reader assumes that such definition is easy, he will perhaps change his mind after shutting his eyes and pondering the matter for ten seconds. Yet, as with "complexity" and "simplicity," "generality" and "specificity" are concepts basic to almost any kind of logical reasoning, including the analysis of power and pluralism.[11]

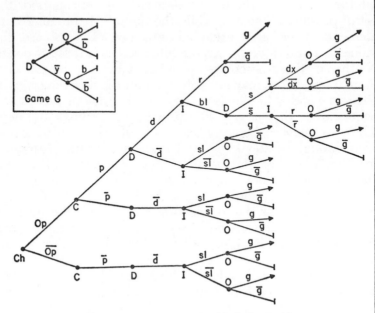

Figure 13. A game tree, as it might be imagined by a "rational" Othello.

The Players

Ch.: Chance	I.: Iago
C.: Cassio	O.: Othello
D.: Desdemona	

The Moves

Op.: Chance gives Cassio an opportunity to attempt to seduce Desdemona.

p: Cassio attempts to seduce Desdemona

d: Desdemona deceives Othello

r: Iago reports Desdemona's infidelity to Othello

bl: Iago blackmails guilty Desdemona

sl: Iago slanders innocent Desdemona

s: Desdemona succumbs to Iago

dx: Iago doublecrosses Desdemona (reports anyway)

g: Othello initiates game G (see inset)

The barred letters are negations of the moves listed above: $\bar{d}$, Desdemona does not deceive Othello, etc.

Figure 2

98

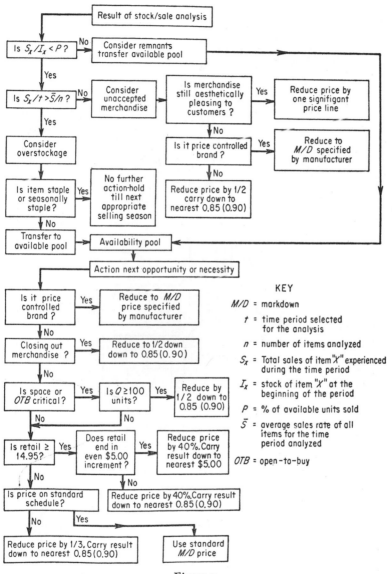

Figure 3

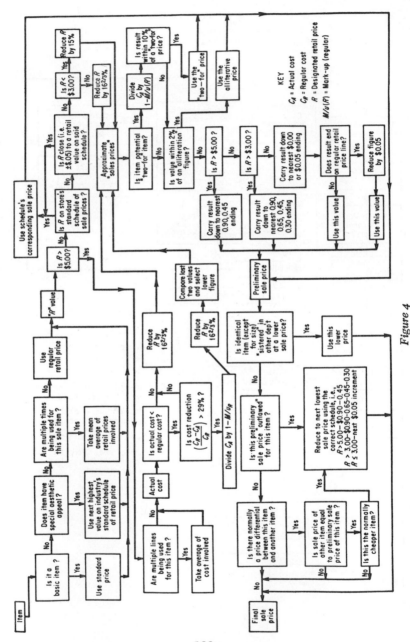

Figure 4

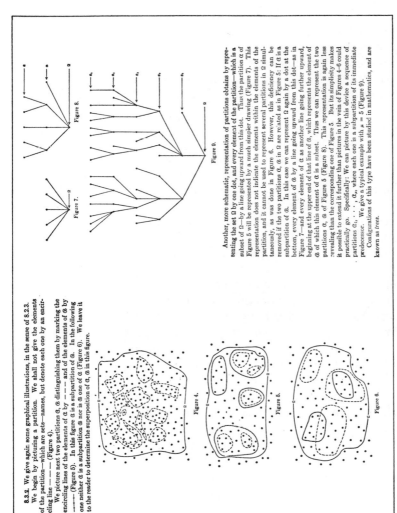

8.3.2. We give again some graphical illustrations, in the sense of 8.2.3.

We begin by picturing a partition. We shall not give the elements of the partition—which are sets—names, but denote each one by an encircling line———(Figure 4).

We picture next two partitions α, β, distinguishing them by marking the encircling lines of the elements of α by — — — and of the elements of β by ——— (Figure 5). In this figure α is a subpartition of β. In the following one neither α is a subpartition β nor is β one of α (Figure 6). We leave it to the reader to determine the superposition of α, β in this figure.

Figure 4.

Figure 5.

Figure 6.

Figure 7.

Figure 8.

Figure 9.

Another, more schematic, representation of partitions obtains by representing the set Ω by one dot, and every element of the partition—which is a subset of Ω—by a line going upward from this dot. Thus the partition α of Figure 5 will be represented by a much simpler drawing (Figure 7). This representation does not indicate the elements within the elements of the partition, and it cannot be used to represent several partitions in Ω simultaneously, as was done in Figure 6. However, this deficiency can be removed if the two partitions α, β in Ω are related as in Figure 5: If α is a subpartition of β. In this case we can represent Ω again by a dot at the bottom, every element of β by a line going upward from this dot—as in Figure 7—and every element of α as another line going further upward, beginning at the upper end of that line of β, which represents the element of β of which this element of α is a subset. Thus we can represent the two partitions α, β of Figure 5 (Figure 8). This representation is again less revealing than the corresponding one of Figure 5. But its simplicity makes it possible to extend it further than pictures in the vein of Figures 4–6 could practically go. Specifically: We can picture by this device a sequence of partitions $\alpha_1, \cdots, \alpha_\mu$, where each one is a subpartition of its immediate predecessor. We give a typical example with $\mu = 5$ (Figure 9).

Configurations of this type have been studied in mathematics, and are known as *trees*.

Figure 5

101

One way to define "generality" and "specificity" is in terms
of sets. If subset S_1 is completely included within set S, then
we can say that S *is more general than* S_1, *and that* S_1 *is more
specific than* S. However, if one element of subset S is *not*
included within superset S, then, strictly speaking, we could
not say that S is a more general set than S_1. As a corollary, my
definition of "generality" is a relative one. Thus, one must ask
"General relative to what?," as one must inquire "Efficient
relative to what?"

We may imagine a *hierarchy of generality as a hierarchy of
sets*. Thus we can postulate a situation in which all the elements of subset S_1 are included within superset S_2, while all
the elements of superset S_2 may be viewed as a subset of superset S_3, and so forth. S_1, S_2, S_3 . . . S_i then represents a progression from specificity to generality, each S_i being more
general than each $S_{(i-1)}$.

Herbert Simon's means-ends chains may be viewed as a
specific type of the hierarchy of generality as a hierarchy of
sets.[12] ("Specific" here indicates that the means-ends concept
is only one of the set of concepts that may be expressed in this
form.) A geologist sets up seismological equipment to sound
for oil; his crew is sounding for oil as part of a natural resources survey; the natural resources survey is part of a program for economic development; this program was established so that a particular political party could maintain itself
in office. Each activity is a means to a more inclusive end,
which is in turn a means to a still more inclusive end. One
may represent this means-ends chain by set theory. Thus,
staying in political office implies a set of activities, one of
which is conducting a program for economic development,
which implies a set of activities, one of which is the particular natural resources survey, and so forth. We may relate the
sets of activities to a concept of generality-specificity. Thus,
staying in office may be viewed as the most general end or
goal because it is the most inclusive set of activities, and so
forth. The means-ends chain, hierarchy of sets, and hierarchy
of generality are illustrated in Figure 6, which also indicates
that the behavior tree is easily related to these concepts.

However, we must realize that a hierarchy of sets, a hierarchy of generality, means-ends chains, and their representa-

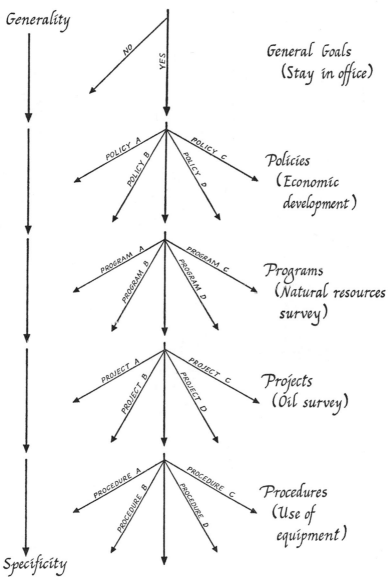

Figure 6

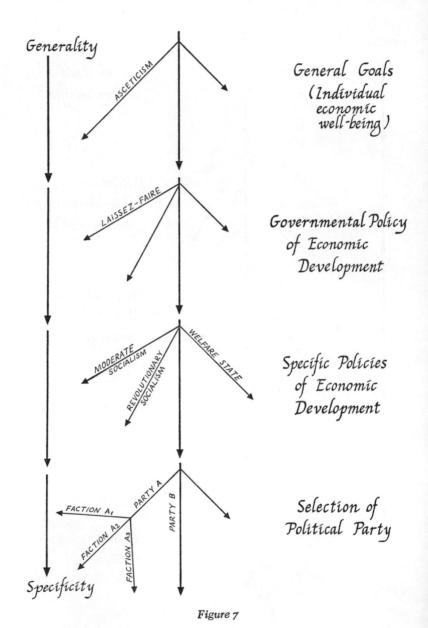

Figure 7

tions are relative to the values of observers. Thus, in the above example, most voters may conceive their own economic well-being as the most general end, implying more specific sets of activities including a national program for economic develop-ment, which in turn implies a set of political policies, which implies that a certain political party should continue in office, and so on. This alternative hierarchy of generalities and sets, of means-ends chains, is represented in the behavior tree of Figure 7. The reader may now catch a glimmer of the relation-ship of the hierarchies of generality and sets, means-ends chains, and the behavior tree to much of what is meant by "values." This relationship will become increasingly apparent.

Simon's position on politics and administration is essentially that less general activities, relatively specific means and ends, are more subject to administrative rationality than more gen-eral activities, relatively general means and ends. Dwight Waldo evolved a similar idea independently of Simon, and ex-presses himself quite lucidly in terms of "a hierarchy of pur-poses" and a "pyramid of values."[13] Waldo states that "the con-cept of *a hierarchy of purposes*" is valuable as a "tool in deal-ing with efficiency."[14] (We may equate "efficiency" with "ad-ministration.") Waldo then develops the concept of a hier-archy of purposes, which is identical to the concept of "means-ends chains" in terms of implicit concepts of a hierarchy of sets as a hierarchy of generalities. He does not recognize this explicitly as do I; hence, he sets off "levels," "lower levels," and "higher levels" with quotation marks. Waldo states that his proposal for dealing with politics and administration in terms of a hierarchy of purposes

can be stated in the form of a series of theses: that efficiency can be measured at various "levels" of human purpose; that on the "lower levels" the purposes of various individuals and groups are much the same, but that there is increasingly important disparity in purposes entertained, values pursued, in the "higher levels"; that the "efficiency" of various instruments and procedures at the lower levels of purpose is likely to be the same or nearly the same for various persons and groups, because the purposes are the same or nearly the same, i.e. the frame of reference is constant; but that in the higher levels of human purpose the "efficiency" of various instruments and procedures tends to differ because the purposes differ significantly—the frame of reference is not constant.[15]

We may suppose that questions of efficiency are inseparably intertwined with questions of administration as opposed to questions of politics. Like Simon, Waldo sees a greater element of efficiency, administration, value agreement, and value specificity at the lower levels of a hierarchy of purposes (means-ends chain) than at the higher levels of such a hierarchy. In my terms, "higher levels" become generality, defined in terms of set theory, whereas "lower levels" refer to specificity, defined in the same way.

Continuing his discussion, Waldo refers to concepts of "unimportant" purposes, as opposed to "higher," "ultimate" purposes.

In practice, the proposed scheme means that the efficiency of various instruments and procedures of a mechanical and routine nature, those that serve "unimportant" purposes *or that serve ends that are important only in terms of other or higher ends,* will be approximately constant in all organizations; but that the less mechanical and routine the instruments and procedures, and the more important *or more nearly ultimate* the purposes they serve, the less likely is their efficiency to be constant. The efficiency of a given typewriter under given operating conditions is the same for all organizations. It is the same for the Eureka Shoe Company as for Field Headquarters of the British Army or for the office staff of the *Daily Worker.* It is the same because the immediate purpose is the same: the production of typewritten words.[16]

Here we note that Waldo identifies questions of administrative efficiency with routine procedures, which are linked to " 'unimportant' purposes." In other words, because routine procedures, routine activities, and *routine issues* are much the same thing, Waldo is saying that administration deals with routine issues. On the other hand, Waldo identifies non-routine issues with "higher ends" and ultimate purposes, which have the properties of importance and generality. We might say that *critical issues and decisions* (i.e., non-routine issues and decisions) are linked with higher ends, ultimate purposes, importance, and generality. Critical issues and decisions, higher ends, ultimate purposes, and generality are represented by the more inclusive sets in a hierarchy of sets or the more inclusive choices in a behavior tree. To most people, as to Waldo, such highly inclusive, general choices are "significant" or *"important."* Furthermore, the meaning of "value" becomes clearer, for most observers would consider a "value" an ultimate purpose, a critical choice. Moreover, the discussions of politics and administration in terms of an elementary set theory and critiques of spurious pluralism are converging, for we see that both involve the concepts of critical and routine decisions and issues.

Waldo suggests in closing "that the notion of a 'pyramid of values' may be of value in evolving a new philosophy of the relationship of the student of administration to his subject matter."[17] He views the pyramid as inverted; the apex is at the lower level, with the base at the highest level. For instance, "as one's frame of reference widens and disagreement about ends becomes important, 'science' and 'objectivity' are more difficult, judgments of 'efficiency' less accurate, more controversial."[18] This may be stated in terms of set theory. First, let us imagine a pyramid that is inverted and balanced on its apex—an image, I must say, which exhibits a certain recalcitrant mischief. If we slice the pyramid with planes perpendicular to the axis from the center of the base to the apex, we derive a succession of triangles. Those triangles sliced from the top are larger than those triangles sliced from the bottom; if we represent a possible decision by a point on a triangle, then the set of possible decisions decreases from base to apex, until we slice down to a single point, the apex. We might call each triangle a "frame of reference" as Waldo does, and thus see what Waldo means by a widening frame of reference in a pyramid of values. Alternatively, we could call each triangle a "range of discretion," as Luther Gulick might,[19] and then we would say that the top slices include a greater range of discretion than the bottom slices, as is clearly indicated by the lowest slice, which takes in only a single point, an image that we can identify with absolute specificity. Clearly, as we slice downward, each set of activities is a superset of a subsequent triangular slice. Thus we see that Waldo's image of an inverted pyramid of values implicitly embodies concepts of a hierarchy of sets and a hierarchy of generality.

Waldo's idea of a pyramid of values, inverted and balanced

on its apex, is not intended to convey an image of invariable predetermination of a specific activity because of the pictorial focus on a single point. Rather, this image conveys the idea of increasing exclusiveness and specificity of decisions and activities, but it does not imply *which* specific activity will result.

As we have noted, Waldo perceives that questions of efficiency and administration become more meaningful as one proceeds to the lower levels of a hierarchy of purposes, or, in other words, questions of efficiency are most relevant when goals are specific. (Simon also takes this point of view, seeing efficiency as most relevant to the more specific levels of the means-ends chains.) Thus we see that the question "Efficient for *what?*" is best answered in terms of some particular goal, especially if it is specific in relation to a hierarchy of sets of activities. (Usually one would say that organizing a secretarial pool is a more specific activity, implying a narrower range of discretion, than building a "Great Society," for example.) Thus we realize that there is much overlap of specific activities among greatly differing types of organizations, and by analogy, among greatly differing political systems. In terms of set theory, we have a considerable degree of intersection among the various sets of activities in the organizations and polities being compared. For instance, the activity of typing is a common element of a shoe company, an army, and a radical newspaper. This indicates the necessity of differentiating organizations and political systems at a more general level than that of the relatively specific, routine activities.

We have already seen an example of such a need for differentiating at the level of general choices. Lindblom's incremental decision making, characterized by partisan mutual adjustment, can be found in both Soviet and American politics and administration. But *it is the more general levels of politics and administration that count.* From available evidence, we can conclude that there is more centralization, more comprehensive rationality, in drawing up the Soviet plans and annual budgets than there is at the equivalent level of American decision making.[20] Furthermore, the American "economic plan" is chosen not just by politicians and governmental executives;

leading corporation executives, financial officials, labor leaders, and even consumers have important roles in deciding the economic future of America too. Moreover, incrementalism and bargaining are important characteristics of such decision making, both inside and outside our government. Yet both tacit bargaining without overt communications[21] (a bane of the trust-buster) and "uncertainty avoidance"[22] reduce the degree of conflict and competition in the formulation of the American "economic plan." In summary, we note that the application of Lindblom's theories illustrates the need to distinguish between degrees of generality in political decisions if we wish to construct a comparative theory.

Selznick's perspective on leadership and administration is congruent with the point of view I am presenting. A basic distinction in his book is the distinction between "critical" and "routine" decisions. Critical decision making is identified with leadership, hence implicitly identified with politics; routine decision making is identified with administration.[23] Selznick's ideas may be expressed in the form of the behavior tree and a hierarchy of sets, as can be understood from the following quotation:

We have suggested that "critical" experience is closely related to organizational self-definition and self-reconstruction. This experience reflects the "open-endedness" of organizational life—the existence of alternative ways of responding and changing. Critical experience calls for leadership. Experience is less critical, and leadership is more dispensable, when the range of alternatives is limited by rigid technical criteria. The more limited and defined the task, the more readily can technical criteria prevail in decision-making. That is one reason why critical experience increases as *we ascend the echelons of administration,* where decisions based on broader interests must be made. But when the organization is not so limited, when it has the leeway to respond in alternative ways, there is room for character-formation, which enters to give structure to precisely this area of freedom.[24] [Emphasis added.]

Thus Selznick links together leadership, critical decisions, higher echelons (levels) of administration, organizational self-definition (character formation), and general, structural decisions. As noted above, such concepts can be related to ideas of generality and importance and represented by a hierarchy of sets or a behavior tree. Inversely, Selznick relates administration, routine decisions, lower echelons (levels) of administration, and limited, clearly defined tasks.

Much of Selznick's thinking in *Leadership in Administration* makes use of the analogy of organizational "character" to psychological character.[25] This analogy seemed inappropriate to me at first, but after reflection I found it useful as an illustration of generality versus specificity. For example, we indicate by a person's "character" his most general decision premises, his most general choices concerning behavior, or something very similar to his "values." In this respect, Selznick cites Erich Fromm for an example of the differences between critical and routine decisions and activities in human psychology: "By static adaptation we mean such an adaptation to patterns as leaves the whole character structure unchanged and implies only the adoption of a new habit. An example of this kind of adaptation is the change from the Chinese habit of eating to the Western habit of using fork and knife. A Chinese coming to America will adapt himself to this new pattern, but this adaptation in itself will have little effect on his personality; it does not arouse new drives or character traits."[26] In this case, a specific activity is changed, but there is little effect on the general structures and choices of personality.

Certain ideas concerning leadership may be represented by the behavior tree. Selznick observes that leaders may make very few critical choices, but that these are crucial for determining policy outcomes. These can be represented by the first few nodes on a behavior tree. (See Figures 1, 2, 5.)

Group leadership is . . . the function of the *leader-statesman*—whether of a nation or a private association—to define the ends of group existence, to design an enterprise distinctively adapted to these ends, and to see that that design becomes a living reality. These tasks are not routine; they call for continuous self-appraisal on the part of the leaders; and they may require only a few critical decisions over a long period of time. "Mere speed, frequency, and vigor in coming to decisions may have little relevance at the top executive level, where a man's basic contribution to the enterprise may turn on his making two or three significant decisions a year."[27] [Emphasis added.]

Note here that Selznick's concept of leadership includes political leadership ("the function of the leader-statesman—
whether of a nation or a private association"). Thus, as stated
above, we can apply Selznick's concepts to a theory of political power as well as to a theory of organizations. We should
also note here that Selznick focuses on key decisions on important issues as central to the understanding of leadership
within organizations. ("These tasks [of leadership] are not
routine; . . . they may require only a few critical decisions over
a long period of time.")

Selznick identifies leadership and critical decisions on important issues with the selection of "values":

> The formation of an institution is marked by the making of value
> commitments, that is, choices which fix the assumptions of policy-
> makers as to the nature of the enterprise—its distinctive aims,
> methods, and role in the community. . . . When such commitments
> are made, the values in question are actually built into the social
> structure. . . . But where leadership is required . . . the problem is
> always *to choose key values and to create a social structure that
> embodies them.* . . . Only after key choices have been made and
> related policies firmly established can criteria of efficient admin-
> istration play a significant role. . . . Leadership creates and molds
> an organization embodying—in thought and feeling and habit—
> the value premises of policy.[28]

Here we see how to map "values" onto the behavior tree and
the hierarchy of sets. Thus Selznick identifies "value commitments" with "choices which fix the assumptions of policy-
makers as to the nature of the enterprise." "Value," as I have
noted, often indicates "a generalized imperative concerning
scope of activity." Selznick's definition and mine amount to
the same thing; both refer to the most general choices in a behavior tree or the most inclusive sets in a hierarchy of sets. In
my definition of "value," the idea of generality must be expressed in terms of a hierarchy of sets. A generalized imperative ("Do this." "Don't do that.") refers to a command regarding a choice, and to be congruent with common usage, this
should be a *general* choice. In addition, Waldo pictures a
value in the same way—as a choice related to ultimate purposes, as a choice at the top level of a hierarchy of purposes or
a means-ends chain. Thus we see that a "value" is a general-

ized imperative concerning the proper scope of action, the most general choice in a hierarchical set of choices, a choice related to ultimate purposes, the basic decisions in a behavior tree. Thus, values embodied in social structure are critical decisions, even though they may not have been made consciously by some group of decision makers.

The behavior tree and the hierarchy of sets have been used to clarify the concepts of generality and specificity, the pyramid of values, the means-ends chain, values, critical-versus-routine decisions, and other associated ideas. In later sections of this chapter, other concepts will be expressed in terms of the behavior tree and the hierarchy of sets. But first some of the limitations of these models for human behavior in politics and administration will be noted.

LIMITATIONS OF THE BEHAVIOR-TREE MODEL

A first limitation of the model is rather obvious—a coherent structure of choices, ranging from ultimate purposes to specific activities, usually does not exist in organizations or in individual psyches. Such coherent structures are often ascertained in situations in which assumptions radically simplify reality (as in game theory), or in which coherent structure is found at the lower (more specific) levels of choice (as in Cyert and March's program for pricing decisions in a department-store sale). Herbert Simon's discussion of structural incoherence in means-ends chains and his version of the behavior tree and the hierarchy of sets are similar to the ideas presented here.

The fact that goals may be dependent for their force on other more distant ends leads to the arrangement of these goals in a hierarchy—each level to be considered as an end relative to the levels below it and as a means relative to the levels above it. Through the hierarchical structure of ends, behavior attains integration and consistency, for each member of a set of behavior alternatives is then weighed in terms of a comprehensive scale of values—the "ultimate" ends.[29]

Simon then comments:

In actual behavior, a high degree of conscious integration is seldom attained. Instead of a single branching hierarchy, the structure of conscious motives is usually a tangled web or, more precisely, a disconnected collection of elements only weakly and incompletely tied together; and the integration of these elements becomes progressively weaker as the higher levels of the hierarchy —the more final ends—are reached.[30]

Thus a coherent behavior tree, an integrated structure of choices, or a simple pattern of overlapping sets is seldom found in organizations, political systems, or personalities. (Simon, like Selznick, uses analogies to personality theory to illustrate the concept of means-ends chains; his concept is much the same as Selznick's image of leadership representing the level of general ends and administration representing the level of specific ends.)[31] Simon gives typical examples of incoherence of choice structure within organizations:

It is also as true of organizational as of individual behavior that the means-end hierarchy is seldom an integrated, completely connected chain. Often the connections between organization activities and ultimate objectives is obscure, or these ultimate objectives are incompletely formulated, or there are internal conflicts and contradictions among the ultimate objectives, or among the means selected to attain them. Thus, decision-making in the Works Projects Administration was complicated by the competing claims of "pump-priming" and immediate relief to the unemployed as agency objectives. In War Production Board decision-making, it was necessary to balance war needs against civilian requirements.

Sometimes the lack of integration in an organization's means-end hierarchy is due to refusal of the policy-making body to decide a "hot" issue of policy—Congress' refusal, for example, to determine for Selective Service the relative weight to be given to family status and occupation in deferments from military service. Sometimes the means-end connections themselves are obscure. For example, to say that it is the objective of an army to defeat the enemy leaves a great deal of room for dispute and inconsistency as to the proper strategies for achieving this end. (The controversy in this country between the "Germany first" and "Japan first" factions comes to mind in this connection.)

Both organizations and individuals, then, fail to attain a complete integration of their behavior through consideration of these means-end relationships. Nevertheless, what remains of rationality in their behavior is precisely the incomplete, and sometimes inconsistent, hierarchy that has just been described.[32]

A second limitation of the behavior-tree and the hierarchy-of-sets models is the overlap of sets of specific activities and specific choices. Waldo noted that typing is much the same in a shoe factory, in an army, or in a radical newspaper. I have stated above that there is much overlap of specific activities among greatly differing types of organizations, and by analogy among greatly differing political systems. Thus, in terms of set theory, we have a considerable degree of intersection among the various sets of activities in the organizations and polities being compared, just as the activity of typing is a common element in the sets of activities organized into a shoe factory, an army, or a propaganda group. Thus it is necessary to differentiate organizations and political systems at a general level rather than at a level of relatively specific, routine activities. Differentiating at the level of general, critical choices enables us to use Lindblom's theories to compare the American and Soviet political and administrative systems, theories which we could not otherwise use for this purpose.

The intersection of specific activities is a limitation on the neat orderly patterns of the behavior tree and the hierarchy of sets. In terms of the tree, we find that originally divergent branches spawn convergent networks at the level of specific choices (e.g. typing). In terms of sets, at a more general level of analysis the characteristics of certain decisions and activities might not overlap, but at the levels of specific choices the amount of intersection can become very considerable. In both the tree and the set models, the intersection of specific activities confuses and complicates the picture, but the overlap problem does not seriously lessen the value of the models.

A third limitation of the behavior-tree and hierarchy-of-sets models is their implication that choices are made sequentially in time, with the most general choice coming first, and less general choices up to the most specific decisions occurring successively. In other words, specificity of decision is implied to be a function of time, with the degree of specificity proportional to the length of time after the first decision. This concept can be represented by the image of a "specificity funnel." Thus, if a right triangle is revolved around an axis containing one of its sides, we could mark off intervals of time on this axis, now the line from the apex of the cone (or funnel) to the center of its circular base. Let us presume that the base is at the left, with the apex at the right. We can mark off time intervals on the axis, with the first intervals in the sequence at the left, and later intervals in the sequence to the right. Now let us suppose that the cone is cut at each time interval with a plane perpendicular to the plane of the axis. The intersecting planes then create a succession of circles of lessening diameter, from left to right, with the diameters inversely proportional to the length of time. Then if the areas of the circles are presumed to represent the generality of decisions (i.e. the set of included activities and choices), we have a picture of a specificity funnel, with the most general decisions coming first and the most specific ones coming last. (See Figure 8.)

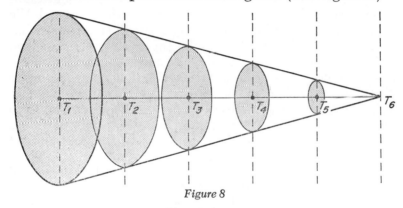

Figure 8

But decision making often cannot be represented by such a specificity funnel. This model of *sequential* decision making is similar to a model of *deductive* decision making, which we know does not correspond to human behavior in many instances. Thus, specific, incremental decisions can add up to a general, structural decision, as in American foreign policy decisions concerning the war in Vietnam. Or general, structural decisions may be *reversible*: they may not lead to *commitment*. For example, during the 1932 American presidential campaign, Franklin Delano Roosevelt made a general, structural decision that the federal budget should be reduced by 25 percent. This decision, however, did not lead to commitment; instead it proved to be reversible, as particular contingencies led him to adopt pump-priming, spending projects. This is only one example of the reversibility of general decisions in political, organizational, and personal life.

The image of the specificity funnel is useful in describing the behavior of organizations and of mobilization states[33] in their early revolutionary stages. The establishment of an organization is usually coincidental with the establishment of the organization's most general purposes. Herbert Simon's description of the founding of the European Co-operation Administration (the E.C.A.),[34] Lenin's founding of the Soviet state, Touré's founding of Guinea, Joseph Smith's blueprint and Brigham Young's founding of "Zion" (Mormon Utah), and the Puritan leaders' settling of Massachusetts Bay all exhibit the type of behavior represented by a specificity funnel. We see that the revolutionary founding of mobilization states has much in common with the founding of organizations: general values and decisions are made first, according to "the plan"; subsequently, more specific decisions are made according to these general values of the plan; a social structure is established to embody the values of the plan, although according to the models of the tree and the hierarchy of sets, the values and the plan are equivalent, since they are identical to the set of most general choices. Such behavior is in contrast to Burkean or incremental decision making, in which the structural outlines of a polity or an organization are established through incremental changes in the most general political and social values. (Such values may not be consciously held.) Here we have the reformist, gradualist, common-law approach to the establishing of political structure, which may be contrasted to the revolutionary, rapid, deductive-law approach to the construction of political structure. (Lindblom denies that incremental decision making is inherently conservative, but I am struck by its Burkean quality of adaptive conservatism or reformism, as opposed to radical decision making, involving revolutionary, structural change. However, I also think that numerous incremental changes may eventually add up to a revolutionary, structural change.)[35]

The fourth limitation of the tree and sets models is the most important. Consider this question: how may we derive a theory of types by which we can arrange activities into a hierarchy of sets?[36] In other words: what criteria can we use to say that one decision is more general than another? In many cases, there seems to be no such problem. For example, we can agree that the decisions embodied in a Soviet national plan are more general than the decisions concerning the establishment of the annual production quota for a single industrial firm. But I stated in my discussion of means-ends chains that a hierarchy of sets, a hierarchy of generality, means-ends chains, and their representations are relative to the values of observers. In other words, all those concepts mapped onto the model of the tree and the hierarchy of sets have a certain value relativity, implicit in the tree and set models. In the example I gave, most voters conceived economic well-being as an end more general than the continuation of a particular political party in office. On the other hand, leaders of political parties may view continuation in office (or gaining office) as the more general end, implying that the promotion of economic development may be a particular means to a more inclusive end.

To suggest another example: are a community's taxation decisions more general than its decisions concerning the construction of schools and the salary of teachers?[37] Sometimes taxation decisions could be the more general decisions, hence the more important issues for the analysis of power. In such cases, educational policy is circumscribed by the amount of money available. (Note that ideas such as "circumscribed" can be mapped into a hierarchy of sets.) In other cases, educational policy may be decided first, with the taxpayers choosing to pay the costs, no matter how high, to produce a first-class educational system. Here, educational policy circumscribes (limits) taxation decisions and is therefore the more general, important decision. But in most such cases, there would be interchange between the two issue areas. Taxation decisions would be made in terms of educational decisions, and vice versa. Consequently, the dichotomy between taxation and education decisions becomes meaningless, as such decisions are made interdependently.[38] Hence in speaking of generality and importance of decisions, we do have a category of general decisions that in this case are a mixture of fiscal and policy decisions. Thus when we are unable to decide which of two or more types of decisions are more general, we may find that the decisions are inseparably linked, giving us a category of general decisions that involves more than one specific issue area.

Associated with this fourth limitation of the tree and hierarchy-of-sets model is the problem of ordering sets, a conundrum which I shall term "the paradox of transfinity." Consider the following problem in ordering personal decisions according to a hierarchy of generality. Certainly, one of the most important decisions a person makes is his choice of vocation. If a person has decided to be a political scientist, it might seem that such a decision is very exclusive in terms of the multitude of possible alternative choices available to him. In other words, this decision apparently excludes a huge range of possible activities, while including a relatively small range of activities and alternatives. But we may view such a decision in a different perspective. Even though he has chosen to engage in activities called "political science," we can say that he still has an infinite range of possible activities open to him. Thus, according to this perspective, there is an infinite variety of ways he could teach his political science courses, as there is an infinite range of possible lectures he could give, each alternative slightly different from the others. Indeed, we can say that there is an infinity of possibility open in teaching only one course. (One could argue that there is not an infinity of possibility, because the political scientist would be fired if he discussed contemporary sexual mores or analyzed the lives of movie actors instead of teaching political science. But we can say that these possibilities are still open, even though the lecturer would be punished if he were to select them.) Furthermore—and this is very important—the lecturer could teach within the range of what his profession defines as appropriate for a given course, and still have an infinity of possibility open. Thus even though his range of lecture possibilities is limited by social sanctions (probably internalized within the lecturer), the professor could yet give an infinite number of slightly differing lectures.

Even more apparent is the infinite range of possibility open to a political scientist in his research. It might seem that choosing the vocation of political science would eliminate 95 percent of the research projects in the current universe of research. Nevertheless, this vocational decision still includes an infinite range of alternative books, monographs, and articles that the political scientist might write. There even remains an infinite range of possibility included within the decision to engage in a "specific" research project. For example, if someone gave me a detailed outline for this book and commanded me to follow the outline, I could still write an infinite number of slightly different books. Thus, there are a multitude of different ways I could write each sentence, let alone the infinite number of alternatives available in combining the various sentences. Moreover, when I select an example to illustrate a "particular" idea, there remains an infinite range of alternative examples that I could use. Furthermore, even after I have selected a "specific" example, I can still express this example in a huge number of different ways. In the "paradox of transfinity" lies the madness of the famous image of the man in the barber's chair looking at his reflection in the mirror facing him, which reflects the image in the mirror behind him, while the front mirror reflects the image in the back mirror reflecting the image in the front mirror, etc.

Now let me relate this paradox of transfinity to my previous ideas concerning politics and administration, generality-specificity of decisions, and analogous concepts mapped onto the behavior tree and the hierarchy of sets. First we realize that an infinity of possible alternatives can be available even within very specific, routine decisions. Examples include the infinite number of slightly differing ways of teaching a specific course, writing a dissertation previously outlined in detail, selecting examples to illustrate a given idea, or expressing such examples once they are selected. Ordinarily, such activities would be considered to be at a very specific level of administration, where the range of discretion is severely limited. (The example of teaching a university course is especially interesting. A professor, after being assigned a given course by his curriculum chairman, usually does not picture himself as an operative in an administrative hierarchy, because he feels he has a relatively wider range of discretion in carrying out this activity than the classroom janitor has in carrying out that particular role. Nevertheless, the chancellor of his campus and the president of his multiversity would look upon the professor as an operative in an administrative hierarchy, whether they admitted this or not. Similarly, the janitor might point to his freedom of movement, pitying the professor who must lecture in a certain physical space and spend much time cooped up in an office.)

In terms of the behavior tree, this transfinite paradox is represented by an infinite number of lines (alternatives) branching out from the most specific nodes. In addition, we can imagine an infinite number of alternatives at nodes at higher levels of generality. In other words, at each node, there would be an infinite number of lines, an infinite set of alternatives. However, the node pictorially represents the concept of a choice that limits subsequent choices, includes a realm of possible alternatives, and excludes another realm of alternatives. (For example, in a behavior tree illustrating vocational choice, a general node might indicate college teaching and research, thereby excluding possibilities such as business management, banking, the Civil Service, and so on. A more specific node, included within college teaching and research, would represent the choice of political science. This decision would include a certain range of alternatives, but would exclude alternatives such as mathematics and literature.) But we now see that *at each node, there is an infinity of excluded choices.** For example, in deciding to become a political scientist, our decision maker has excluded an infinite range of possible vocational activity, yet the decision includes another infinite range of activity, as indicated in my previous discussion. Furthermore, one intuitively feels that these are different types of infinities.† Now we are left with

---

* This also applies to prediction from hypotheses. Thus any hypothesis both includes and excludes an infinite range of events, and such included and excluded infinities also characterize prediction from a hypothesis. See Chapter 7 below.

† I am aware of the existence of transfinite numbers, but analysis in this realm is beyond my present competence. I am also aware that in some cases I may not be referring to infinities, but to finite numbers of huge magnitude.

the image of a behavior tree with an infinite set of lines (alternatives) at many, perhaps most, of the nodes (decisions).

What happens to the model of a hierarchy of sets? First, we see that there are an infinite number of elements in the more "specific" sets, such as teaching a particular political science course, writing a particular political science dissertation, selecting an example to illustrate an idea within a dissertation, or expressing such an example. Yet once more we intuitively feel that there are different types of infinity. For example, selecting college teaching and research evidently includes one type of infinity of possible alternatives. Choosing political science as a specific vocation includes a second, more "specific," type of infinity of possible alternatives. Selecting a particular dissertation seems to include a third, yet more "specific," type of infinity; the outline of this dissertation would include a fourth type, yet more "specific"; selecting an example to illustrate a particular idea would be a fifth type; selecting a particular mode of expressing such an example would be a sixth type. Moreover, each decision also *excludes* a range of possible alternatives that has an infinite magnitude, and by analogous reasoning, we see that there is also a hierarchy of infinities among the *excluded* alternatives. This paradox of transfinity has important implications for the normative theory of freedom and for the empirical theory of power. However, its further exploration involves higher mathematics and logic, and is beyond the scope of this book.

Dilemmas of spurious pluralism, as outlined in Chapter 4, can be related to the paradox of transfinity. We have seen that even when decision making is highly restricted, one can show an infinity of remaining possibilities. For example, even if I were commanded to follow a detailed outline of a book, I could still choose among an infinite number of slightly different acceptable theses. Even though I could be imprisoned for writing on a different topic, I could claim to have an infinite range of choice, and thus freedom! Or if I am instructed to write short stories only in the vein of socialist realism, even though I am greatly restricted, I still have the *freedom* to write an infinite number of slightly different stories in this vein. Similarly, the Forest Service Ranger may be controlled by his indoctrination into the professional values (ideology) of forestry, and yet we could say that he has a wide range of discretion in managing his local district. Or the manager of a Soviet industrial firm may be restricted by the national economic plan, the annual budget, and numerous control agencies, and yet we could say that he has an infinite number of alternative activities available in fulfilling his production quotas. Moreover, the manager of the Soviet firm may gain acceptance of some of his preferred alternatives by bargaining with superiors, and thus we might say that he has a significant amount of "power" in Dahl's terms. Thus, in general, even the most totalitarian system leaves an infinite range of choice according to *some* perspective. But then the important question is: Choice between what? We might say that a prisoner in a maximum security cell still has an infinity of alternatives open to him. He can pace the cell in different ways; he can sleep at different times; he can engage in an infinite number of different reveries. He may even exert interpersonal power, perhaps by persuading the guards to grant him cigarettes at less than the usual bribe. An infinity of possibility is still open, even though the choices of the prisoner are extremely restricted.

The paradox of transfinity is a conceptual dilemma comparable in difficulty and importance to the problem of non-issues. Non-issues refer to the alternatives excluded by certain choices, which may not be conscious. (Remember an *issue* is a type of *alternative*. I could equate the two concepts, but common connotations of "issue" include some amount of controversy or confusion. An "issue" usually indicates a prominent alternative, relative to some frame of reference.) We have seen that non-issues themselves are subject to the transfinite paradox, because the prisoner's infinity of excluded alternatives seems much "smaller" than Aristotle Onassis' infinity of excluded alternatives.

However, as with the non-issues problem, we can make useful progress without really solving the paradox of transfinity. Thus, in most cases, a hierarchy of generality seems obvious, non-controversial, and defensible. Thus, the six types of generality involved in being a political scientist and writing a book can be ranked in a hierarchy of sets and a hierarchy of generality, in means-ends chains, in a behavior tree, only now one must recognize the problems incurred by the included infinities. Similarly, we can recognize the relativity of some hierarchies of generality, as in the example in which winning office was more general to politicians and gaining economic well-being was more general to most voters. In some cases, insights derived from "modern" mathematics (i.e. developed in the last hundred years) might help our theoretical advance. Finally, the paradox of transfinity indicates the wisdom of explicitly stating one's criteria for establishing a hierarchy of sets.

SUMMARY

In this and the previous chapter, I have emphasized the need to make a distinction between critical and routine decisions for a theory of power and democracy. Students of organization theory and public administration have devoted much thought to the distinction between critical and routine issues and decisions, for such concepts are the basis for distinguishing political decisions and administrative decisions. Taking a cue from Herbert Simon, I discussed the distinction between critical and routine decisions and issues in terms of the behavior tree of game theory, a concept central to much theorizing about decision making. Further, we saw that the behavior tree is a representation of the simpler ideas of mathematical set theory.

I have noted that many valuable concepts can be stated and clarified in terms of the behavior tree and the hierarchy of sets. Such concepts include: generality-specificity; values and key decisions; means-ends chains; the Waldo pyramid, i.e. politics-administration as a hierarchy of purposes; Selznick's concept of organizational character-formation as illustrated by the founding of both organizations and revolutionary, mobilization polities; Cyert and March's flow diagrams and hence the computer simulation of decision making. It is apparent that "importance" is usually linked to the more general, inclusive sets in a hierarchy of sets. Moreover, we see that theorists of comparative politics must avoid the error of comparing low-level decisions in some cases. For example, Lindblom's theories of bargaining and decentralization of power are useful in comparing general decisions, but such concepts are misleading if applied at a specific level of decision making. Findings of pluralism can be clarified or tested against the logical structure of the behavior tree and the hierarchy of sets. Ideological consensus can close general choices and leave only routine decisions, as in the case of the Forest Ranger. Finding pluralism within totalitarian systems (even prisons) is a case of analysis on an excessively specific level.

However, I described four limitations on the behavior tree and hierarchy of sets as logical structures for the analysis of decision making and political power: the ubiquity of structural incoherence; the intersection of sets of specific activities included within more general decisions and activities; the possible misapprehension of a specificity funnel; and the more important limitation of the paradox of transfinity, which leads us to see an infinite number of possible alternatives radiating from specific nodes (decisions) on the behavior tree.

We may recall that Herbert Simon emphasizes the importance of the concept of the behavior tree: "The fact that this concept has been seized upon independently in such a variety of contexts to provide a framework for a theory of behavior suggests that it represents the real core of the new behavioral Zeitgeist."[39] I agree with Simon, although I would express his idea differently: the behavior tree is a representation of the simple ideas of set theory, which are necessary for almost every type of logical reasoning, as is seen in symbolic logic and Boolean algebra. Thus the use of the behavior tree as a central concept in theories of decision making is an affirmation of the value of logical organization and reasoning.

7. Structure and Behavior

THE DICHOTOMY

In the preceding chapter, concepts concerning generality and decisions were related to the logical structures of the game tree and the hierarchy of sets. Among such concepts was the decision premise, organized by Cyert and March into flow diagrams (similar to the game tree), which can be simulated by computer. If we wish, we can use decision premises and computer programming to represent a deterministic view of human activity. For instance, we may imagine that all men have programs inside their heads, and that these programs flip the switches controlling the biochemical and mechanical forces that constitute all human behavior. In such a case, we could say that the programs inside men's heads *caused* human behavior, and accordingly, social science would consist of the discovery and analysis of these programs. Power would be defined and measured by a person's capacity to rewrite other persons' programs.

We can call a programmed decision premise "an imperative";* some imperatives may be viewed as more general than others, as in the Cyert and March flow diagrams, or in the game-tree and the hierarchy-of-sets models. In our metaphor of programmed people, we have assumed that programs in heads trip biochemical switches and hence cause human activity. In summary, we see that "value" defined as "a generalized imperative concerning scope of activity" may be viewed as a *general decision premise* or as a *general cause*. Recalling that power is a type of social causation, we can see that there

---

* Here I am purposely Weberian in using the term "imperative."

would be greatest power in the capacity to determine the critical decisions, the general causes, the values, in other persons' programs.

Values or general decision premises can be called structural decisions. For example, in the concluding chapter of *Comparative Politics,* Apter divides theory of comparative government into "structural" and "behavioral" analysis. He writes: "The structure may be defined as the relationships in a social situation which limit the choice process to a particular range of alternatives. The behavioral may be defined as the selection process in choice, i.e., deciding between alternatives." The "point of contact" of these modes of analysis "is the choice process," according to Apter.[1]

The following is a summary of what I consider to be the best ideas in Apter's analysis.[*] The parenthetical words are my own extrapolations and additions to Apter's presentation.[2]

Behavioral	*Structural*
More experimental; more objective. Inductive and quantitative. More cases to test theories.	Less of these things. Deductive; qualitative. Greater use of subjective, experiential verification.
Use of psychological theory. Focus on individual behavior.	(Use of sociological theory. Focus on large social aggregates, e.g. class analysis.) Structural-functional theory of Parsons, Merton, Levy, etc. The historical-sociological approach to international relations, as in the work of Stanley Hoffmann.[3]
Emphasis on motivations, attitudes, perceptions. Concern with cognition and efficiency. Decision-making theory in international relations and in organization theory, in Snyder, Bruck, and Sapin; Herbert Simon.[4]	
The psychological functions of attitudes; e.g. Smith *et al.*	(The sociology of knowledge; e.g. Mannheim.)
In comparative politics, comparison involves many units, has greater verifiability and replicability. E.g. Almond and Verba.	Less of these things.

[*] Complete titles and publication data for works referred to in the outline are given in the Bibliography, pp. 253–65.

Behavioral	Structural
(But the behavioral focus on attitudes, often having an indefinable relationship with actual activity and its focus on actions of the individual, tends to treat questions that seem less significant for purposes of comparison.)	The structural emphasis treats questions of greater comparative significance, although its hypotheses are harder to verify. E.g. theories of revolution; Hartz, Tocqueville on American politics.[5]
Modal political events may be treated within a psychological framework, as in the work of Lucian Pye on revolution and social change.	Modal political events are treated from a perspective of generalized social theory. For example, Chalmers Johnson's explicit rejection of psychodynamic theories of revolution and his substitution of functional and ideal-typical analysis.[6]
Psychological theories of voting behavior: Campbell *et al.*	(Theories of party systems and electoral institutions, such as Duverger's treatment of the "functions of party systems," as in Rossiter, *Parties and Politics*; Schattschneider, *Party Government*.)
Symbolic interactionist sociological theory.[7]	Structural sociological theory.
"Political material is perceived and has an influence to the extent that it serves a need for the individual, i.e., if it provides: information useful in solving a career or other objective problem; means of social adjustment to others; or opportunity for the release of psychic tension." Lane, *Political Life*, p. 298.[8]	"Weakening of values may characterize significant segments of a society before a radical decay is observable in the entire social body." Selznick, *Organizational Weapon*, p. 308.[9]
Lasswell's thesis in *Psychopathology and Politics*[10] that private motives displaced upon a public object, rationalized in terms of the public interest, produce political man.	

Behavioral	Structural
In organization theory, emphasis on decision making or choice making, motivation on an individual basis, and cognitive and calculative matters.* Simon, *Administrative Behavior*; Barnard; March and Simon; Cyert and March; Braybrooke and Lindblom (pp. 3–143).	In organization theory, emphasis on the total organizational structure, the role of values, and Weber's ideal-type of bureaucracy.* Weber, Merton, Gouldner, Parsons, Selznick, Etzioni (pp. 20–57), Blau and Scott, Bendix.
Utilitarian political theory, e.g. Bentham. Adam Smith.	Marxist political theory. Plato. St. Thomas Aquinas.

Surely most observers, after contemplating Apter's structural and behavioral distinction, would favor the study of both structural and behavioral variables in theorizing about a political system, an organization, or a system of international relations.

As we have seen, the structural decision (the same thing as a critical decision) can be defined as the set of general choices "which limit the choice process to a particular range of alternatives." Further, we may recall that an issue is a type of alternative—an issue refers to an alternative that many people perceive as both prominent and controversial. Thus, because a structural or critical decision limits available alternatives, *such decisions limit available issues.* Clearly, the structural-behavioral distinction is related to the non-issues controversy in the community-power literature. In these terms, Bachrach and Baratz are criticizing Dahl for studying only behavioral factors and for neglecting structural factors, which limit the available issues. (This is probably an inaccurate criticism

---

* Organization theory may be applied to political parties and other political groups (e.g., McKenzie's use of Michels or Michels himself) and to institutions such as legislatures and national administrative bureaucracies. For example, Michels could be used to treat the inner-club thesis of senatorial power, or an organization-theory decision-making analysis might be made of the executive branch by combining Simon *et al.* and Neustadt, *Presidential Power.* Wildavsky makes such an analysis of the Presidency in unpublished lectures.

of *Who Governs?*, because the first section of the book is a structural analysis of the polity of New Haven. Dahl traces the historical development of this local political system "from oligarchy to pluralism" in periods differentiated according to extent and content of participation and the class backgrounds of the ruling elites: Patricians, Entrepreneurs, Ex-Plebes.)[11]

The concept of the boundary decision relates the structural and the behavioral perspectives.* Thus one could study the decision processes on a boundary issue (which might rank low according to participant-activity criteria) in order to consider how the decision processes affect the structure of the particular political system, conceiving "structure" in the sense of generalized imperatives, the most general "do's" and "don'ts." Examples include the numerous, relatively quiet instances of Negroes challenging, in some peripheral way, the dominant sociopolitical values of the Deep South in the years before the impact of the Civil Rights Movement.

STRUCTURE AND BEHAVIOR: EXAMPLES

In this section, I describe the differing approaches of the structuralists and the behaviorists by comparing the way they would analyze the same political situation (the so-called Bay-fill problem). Then I illustrate this difference in terms of two exemplary situations. Initially I refer without explanation to the structuralists' use of the concepts "class" and "ideology"; however, later in this section, I note certain convergences between "class" and "ideology" and the conceptual frameworks of the game tree and the hierarchy of sets.

For many years, numerous politically informed citizens of the San Francisco Bay Area have been concerned about the unchecked filling of their Bay, the most distinctive feature of their natural environment. Nevertheless, local government

---

* In a personal communication, Aaron Wildavsky maintained that structure and behavior should be linked through hypotheses relating past value commitments to present choices. The boundary decision is such a hypothesis, for it relates the past value commitment of defining the political system's issue scope to the present choice of possibly changing this issue scope.

proved only partially capable of stopping the pouring of dredged dried mud and garbage into that pure inlet of the Pacific. The structuralist would describe this situation by applying concepts of class and ideology. He would note that the municipalities of Berkeley and Sausalito had ordered a stop to indiscriminate filling of the Bay within their local jurisdictions before the passage of the Petris-McAteer anti-fill law by the California state legislature in 1965. The structural analyst would note that Berkeley and Sausalito have an unusual proportion of upper-middle-class professional people, unusually imbued with the values of attentiveness to the public interest and concern for the conservation of natural resources, both of which may be viewed as ideologies of medium-range generality. The structuralist would then state his hypotheses, relating municipal anti-fill ordinances to class and ideology, and apply them to other communities. By using indices of occupation and education, he would ascertain whether other communities fell into the same category as Berkeley and Sausalito. Using content analysis of newspaper editorials or other indices of the local strength of ideology, he would rank communities according to the strength of public-interest consciousness and conservationism. Then, the structural analyst might study the opposition to anti-fill ordinances according to concepts of class and ideology. He would note that the Bay fillers consisted mostly of certain business interests that could be divided into two groups: landowners, including various corporate interests and real-estate speculators who had acquired title to the Bay's shores and to the accompanying filling rights; and land developers, including subdivision builders and, more importantly, city governments that want cheap land to attract industry and thereby reduce taxes. The structuralist might note that, in this situation, municipal government acted in accordance with the interests of certain capitalists and property-owning taxpayers. On the other hand, some of the leading opponents of Bay filling were businessmen and other members of upper-income groups; in other words, as usual in American society, the observer would find splits within economically defined classes. The structural analyst would find that the existence of scores of independent local governmental authorities, together with tax reduction as a preeminent local political issue, caused competition among local governments for the acquisition of new industry; as a result, local governments became important Bay-filling developer-capitalists (entrepreneurs and financiers) themselves. This situation predominated unless a local community had an unusually high proportion of middle-class professionals and important currents of conservationism and public-interest consciousness. Then the anti-fill position would triumph. The sophisticated structural analyst would note that the fragmentation of local government worked both ways, for it permitted the conservationist forces to pass three local anti-fill ordinances. Finally, the structuralist would correlate his various social structural and ideological indices with the presence of anti-fill ordinances, and if the correlation were reasonably high, the structural analyst would consider his study finished.

The behaviorist, on the other hand, would approach the Bay-fill situation in a quite different way. Perhaps criticizing the structuralist for insufficient consideration of the decision-making processes involved, the behaviorist would devote considerable attention to the details of the decision making on the anti-fill ordinances passed by the Berkeley, Sausalito, and San Leandro (the third city to pass such an ordinance) city councils. He would identify the primary actors and observe who initiated, modified, and vetoed proposals in the anti-fill issue area. The behaviorist would study the defeat of proposed anti-fill legislation in other municipalities. He would probably find fragmented power in the Bay-fill issue area, and decisively reject power-clite hypotheses, which would posit near-complete control by business interests in this sector of policy making. The behaviorist would explore more thoroughly the activities of pressure groups, but would probably de-emphasize a structural interpretation of class interests. He would pay greater attention to the role of elections in deciding Bay-fill proposals. The behaviorist would study the intergovernmental relations between the dozens of relevant local governments, ranging from cities to port authorities, to sanitation districts, to junior college districts desiring cheap land for new campuses. Not content with generalities about the frag-

mentation of local government and its relation to class interests, he would study the discussion and bargaining among
the numerous local governments when considering the Bay-
fill issue. The behaviorist would not content himself with
general observations, perhaps verified by indices, concerning
the class and ideological structuring of public attitudes toward regulation of Bay filling. Instead, he might carry out
public attitude surveys to discover the extent of information, concern, and activity on this issue.

Primarily interested in social class and ideological factors
that structure the consideration of political issues, the structural analyst might regard the behaviorist's study as trivial,
or as missing the central points (e.g., Bachrach and Baratz's
criticism of *Who Governs?*). The behaviorist, on the other
hand, would consider the structural analysis too general, too
poorly verified, and gravely lacking in details of the actual
political processes involved in the decision-making processes
on this issue. Each would be dissatisfied with the other's explanation, although each explanation could be based on considerable evidence.

Now let us consider two other illustrations of the differences between the structural approach and the behavioral
approach. First, let us suppose that two observers wish to
study the movements and feeding patterns of cattle on a
western ranch. The behavioral analyst would focus on the
activities of the cattle themselves; he would divide them into
groups, observe patterns of domination within the groups of
cattle, see whether groups followed the movements of the
lead animal in feeding and in responding to perceived dan-
ger, etc. The structural analyst, on the other hand, would be
less interested in direct observation of the cattle's activities.
Instead, he would interest himself in the patterns of fence
building, which limit the possible movements and feeding
activities of the cattle. The structuralist might leave the field
altogether, ignore the possibilities of observing, counting,
grouping, and charting the movements of the cattle, and instead, check the public records at the county courthouse to
develop a theory of land ownership and bounding and its
relationship to fence construction.

Second, let us consider a famous poem by Robert Frost, "The Road Not Taken."*

> Two roads diverged in a yellow wood,
> And sorry I could not travel both
> And be one traveler, long I stood
> And looked down one as far as I could
> To where it bent in the undergrowth;
>
> Then took the other, as just as fair,
> And having perhaps the better claim,
> Because it was grassy and wanted wear;
> Though as for that the passing there
> Had worn them really about the same,
>
> And both that morning equally lay
> In leaves no step had trodden black.
> Oh, I kept the first for another day!
> Yet knowing how way leads on to way,
> I doubted if I should ever come back.
>
> I shall be telling this with a sigh
> Somewhere ages and ages hence:
> Two roads diverged in a wood, and I—
> I took the one less traveled by,
> And that has made all the difference.

Studying this situation, the behaviorist would concentrate on "the selection process in choice, i.e., deciding between alternatives." The behaviorist would conduct a "decision-making" study. He would interview the poetic traveler and attempt to ascertain the wayfarer's perception of the decision-making situation and the concomitant information-gathering process:

> Two roads diverged in a yellow wood,
> And sorry I could not travel both
> And be one traveler, long I stood
> And looked down one as far as I could
> To where it bent in the undergrowth

---

* "The Road Not Taken," from *Complete Poems of Robert Frost.* Copyright 1916 by Holt, Rinehart and Winston, Inc. Copyright 1944 by Robert Frost. Reprinted by permission of Holt, Rinehart and Winston, Inc.

The behaviorist then would attempt to ascertain the traveler's motives for choosing one rather than the other road:

> Then took the other, as just as fair,
> And having perhaps the better claim,
> Because it was grassy and wanted wear

The behaviorist would note the poet's values of estheticism ("because it was grassy") and moderately experimental nonconformity ("and wanted wear"). Perhaps influenced by writers such as Harold Lasswell, Erich Fromm, Robert Lane, Fred Greenstein, and other students of "socialization,"[12] the behavioral decision-making theorist might conduct a "depth interview" and trace the poetic traveler's values of estheticism and moderate nonconformity to "primary-group influences," especially his family background.

The structural analyst, on the other hand, would not emphasize decision making, perceptions, information gathering, the goals of specific individuals, and socialization. Instead, he would concentrate on the structure, which "may be defined as the relationships in a social situation which limit the choice process to a particular range of alternatives." The structuralist would ask such questions as the following: Why was there a crossroads in the first place? Who designed the respective courses of the two roads and why? Why wasn't there a third road at the crossroads? (Cf., Why isn't there a strong socialist or fascist movement in the United States?) Why isn't there a connecting road between the two roads, so that the poet could more easily go back to travel on the second road?

After interviewing additional travelers about their decision-making processes, the behaviorist would draw his conclusions and criticize those of the structural study as dealing in vague generalities and missing the central point, i.e., why certain types of people choose one road rather than another (as when they vote for one party rather than another). The structuralist, on the other hand, would maintain that the analysis of the origins and development of the structure of the choice situation is more important than the analysis of individual decision making.

Although the effort may seem esthetically barbaric, one

can easily translate Frost's image into the game tree and the hierarchy of sets. "Two roads diverged" and the poet realizes:

> Yet knowing how way leads on to way,
> I doubted if I should ever come back.

This image is the same as that of a game tree, with an original choice between two alternatives, each alternative leading to subsequent nodes (decisions) with subsequent branching alternatives. Indeed, the traveling poet sees his decision as important, general, key, crucial, etc., in terms of its eventual effect upon his "journey." In Selznick's terms, this decision involves commitment, self-definition, and the setting of a basic value.[13]

> Yet knowing how way leads on to way,
> I doubted if I should ever come back.
>
> I shall be telling this with a sigh
> Somewhere ages and ages hence:
> Two roads diverged in a wood, and I—
> I took the one less traveled by,
> And that has made all the difference.

Yet we know that Frost's image, like the game tree, should not imply the specificity funnel and that it is subject to the paradox of transfinity, as we can readily imagine an infinity of possible sensations and activities available to the poet on *either* road.

But how does this discussion relate to pluralist theory? We have seen that to analyze the Bay-fill issue, the structuralist would emphasize the bounding of political activity by social structure (including class) and values (including ideology). The behaviorist would emphasize political decision making within these bounds. The structuralist would study the fence around the cattle; the behaviorist would study the activity of the cattle within the bounds of the fence. Studying decision making at the fork in the road, the structuralist would emphasize the general limitations on behavior set by the configuration of the roadways. The behaviorist would study decision making within the bounds set by the configuration of the roadways.

Analyzing the Bay-fill issue, the structuralist concentrates on social structure (including class) and values (including ideology), and hence his findings omit the complex welter of political behavior within the bounds set by social structure and values. He uses fewer variables in comparison with the behaviorist, whose variables include all important political actors, political roles, and political groups. Thus, it is more likely that the structuralist will develop a simpler explanatory system, having fewer variables, fewer relationships, and less interdependence among variables (especially as there are fewer variables to begin with), and greater stability in the relationships between the variables.* For example, he may conclude that capitalism, laissez-faire ideology, fragmentation of local government, and typical configurations of social structure correlate with the degree of Bay-filling activity. On the other hand, he may conclude that upper-middle-class professionalism and the ideologies of conservationism and attention to the public interest correlate with the regulation of Bay-filling activity. Quite likely the structuralist would conclude that these relationships would be stable over a "short" period of time, say ten years. Hence, he posits a relatively simple system.

The behaviorist, studying the kaleidoscopic complexities of political behavior within the bounds set by social structure and values, includes as variables all individuals and groups exhibiting significant power (causal impact) within this particular issue area. Thus, it is more likely that the behaviorist will develop a complex explanatory system, having numerous and diverse variables, numerous relationships and great interdependence among variables (especially as there are numerous variables to begin with), and less stability in the relationships between the variables. If he attempts a complete study, the behaviorist must examine political activity within scores of local governments—cities, villages, counties, sanita-

---

* Of course, a simple theory is better than a complex theory, if their predictive values are equivalent.

tion districts, port authorities, junior college districts, etc. (The judicious behaviorist would probably sample the jurisdictions, however.) In addition, he must analyze the impact of federal and state regulation on the Bay-fill issue area within the scores of local jurisdictions. Then the behaviorist must discover which persons and groups have power (causal impact) over Bay-fill decisions within the various governmental jurisdictions. He must analyze Bay filling as an issue area in the complex system of intergovernmental relations among the scores of local governments, the state government, and the federal government. Finally, the behaviorist discovers which political actors, political roles, and political groups have power over decisions within this issue area. Probably he will find a complex system of decision making within the issue area.

Now we begin to see how the structuralist and the behaviorist can develop seemingly contradictory conclusions. Thus, if the structuralist is incautious, we could criticize him for committing the gross errors of the stratificationists, as analyzed by Nelson Polsby.[14] The structuralist's simple system, correlating capitalist social structure and fragmented governmental structure with Bay filling, might carry the implication that a power elite of capitalists and their political "legmen" consciously manipulated the public.[15] (This is a simple system, with simple causation, having power concentrated in a single, independent variable.) Furthermore, his emphasis on economic classes could imply that economic *resources* are political power. However, the pluralist, following Robert Dahl's political analysis, would view economic goods as means (resources) which may or may not be successfully converted into political power, i.e., cause desired political effects. As in the community-power literature, controversy might develop between the structuralist, who argues that the distribution of economic resources is equivalent to the distribution of political power, and the pluralist-behaviorist, who argues that potential power in terms of resources may not be converted into actual power, conceived as political causality.[16] Such controversy results from the following factors.

1. There is a confusion over terms. For example, what is

138   THE STRUCTURE OF POWER

"power"? The pluralist-behaviorist defines power as political causation by individuals and groups. The structuralist may define power as resources, which have an uncertain correlation with power as causation.[17]

2. The structuralist may draw unwarranted conclusions, or an observer may draw unwarranted inferences, from such a study. For example, the finding of a simple systemic structure does not imply that political behavior may be explained by a simple system such as the power-elite, single-independent-variable theory.

3. The structuralist studies the bounding of political activity by social structure (including class) and values (including ideology). The pluralist-behaviorist studies political decision making within these bounds.

The pluralist-behaviorist tends to find a complex pattern of interaction characterized by decentralized power and complex causation at the crossroads of political decision making. However, the structuralist then may charge that the finding of kaleidoscopic diversity is the discovery of spurious pluralism because the study of critical decisions has been neglected.

In studying community power, the pluralist-behaviorist concludes that the distribution of power in New Haven, or in most other American communities, evidences the characteristics of a complex system—pluralism, complex causation, fragmented power.[18] A sophisticated structuralist might agree with this assertion, although most of the stratification theorists, reviewed by Polsby, would not agree. The structuralist would qualify the pluralists' generalizations by stating that the observed pluralism is bounded by social structure and ideology (or values), which limit the issue scope of the political process. Similarly, the pluralist-behaviorist would hold that power in the American political system is fragmented, dispersed, and widely shared. On the other hand, the structuralist would contend that such complexity and dispersion of power is limited by social structure and ideology (or values), which set the issue scope, concentrate power resources, and simplify analysis. The structuralist sees structure and boundaries; the behaviorist sees choice (decision making) within the structure and boundaries.

STRUCTURE AND SOME SOCIOLOGICAL CONCEPTS

At this point, let us note some of the central concepts of structural sociology—social structure, class, role, ideology, values, and organization—and the ways they may be mapped onto the model of the game tree and the hierarchy of sets. First, ideology and values can be called decision premises, even general decision premises: the initial choices on the game tree, the most inclusive sets in a hierarchy of sets of decision premises and activities.*

Second, organization can be viewed as a system of decision premises and activities, or means-ends chains, and thus can fit the model of the game tree and the hierarchy of sets. Thus, we can picture an organization as a set of relationships between general decision premises and specific decision premises in the manner of Herbert Simon.[19] The game tree and the hierarchy of sets can also be viewed as a set of relationships between general and specific decision premises (choices), and thus these models accord with Simon's model of organization.

It is somewhat more difficult to map social structure, class, and role onto the models. Social structure can denote class structure, so let us examine the concept of class as an example. The term and concept "class" is identical to the logical term and concept "set," and in fact these terms are often used interchangeably in mathematics and logic. Consequently, because "class" indicates *classification* of data according to the possession of common *properties,* one can delineate classes in any terms one chooses, e.g., occupation, education. Of course, one can classify social data according to aggregations of single criteria; a class may be defined as the composite of economic, occupational, and educational attributes, for example. The criteria for classification into classes (sets of data) may

---

* Here I am dealing with "ideology" as an operational reality, rather than as an evanescent political strategy having little or no relation to the actor's values and beliefs. In other words, ideology in these terms is an independent variable rather than a dependent variable, although, of course, ideology is not necessarily the sole variable having significant effects within a systemic construct.

be objective (not perceived by the actors themselves) or subjective (perceived by the actors themselves).

Although the concept "class" most specifically denotes a logical operation, the term has come to mean the general structure of possession of economic goods and relationships to the means of production. Observation has shown the importance of correlating the general structure of possession of economic goods with various social (including political) events. However, as Dahl has emphasized, potential power in terms of economic resources often is not correlated with actual power in terms of political decisions, because economic goods are only one of several important power resources.[20] Thus, following Dahl, I view the possession of economic goods as a resource that may be utilized for the successful exercise of power, a situation that can be expressed as writing the decision premises on the programs of others. Consequently, economic goods as means to the end of successfully exercising political power, and classification schemes based on the possession of economic goods, are variables that may be related to the exercise of political power in particular hypotheses. In summary, economic classifications may be related to the game tree and the hierarchy of sets as variables related to the exercise of power.

Other connotations of social structure include national, racial, religious, and other identifications that are primary in an actor's hierarchy of loyalties. Such primary loyalties may be related to decision premises in specific hypotheses; certainly they are among the most general choices in terms of values, self-definition, commitment, and implications for political action. Thus such classifications usually have an important relationship to the more general decisions in the game tree and in the hierarchy of sets. Social structure may also denote other, perhaps secondary, loyalties, such as identification with specific geographical areas smaller than the state, one's occupational or professional group, and various political interest groups. (Of course, such loyalties can take precedence over national, racial, and religious loyalties for some people. The question of which are primary loyalties is an empirical matter.) Such secondary loyalties, whatever they are, can be seen as more specific choices or decision premises than primary loyalties. As such, they may be mapped onto the game tree and the hierarchy of sets.

Social structure also may denote a system of roles. Although "role" is defined in many differing ways,[21] the following definition expresses the central idea that most scholars have in mind: a "role" is a regularly recurring pattern of interaction that can be described by (1) who expects (2) whom (3) to do what (4) in which situation (5) and the actors' expectations of social rewards for conformity and social sanctions for deviance. Consequently, a role can be expressed in terms of shared expectations about behavior, including shared understandings concerning the social sanctioning of behavior. Such a pattern of shared information can be viewed in terms of decision premises, and hence mapped onto the unifying model. For example, one can view an organization as a structure of roles, hence as a structure of shared information about expected behavior, hence as a structure of decision premises concerning one's own behavior in relation to others. We may regard a social system in an analogous fashion, although here the importance of conscious direction is less than in an organization.

Alternatively, we can view roles as parts (variables, factors, etc.) of a social system. Thus a role is an element of the total social system or a part of a whole.[22] Part-whole is logically the same as subset-superset. Hence a social system is a superset, of which each role is a subset. We can view both superset and subset (a set and its partitions) as patterns of information.[23] Thus a social system is described by a more general pattern of information than is a component role. These patterns of information are descriptions of human decisions and activities, or decision premises, which may or may not be perceived by the actors themselves. Hence a social system may be viewed as a general pattern of information concerning decision premises, while a role may be viewed as a specific pattern of information concerning decision premises. This is a restatement of the idea of the game tree and the hierarchy of sets.

To analyze another concept, a value (a critical decision, a general choice, an ultimate purpose, etc.), in these terms, we do not necessarily describe power, because a value does not necessarily reflect someone's conscious design (intentions). Insofar as the value reflects the social causation of some activity, however, we are describing *influence*. However, such influence may result from the actions of many individuals, rather than from the actions of one or several. Further, such influence may result from the accretion of many events, rather than from one or several events. We see, then, that the important sociological concepts of value, ideology, organization, social structure, class, and role can be mapped onto the unifying models of the game tree and the hierarchy of sets. Thus we can map the central concepts of the sociologist-structuralist onto the unifying framework.

In summary, we can speak of "structural decisions," which, like critical decisions, values, power over general decisions, ultimate purposes, leadership, organizational definition, commitment, and so forth, refer to the general nodes in the game tree and the general choices in a hierarchy of sets of choices. For example, in the crossroads situation, the decision to construct the crossroad in a particular form becomes a general node on the game tree and a general decision in the hierarchy of sets of decisions. Similarly, in the cattle ranch illustration, the construction of fences becomes the general decision in the sense of the game tree or the hierachy of sets, whereas the specific "decisions" of the cowboys and cattle are specific nodes or specific sets, analogous to administration in the politics-administration dichotomy. A theory of power and democracy, embodying a critical-routine-decisions distinction, must be sensitive to these theoretical considerations.

HYPOTHESES AND PREDICTION

Here I shall remark on certain implications of prediction that concern significance, the structural and the behavioral approaches, and the game tree. First, let us observe that because of the multiplicity of variables involved in social analyses and the practical impossibility of controlled experimentation, hypotheses in social science may be viewed as probabilistic statements when related to particular situations. Thus, if we match a hypothesis with each one of the entire realm of events considered, we can associate the matching with a particular probability coefficient, stating the likelihood that the given event will occur. In the distribution of probability coefficients, a very few will approximate 1, while most will approximate 0. However, the reader will see that we are approaching another one of the paradoxes of infinity. Social scientific hypotheses may be viewed as excluding numerous events, really an infinity of possible events, as highly improbable or nearly impossible. In such cases, when a given event is matched with a hypothesis, the probability coefficient stating the likelihood of the event's occurrence is near zero. On the other hand, *for another infinity of possibility*, a hypothesis may state only that any one of these events is quite likely to occur. In this case, the probability coefficient associated with the matching and stating the likelihood of the event's occurrence is near 1.

This situation is conceptually similar to the paradox of transfinity mentioned in an earlier chapter. There we saw that a particular actor made a choice (C_1), say choosing the vocation of political science. Choice C_1 both excluded and included an infinity of possible events. After choosing C_1, the actor might make a more "specific" choice (C_2), included within C_1. Such a choice (C_2) might be the selection of teaching and research within political science. Yet again, we saw that C_2 both excluded and included an infinity of possible events. This sequence toward specificity may be continued indefinitely, unless one can somehow define an *indivisible* choice, conceptually analogous to a basic particle of matter.

Prediction from hypotheses is subject to a similar paradox of transfinity. When predictions are derived from a hypothesis having a certain level of generality, such predictions both exclude and include an infinity of possible events. Even predictions derived from hypotheses having narrower ranges of generality each exclude and include an infinity of possible events, unless we somehow arrive at a hypothesis having indivisible specificity. This idea can be mapped onto the game tree because the hypotheses refer to human choices, whether or not such decisions are perceived by the actors. This generality-specificity hierarchy of prediction is a hierarchy of sets.

Whether or not one considers a hypothesis significant involves one's views about the significance of the infinities excluded and included by the implied predictions. For example, I have stated that hypotheses describing pluralist, complex-systemic power in a given sphere are significant mainly in relation to power-elitist, simple-systemic descriptions of power. If an observer considers the power-elite theories to be silly or trivial, then the observer will not be particularly impressed with the pluralist hypotheses, which seemed evident to him in the first place. In this case, a hypothesis of pluralism excludes an infinite number of imaginable power elites and single-independent-variable systems. Nevertheless, the pluralist hypothesis includes an infinity of possible pluralist systems, complex systems with decentralized power and fragmented causation. Consequently, if an observer is highly impressed with a finding that excludes the possibility of the operation of a power-elite system, then he will view pluralism as a significant finding. On the other hand, if an observer is much more concerned about the *type* of included, complex, pluralist system, then he will not view the finding of pluralism as significant. In other words, the significance of the hypothesis varies according to the observer's interest in the excluded versus the included range of possibilities.

This view of hypotheses has important implications for our concern with the structural and behavioral approaches. In Louis Hartz's structural theory of American politics,[24] for example, he states that there is a Lockean liberal tradition in America—an ideology that precludes certain outcomes and issues from occurring in American politics. Hartz's portrait of American political behavior, as bounded by the structural constraint of liberal ideology, seems very significant to many scholars who are impressed with the non-alternatives (non-issues) of feudalism and other forms of aristocracy (except in the South, a matter treated by Hartz),[25] socialism, communism, fascism, and populist authoritarianism such as Peronism. Other scholars, less interested in these questions, would be less impressed by Hartz's ideas, because liberal ideology can be manifested in a huge number of forms that may be of greater interest to this group of students. For instance, the theory of the liberal consensus bounding pluralist diversity says little about the national appropriation process, the one-party South, or the career patterns of legislators. Such phenomena are within the range of possibilities *included* by Hartz's conclusions. Again, the significance of the hypothesis varies according to whether the observer is interested in the excluded possibilities (socialism, fascism) or in the included possibilities (one-party South, legislators' careers). If one is chiefly interested in the *excluded* possibilities (socialism, fascism), one views the hypothesis as *significant*. If one is chiefly interested in the *included* possibilities (one-party South, legislators' careers), one views the hypothesis as *insignificant* or irrelevant. This situation is similar to the relative significance of pluralist findings: if one is chiefly interested in the excluded possibilities (i.e., power-elite systems), one views the pluralist conclusion as significant.

Those concerned with the included possibilities of a hypothesis can maintain, quite correctly from their perspective, that the given hypothesis is trivial. Consequently, the significant matters become the more general phenomena included within the first hypothesis. Thus, a pluralist-behaviorist might say that Hartz's theory of the Lockean liberal consensus is obvious, and that more significant (and not obvious) propositions can be gained by generalizing about the national appropriations process or the career patterns of legislators. However, as Simon has noted, commonsense parables are often contradictory, and "obvious" generalities may cancel each other out, leaving confusion. Thus the "obviousness" of Hartz's finding of a Lockean liberal consensus is canceled out by the "obvious" generality that American politics exhibits tremendous diversity, in the multitude of groups, in the multitude of interests articulated, and so forth.

We see that a hypothesis not only predicts that something will happen—certain events are *included*; it also predicts that something will *not* happen—certain events are *excluded*. However, if the predictions or included events are "obvious" or uselessly general, relative to the interests of an observer, then that observer will view the hypothesis as insignificant. This would be the attitude of many pluralist-behaviorists toward structural propositions, such as Hartz's theory of the Lockean liberal consensus bounding pluralism. Moreover, some observers might regard a hypothesis as trivial or insignificant, *both* in its range of excluded events *and* in its range of included events. Such an observer might regard such a hypothesis as "too specific," "lacking explanatory power" (range of causes-effects covered), "lacking theoretical interest" (excessively low-level for theoretical purposes). This might be the attitude of many structuralists toward pluralist-behaviorist propositions concerning the national appropriations process, legislator's career patterns, and so forth. Excepting questions of verifiability, the structuralist's attitude toward the pluralist-behaviorist's work would be similar to the latter's attitude toward the descriptive-historical approach.

THE STUDY OF POLITICAL CULTURE

Studies of the origin and development of political structure are difficult to verify. Although in some instances the decisions of a few persons within a brief interval of time may have a great effect on the development of a political structure, in more instances structural development results from a multitude of decisions by numerous actors over a long period of time. The first case requires a simple explanatory system, but the second, more common, case requires a complex explanatory system. Furthermore, such decisions are in the past and thus cannot be observed directly. Consequently, the analyst must rely on historical records and interpretations, which may be sketchy or biased. Hence, interpreting the origins and the development of political structure may necessitate complex hypotheses, based on sketchy, and perhaps biased evidence. In terms of the illustration of the crossroads, the structuralist must study courthouse records that may only vaguely describe road building in the era of the community's founding. The prospect of such labors may be unattractive to the committed empiricist, especially if he is relatively uninterested in structural questions in the first place.

Stanley Rothman has commented on a tendency of students of American politics, interested in both empiricism and the development of a social scientific theory, to overlook structural considerations.[26] Let us review his argument in the light of the structural-behavioral distinction. Citing Hartz, Rothman refers to "a general parochialism on the part of American scholars,"[27] which is "a tendency, not limited to American scholars, to universalize their own political experience."[28]

Thus, almost all Americans, at least verbally, agree with the values of Lockean liberalism, as interpreted by Madison.* One might say that the general decision premises of almost all Americans are identical. Accordingly, many political scientists have ignored these unifying, structural elements, and have concentrated on the analysis of specific, conflicting decision premises (goals, interests). Hence, as Rothman notes, David Truman and other writers emphasize events exhibiting the characteristics of "classical Liberal Utilitarianism" but give little attention to other kinds of political activity.[29] In Apter's terms, "classical Liberal Utilitarianism" is a behavioral (and a prescriptive or a descriptive) theory that concerns the decision making of discrete individuals. Such theory "deals with *which* choices are made by . . . individuals and *why*,"[30] but it places less emphasis on commonly held choices that bind communities together and on the limits of individual rationality, the foremost limitation on the human choice process.

Rothman discusses Truman's de-emphasis of structural factors: "Despite his call for the study of all types of groups, almost all his efforts are expended in dealing with economic interest groups as they pursue their rational self-interest within certain well defined parameters."[31] Rothman continues his discussion of Truman: "And, in fact, the analysis seems quite capable of handling the behavior of these groups until we ask why, indeed, they limit themselves to these parameters."[32] In other words, why is there consensus on the general decision premises with conflict only on specific decision premises? "For example, why do American workers accept the system? Why don't they vote for a Communist Party or join Communist trade unions, as French workers have done? And why is American business generally committed to democracy? Business groups in other countries have not always revealed the same

---

* When asked "Speaking generally, what are the things about this country that you are the most proud of?" 85% of a random sample of 970 Americans mentioned governmental and political institutions. One could term this a consensus valuing Lockean liberalism as interpreted by Madison; the percentage contrasts strikingly with the 46% naming governmental and political institutions in Britain, the 7% in Germany, and the 3% in Italy. See Almond and Verba, *The Civic Culture: Political Attitudes and Democracy in Five Nations*, Princeton, 1963, pp. 102–5.

attachment. Examples could be multiplied."[33] Rothman further comments "that the comprehension of any society, whatever the terms used, will always require an examination of its *culture* and the structure of *values and beliefs* which are held by individuals who compose it."[34] (Emphasis added.)

The last statement is similar to the definition of "political culture" by Beer and Ulam: "As with the general culture of a society, the principal components of the political culture are *values, beliefs,* and *emotional attitudes.*"[35] Rothman urges "the study of the patterns of normatively oriented political action which characterize a given social system" to go beyond the limits of group theory.[36] Similarly, Beer and Ulam make "political culture" one of their four central comparative variables to go beyond the group-theory approach implicit in the other three—"interests, power, policy."[37] In a similar vein, Macridis uses "ideology" to escape the group-theory approach implicit in "decision making," "power," and "political institutions."[38] Taken together, Macridis suggests that these four are "basic concepts that suggest a classificatory scheme of politics."[39]

Likewise, "political culture" provides an escape from the group-theoretic limitations of Almond's seven "political functions." "Political communication" is much the same as "public opinion"; "interest articulation" is much the same as what interest groups do; "interest aggregation" is much the same as what political parties do; the three governmental functions—"rule making, rule application, and rule adjudication"—are familiar from institutional writings.[40] Only "political socialization and recruitment" go beyond group-theory analysis.*

Seemingly, there has been a conceptual evolution in comparative politics from the legal-institutional sphere to that of parties and groups, and then a groping for structural concepts that go beyond the group-theory world. In other words, we have the following conceptual evolution (not in order of profundity).

1. The study of law, constitutions, and institutional frameworks.

---

* The revised and extended comparative framework, set forth in Almond and Powell's *Comparative Politics,* goes beyond these earlier functional categories and accordingly must be exempted from this criticism.

2. The study of institutional politics and policy making.

3. The study of political parties or other extra-governmental interest aggregators.

4. The study of interest groups or other articulation structures.

5. The study of opinion formation and political attitudes.

6. The study of parapolitical attitudes—authoritarian personality, psychopathology and politics, democratic personality, and so forth.

In *The Civic Culture*, Almond and Verba devise structural concepts by aggregating data concerning political attitudes, personality structure, and individual political activity. Political structure is described in terms of the various distributions of participant, subject, and parochial political roles. Such a structural theory is a *contemporary* theory and a theory concerned with *mass behavior*. Because of the nature of its data, it is contemporary, for we cannot travel backward in time to do survey research in the past. However, survey research could indicate the mechanisms of *future structural* changes, if such surveys were made once a decade or generation.

In the subsequent major work on political culture, *Political Culture and Political Development*, Sidney Verba states that the "political culture of a society consists of the system of empirical beliefs, expressive symbols, and values which defines the situation in which political action takes place. It provides the subjective orientation to politics."[41] Verba notes that political culture "is very broadly defined" in his essay and that it "refers to the orientations of all the members of a political system."[42] Thus, Verba would apply the concept to both elite and mass levels. Rather than take a random sample of the population, as in *The Civic Culture*, however, we may prefer for some purposes to separate the political culture of the elite from the total. Then we may concentrate on the values, beliefs, and emotional attitudes of the political *leaders* and their orientations toward the political system.

PART THREE

Power and Leadership

8. The Concept of Leadership

The idea of leadership combines the two important concepts of power and critical decisions (issue salience). Thus, if a leader is defined as a person who exercises considerable power, then the theory of leadership is a theory of power, causation, and issue salience.

In the next two chapters I discuss political leadership* and its relationship to the developing of values and to political innovation, thereby following the sort of analysis made by Philip Selznick in his *Leadership in Administration*. In particular, I will contrast the charismatic hero with the pluralist politician. Such an analysis concerns the relations among past value commitments and present choices, or among present choices and future commitments, and thus links structural and behavioral theory.

LEADERSHIP AS CAUSATION

In ancient times men sat around their campfires at night and listened to tales of tribal founders, the man-gods who defined their way of life. With the development of writing men re-

---

* We may refer to a "restricted" sample of political leaders and an "expanded" sample of political leaders. Discussion of leadership may vary somewhat if one is referring only to "top leaders" (congressmen, governors, etc.), as in the restricted sample, or if one is referring to both top leaders and activists, as in the expanded sample (U.S. national presidential nominating convention delegates, etc.). For example, whereas the ideological position of the expanded sample of leadership may be more extreme than that of the average party voter, the ideological position of the restricted sample may be less extreme than that of the average leader in the expanded sample. In other words, the M.P. may "sell out" the party activists, as Michels so greatly feared. In discussing leadership in this book, I am generally referring to the top leaders, the restricted sample.

corded the deeds of heroes and kings. Artists of all types have found heroic leaders to be inspiring subject matter, but modern social analysts have had little success designing a theory of social and political leadership.[1] I hope to take a few small steps toward this goal in this work.

From ancient times to modern, men have personified the social-structural forces that shaped their lives. Such personification may have clarity, charm, and artistry, but, of course, it is usually grossly inaccurate from an analytic point of view. How then can we describe the impact of the heroic leader on his society?

When we study an individual leader, we are using behavioral analysis rather than structural analysis, although as always structure and behavior are inextricably linked. Thus, the focus on a leader directly involves a theory that "deals with *which* choices are made by . . . individuals and *why*"[2] (and in this case the individual is a leader). However, the leader's decisions and actions are limited by social structure and values, as the departed Ghanaian Osagyefo's (Savior's) decisions were limited by the structures of tribalism and socioeconomic underdevelopment. In other words, we consider why the leader led his band down one road rather than the other within the limitations set by a crossroads. In analyzing the Bay-fill issue, if we study leadership, we focus on human activity within the bounds of social structure and values. Hence, we would suspect that the behavioral study of American politics could provide a basis for a theory of leadership, and indeed I argue that it does.

A *leader* may be defined as one who has unusual *influence*. Influence may be viewed as one's capacity to make people behave differently than they would have otherwise. A leader may also be defined as one who has unusual *power*. Here we view "power" as a person's capacity to make others do something that they would not do otherwise and that the person specifically wants or intends. (We may perhaps include the dimension of others' resistance.) As we have seen, such definitions of power and influence refer to social causation. When the leader successfully exercises influence, he causes change in human activity.* When the leader exercises power, he causes manifest effects (in Merton's sense) in human activity, i.e., the leader causes changes that he originally desired.[3]

In other words, the leader is one who makes things happen that would not happen otherwise. I think this statement is congruent with commonly held images of leadership. (Note that a leader is exerting influence when he vetoes possibilities, when he stops things from happening that would have happened otherwise. For example, President Hoover was very influential during the Depression, and especially so by clinging to his laissez-faire ideology, which foreclosed possible events that might have happened otherwise.)

Sidney Hook, in *The Hero in History*, depicts the heroic leader as one who makes things happen that would not have happened otherwise. For example, at the end of his introduction, he describes the purpose of his book: "An attempt will be made to work out some generalizations of the types of situations and conditions in which we can justifiably attribute or deny *causal influence* to outstanding personalities."[4] (Emphasis added.) Hook defines "the hero in history" in this way: "The hero in history is the individual to whom we can justifiably attribute preponderant influence in determining an issue or event whose consequences would have been profoundly different if he had not acted as he did."[5] In other words, "the hero is defined as *an event-making individual* who redetermines the course of history."[6] (Emphasis added.)

Such a view is similar to Robert Dahl's scheme in *Who Governs?* for ranking the power of actors. Dahl observes which persons initiate and veto proposed policies; those who initiate

* This definition of leadership is subject to the Oswald Paradox. Lee Harvey Oswald exercised great influence on human events, that is, he significantly altered the behavior of the American national government. Thus, we might say that Oswald was an extraordinarily influential individual, and depending on his intentions, possibly an extraordinarily powerful individual. His influence would seem to be far greater than that of the average senator, for example. On the other hand, Oswald's influence/power is solely dependent on Kennedy's influence. The more independent causal impact on human events Kennedy possessed, the more Oswald possessed. Such a case as the Oswald Paradox arises when we see the person rather than an analytical construct such as the role as the unit of the system.

and veto the most often are said to have the most influence and are the political leaders of the community.[7] This is the same basic view of leadership as Hook's and my own. Thus, when a person initiates a measure, he makes an event happen that would not have happened otherwise. When such an initiative becomes governmental policy, many events occur that otherwise would not have occurred. Similarly, modification means making changes in political events. Vetoing prevents the occurrence of certain events. Initiation, modification, and vetoing all refer to changing the course of human events, in this case through changing the course of governmental policies.

The image of the community political system in *Who Governs?* and Aaron Wildavsky's *Leadership in a Small Town* portrays real people as the units of the system, rather than roles or analytical constructs as the basic units. Dahl and Wildavsky do consider such roles as that of mayor, city manager, and party leaders, but the individual actor is the basic unit they use for analyzing the distribution of power. Thus, if many individual persons in the system or a subsystem are found to exercise influence and power, then the system is said to be decentralized. Analogously, if one or few persons in the system or a subsystem are found to exercise influence and power, then the system is said to be centralized, in Dahl's mode of analysis.[8] Defining power and influence in terms of causality and focusing on the individual actor as the systemic unit combine to make up the conception of leadership that I have just outlined. Accordingly, political studies of this type should provide material for the study of leadership.

A MODE OF ANALYSIS

If we define leadership as influence, in turn defined as causality, what mode of analysis can we use? Certainly, theorizing about leadership, defined as influence, of entire societies involves operational and verificational difficulties of greater magnitude than those encountered in the analysis of influence within small groups. As Hook has stated:

It is not enough, however, for those who believe in the importance of outstanding individuals in history to establish the fact of the *existence* of outstanding individuals. They must present the evidence that these individuals not only existed but had a decisive influence on their respective fields of activity. Further, they must be able to meet reasonably the challenge that if these individuals had not lived and worked as they did, their work would, in all likelihood, have been done by others.[9]

But how are we to establish that a leader had "decisive influence" or that a leader's work would not have been done by others? We have seen the problems of determining "decisive [i.e., great] influence." To consider Hook's next point: if a leader's work would have been duplicated by others, then the leader's activities can be said to have been determined by a social system. And if we can define and understand the mechanisms of social systems and subsystems, we have solved the major problems of social science.

But I do not prescribe a retreat from the analysis of leadership as an escape from the dilemma. The scholar committed to empiricism and strict verification may wish to work on other problems, and, except for the analysis of influence within small groups, he has generally done so. Accordingly, the study of leadership of entire political systems is now carried out by descriptive historians, journalists, and novelists. For example, analytical literature on the American Presidency, perhaps the world's most important political office, is extremely sparse. There is a need to devote more resources to the social-scientific study of leadership, in spite of the extraordinarily difficult problems of operational definition and verification.

Thus, if we wish to analyze leadership, defined as influence, we must rely on a mode of analysis akin to policy analysis. In other words, we must marshal data and theories and apply them to an exceedingly complex situation, using judgment and probabilistic reasoning. When we analyze leadership, we are in effect using the same mode of analysis as leaders must use themselves—marshaling data and theories, relying on judgment and probabilistic reasoning. However, as social scientists, we emphasize concepts, evidence, and the testing of hypotheses. Furthermore, we can choose to deal with only a part of a situation, and we have much more time to gather evidence and theories.

Let us outline some important considerations for the study

of leadership, defined as influence. First, we must establish the limits of a person's action in terms of general social forces, although this is obviously difficult. Second, we "think away" the existence of the particular leader, and consider what might have happened if the leader had not lived. Third, we compare the more probable "might-have-been's" with the actuality in order to assess the magnitude and significance of the influence (causality) the leader has exercised on human events. Finally, such judgmental-probabilistic reasoning need not be restricted to past events but can be applied to future possibilities. Indeed, this is done constantly by policy analysts and other observers of political events. (For example, when we ask what difference it would make if De Gaulle were to die today, we are asking how much influence De Gaulle has.)

A good example of such judgmental-probabilistic reasoning is Hook's argument that Lenin was an event-making man, a leader of extraordinary impact, a person having extraordinary influence.[10] Thus, Hook writes "that had it not been for the work of one man [Lenin] we should be living in a vastly different world today."[11] If we think away the existence of Lenin, then according to one's probabilistic judgments of the relevant historical data and theory "we should be living in a vastly different world today." In other words, Lenin's actions caused very important effects. Lenin exerted extraordinary influence or power, insofar as the effects of his actions were intended or manifest.

Hook continues in this fashion:

There are four stages to the argument. The first is that, next to the World War, the most momentous occurrence of the twentieth century has been the Russian Revolution of October 1917. [Hook writes in 1943.] By "most momentous" we mean that it has had a greater influence on the political, social, and economic history of the world since its occurrence than any other single event. The second step in the argument is that the Russian Revolution was not inevitable. The third is that it was triumphant because of the directing leadership of Lenin and that without him it would have been lost. The fourth is that if the Russian Revolution had not taken place the cultural, political, and, in part, the economic life of the world would have been very different.[12]

The first and the fourth stages of the argument amount to a restatement of the same idea—the Bolshevik Revolution was the cause of very significant effects. The second and third stages of Hook's discussion express the idea that the Bolshevik Revolution, in anything like its actual historical form, could not have occurred without the actions of Lenin. In a way, Hook thinks away the existence of the leader (Lenin), considers what might have happened in such a case, and compares the might-have-been with the actuality in order to assess the significance of the leader. Hook also establishes the limits of the individual person's action in terms of general social forces. Thus, he views the downfall of the tsarist autocracy as inevitable, so obvious that the participants expected such a downfall themselves: "all political groups, except pensioners of the court and other reactionary elements, anticipated the downfall of the autocracy through a 'February' Revolution at almost any moment after the outbreak of the Russo-Japanese War."[13] Such a general outcome may be predicted by structural analysis, by noting the degree of class conflict, social change, and the breakdown of legitimacy.

Where the vital needs of submerged classes are unfilled, where conflicts of interest are so deep that they cannot be negotiated without cutting into the vested powers of men who are firmly convinced of their divine or social right to those powers, where customary political rule becomes increasingly inept or oppressive, where the moral professions of those in the saddle sound hollow in the light of actualities—we can already feel the vibrations of discontent that may suddenly erupt into a cataclysmic flood. We can tell that it is coming, we can predict its approach though not what particular event will set it off.[14]

However, Hook maintains, we cannot predict which choices will be made and why, within the structural limits set by such a situation of potential revolution. "We can predict, in other words, the advent of a revolution or war but *not always what its upshot will be. That upshot may sometimes depend upon the characters of the leading personalities.*"[15] That is to say, specific decisions and outcomes ("upshots") cannot be predicted from structural (class and value) analysis, and we must resort to the behavioral analysis of leaders to explain and predict the choices they make within the structural limits.

In other words, the analysis of leadership, defined as influence, must use both the structural and behavioral approaches. Hook criticizes Trotsky's *History of the Russian Revolution* for taking the position that the October Revolution was inevitably prefigured by the class structure of Russian society. In contrast to such structural determinists as Trotsky and Plekhanov,[16] Hook emphasizes a behavioral dimension, limited by structural factors.

The existence of possible alternatives of development in a historic situation is the presupposition of significant heroic action. The all-important point for our purposes is whether there are such alternatives of development—their nature and duration. The position taken so far commits us to the belief that there have been and are such alternatives in history with mutually incompatible consequences that might have redetermined the course of events in the past, and that might redetermine them in the future.[17]

However, Hook also emphasizes the limits on individual decisions and actions set by general social forces. Thus, his method *"does not assert that all alternatives are possible."*[18] It recognizes limitations on possibilities, including limitations on the possible effect of heroic action, based on the acceptance of generalized descriptions or laws of social behavior.

We have said that Hook follows the mode of reasoning outlined above: he establishes the limits of the individual person's action in terms of general social forces; he conducts the mental experiment of thinking away the existence of a particular leader and considers what might have happened if the leader had not existed; he compares the more probable "might-have-been's" with the actual course of events in order to assess the magnitude and significance of the leader's influence (causal impact) on human events.

The reader bent on verification may object to such judgmental-probabilistic consideration of what might have been, of the difference between what *might have been* and what *was*, or, in short, of considering the "if's" of history. But he who does not consider the "if's" of history is at best a journalist of the duller sort. He who considers the "if's" of history is analyzing; he is considering variations of effects and variations in causes, how one factor in a system varies with another. Considering the "if's" of history is conducting a mental experiment. For example, we might think away the destruction of the U.S.S. Maine in 1898 to consider whether more general social forces were impelling the United States into war with Spain. Or we might imagine that Hitler had been killed in the Munich putsch of 1923 to consider which components of German fascism were the results of the idiosyncrasies of one man and which components were the effects of general social forces.

Dealing with the "if's" of history is analogous to conducting controlled experiments, although of course the verifiability of the conclusions of such mental experiments is extremely tenuous. Thus, in a controlled experiment, the analyst sets up two runs, in which all factors are duplicated except for one, which presumably accounts for any observed differences in the results of the run. In the mental experiment, the analyst may vary a single factor, and relying on judgmental-probabilistic reasoning, posit varying outcomes.*

We see, then, that consideration of the "if's" of history is a form of hypothesizing, while neglecting such "if's" leads to description. However, as Hook has noted: "When we draw the line of possible eventuality too far out of the immediate period, the mind staggers under the cumulative weight of the unforeseen."[19] We must realize that the difficulty of such hypothesizing probably increases exponentially with the passage of time.

---

* Those rejecting such judgmental-probabilistic analysis might consider that much U.S. national defense planning relies on exactly this type of reasoning, projected into the future. For example, we find mental experiments in the writings of the analysts of nuclear-era strategy and diplomacy, as in the scenarios of Herman Kahn and others: "If we do this, the result will be that; but if we do something else, the result will be. . . ." These observers are dealing with the "might-be's," instead of the "might-have-been's"—the "if's" of the future rather than of the past. However, as Aaron Wildavsky pointed out to me, mental experiments are difficult to replicate. The best way of proceeding is to conduct the mental experiment, refine testable hypotheses, and test against data, if this can be done in a given situation.

FUNCTIONALIST AND EQUILIBRIUM MODELS

In many cases the language of structural-functional analysis can be translated into cause-effect terminology. Accordingly, a "structure" is often no more than a variable of a system, and the structure's "functions," in terms of the entire system, are often no more than the descriptions of effects of a variable's actions as a causative agent. The term "dysfunctions" often refers to no more than a causative agent's effects that change the total system's actions. Hence, the following structural-functional terminology can be related to the cause-effect terminology that I am using. Harry M. Johnson notes that "there seem to be three basic methods for arriving at knowledge concerning functions and dysfunctions."[20] The first of these three methods is "the method called 'mental experiment,'" which "is to 'think away' the partial structure in question and ask what would happen in and to the social system without it."[21] I have discussed this method above. Johnson adds that "another basic method of discovering functions and dysfunctions is to compare cases that are similar except for the partial structure in question."[22] The "mental experiment" and the comparative method amount to much the same thing: comparative method focuses directly on concrete data; mental experiments focus on abstract, probabilistic data, which are, however, linked to concrete, observed data. Both methods attempt to set up abstract controlled experiments, in which all factors save one are alike in two or more situations. Relationships are then sought between the salient variable and differences in the situational outcomes.

According to Harry M. Johnson, a third method for analyzing functionality (hence cause-effect relationships) within social systems is the analysis of deviance and social control.[23] This would seemingly have no application to the study of leadership, but considering deviance makes us recognize the need to state assumptions concerning the dynamics of the social system surrounding the leader. For example, let us consider a social system composed of concrete units—the actors themselves—such as Dahl's models of power. Suppose that one of the units, a variable of the system, begins to act in deviant fashion, outside the range of typical actions. What will happen? Either we postulate an equilibrium model or we do not. If we postulate such an equilibrium model, then the deviant behavior of the individual variable will cause counteractivity by other variables, so that the whole system, or a part of it, acts more intensely than usual, until the system returns to equilibrium and the deviant behavior is terminated. On the other hand, if the system does not return to equilibrium, it becomes a new system. In other words, if we postulate an equilibrium model, the deviant behavior will produce what cyberneticians call a negative-feedback action system, i.e., an activity-set for the purpose of control.[24]

However, if we do not postulate an equilibrium model, then we might not presume a negative-feedback action system for social control. Thus, if a variable deviates from a former action pattern, such a variation may not produce intense activity to restore the former action pattern. Instead, the deviant pattern may produce some small changes in the system. (Whether or not such small changes produce a "new" system is a matter of definition.)

As an example, we may ask how much influence Governor Orval Faubus exerted in the Little Rock crisis of 1957–58. Did Faubus exert a significant impact on modern American history, or didn't he? If we postulate an equilibrium model, we would say that Faubus' behavior, deviant from the standpoint of the national legal system, made little difference over a period of five years, because the governor's activity only provoked the federal government to intense counteraction until eventually the normal state of affairs was restored. Here, normality is seen as very gradual racial integration, with only minor disruptive conflict. By 1966 it could be said: "Anti-Faubus sentiment has developed over his increasing moderation on the racial issue (Faubus has appointed more than 100 Negroes to state jobs that were previously held by whites)."[25] Thus, an observer might conclude that Faubus' actions in 1957–58 had little medium- or long-range effect, and hence that the Arkansas governor, who probably provoked the confrontations at Little Rock Central High School to increase his electoral popularity, actually exerted little influence on (caused few changes in) the flow of human events.[26] In other words, the idiosyncratic behavior of Faubus precipitated an increase in the intensity of conflict and the use of measures of control until an equilibrium situation was reestablished.

Parenthetically, we must note that there are problems with using the concept "equilibrium" in such contexts. The idea of equilibrium may be represented by a rectangular block in a motionless position on a flat surface; an unstable equilibrium may be represented by a cone balanced on its apex; a dynamic equilibrium may be represented by a pendulum in motion. Yet in most social situations, we have greater dynamism than in any of these three cases. In many social situations, it is more useful to refer to a system's rate of change with respect to a set of factors.[27] For example, in the Arkansas situation, we did not have oscillation around a central point (complete segregation of schools) in 1957–58. Instead, we had a system of social practices gradually changing toward somewhat greater racial equality, which was temporarily interrupted by Governor Faubus' actions in the Little Rock school crisis. In other words, Faubus tried but failed in his attempt to slow down or halt gradual change in a system of social practices. Thus, deviant behavior and the actions of leaders can be viewed as acting to modify the rate of change of a general system of social action. Consequently, social-control practices may be viewed as attempts to reestablish the previous rate of change. Such a rate-of-change model can be more useful for analysis than the equilibrium model. We see that the analysis of deviance can be linked to the study of causes and effects within systems, and hence to the analysis of the independent causal impact of leadership.

GREAT MAN THEORIES OF LEADERSHIP

Much recent writing about leadership can be related to the "charisma-paradigm" model, which may be summarized as follows: in times of value strain (Smelser), a charismatic hero may appear (Weber, Hook), whose psychological processes are paralleled by his public actions (Lasswell), perhaps in a widely appealing resolution of a personal identity crisis (Erikson, Pye) that provides the critical decisions and values for a new social identity (Selznick), thereby leading to social change through the establishment of new social structures infused with new ideology.[28] I refer to this model as the "charisma-paradigm" model, since it is an extension of Weber's concept of charismatic authority, and in it the leader provides a new paradigm for personal and social identity (in the manner that great natural scientists, through revolutionary experimental and theoretical discoveries, provide the general framework for most subsequent scientific investigation until another "scientific revolution" occurs).[29]

The first five books of the Old Testament provide a prototype for this charisma-paradigm model. In Egypt, the minority Hebraic ethnic group found itself in a position akin to colonial status. In Karl Deutsch's terminology, the Hebrews were not assimilated into the dominant national community, but became increasingly differentiated, in a process similar to some types of modern nationalism.[30] As Haas has noted, in the "nation-before-the state" model of nationalism, a group of intellectuals perpetuates a unifying national myth that, infused with social, linguistic, and religious distinctiveness, accelerates the differentiation of a particular group from other such groups.[31] According to the Old Testament, something like this happened with the Jews in Egypt. Thus, whereas Seymour Martin Lipset refers to the United States as "the first new nation,"[32] I would refer to the ancient Jews as "the first new nation." The Jews broke free from a subordinate social and political status, only to find themselves wandering in the wilderness, for though they felt themselves to be a chosen people, they had yet to establish their promised land. Similarly, many new nations today, after gaining freedom from colonial rule, find themselves "wandering in the wilderness," searching for a promised land of unification and economic development. In this respect, I think that the ancient Jews provide a more pertinent image for the first new nation than America, whose national elites reached agreement comparatively easily on a political constitution, which rapidly became the catalyst and symbol for national unification. George Washington and other members of the political elite performed excellently in solving difficult political problems in the construction of their new nation, but eighteenth-century American political and social conflicts and economic conditions did not pose problems as staggering as those faced by Nehru, Mao, or Sukarno.

As we may take the Pentateuch to be a prototype of emerging nationhood, so we may see Moses as an archetype of the heroic, charismatic leader. Moses' disgust with the worship of the golden calf and his solitary receipt of the Ten Commandments on Mount Sinai can be viewed as psychologically and sociologically symbolic, just as Luther's rebellion against the Catholic Church has been interpreted by Erikson.[33] The Ten Commandments can be seen as coming from God, but one can also view them as the solution of a crisis in personal identity—a solution that had wide appeal for others. Erikson focuses on identity crises occurring in the person's late adolescence or early twenties, but some persons, such as Moses (Gauguin, Goethe), had such crises in later life. Accordingly, we may regard Moses as an archetype of the charisma-paradigm model of leadership. Moses established the critical decisions and values for a new *social* identity, with his new ideology embodied in the Commandments and the other articles of the Torah, which mobilized the wandering people toward their goal of reaching their promised land.

As stated above, a "value" may be "a generalized imperative concerning scope of activity." The Ten Commandments express precisely what I mean by "value." Thus, when Moses brings the Commandments down from the mountain, we have an evocative image of the charismatic leader creating new values (Do this. Don't do that.), making critical decisions, setting a new paradigm for society.

The Old Testament provides an image of a hero in history, a "great" political leader, an image that has three elements corresponding to the three main factors in the psychological and social-psychological study of leadership—the leader, the followers, and the situation of the group.[34] The weight of evidence indicates that in studying leadership, one must consider all three factors. Accordingly, one cannot separate the leader from the followers and the situation and still analyze traits of leadership. One cannot discuss authority without discussing the values and perceptions of followers, as Weber emphasized in his discussion of authority.[35]

In the charisma-paradigm model of leadership, these three factors are considered. In the *situation,* one usually finds a high degree of social and political conflict and/or confusion about basic values (wandering in the wilderness). In the *leader,* one usually finds the resolution of a personal identity crisis, which provides the crucial decisions and values for a new social identity. One must question why one particular leader's paradigm, and not another's, is appealing to the *followers.*

Extraordinary leaders are those who make an extraordinary impact on the course of social events. We would say that such leaders are "revolutionary" because they cause revolutionary social and political changes. Perhaps a theory of leadership is related to a theory of revolution, for indeed both these types of theory are closely linked with almost all other types of social theory. A theory of revolution, like a theory of leadership, must take into account leaders, followers, and situation. To develop a theory of leadership, it seems reasonable to look to theories of revolution, but unfortunately there is much disagreement in this last field of study.

Extraordinary political leaders tend to appear in times of extraordinary political conflict. (This does not mean, however, that such extraordinary conflict will *necessitate* the appearance of an unusually influential leader.) If the group situation is one of wandering in the wilderness, there is more dissatisfaction, more demand for change, hence more leeway for the exercise of influence (the causing of changes), than if the group finds itself in a Garden of Eden, where all are satisfied, no one wants change, and hence no important changes are to be made. In times of turmoil and social conflict, followers want change; hence a leader who causes such changes may appear. The charisma-paradigm model, then, does not apply to a stable political system, with high agreement and low conflict, unless this model of leadership is modified to show differences of degree.

Many writers have made the point that great leaders appear only when the group is wandering in a wilderness. For example, Eric Hoffer writes in *The True Believer*: "There has to be an eagerness to follow and obey, and an intense dissatisfaction with things as they are, before [the mass] movement and leader can make their appearance. When conditions are not ripe, the potential leader, no matter how gifted, and his holy cause, no matter how potent, remain without a following."[36] This applies not only to the development of mass movements, but also to the politics of democracies:

In Britain, too, the leader had to wait for the time to ripen before he could play his role. During the 1930's the potential leader (Churchill) was prominent in the eyes of the people and made himself heard, day in, day out. But the will to follow was not there. It was only when disaster shook the country to its foundation and made autonomous individual lives untenable and meaningless that the leader came into his own.[37]

Sidney Hook also finds a relationship between the appearance of the heroes of history and times of "a sharp crisis in social and political affairs."

Whoever saves us is a hero; and in the exigencies of political action men are always looking for someone to save them. A sharp crisis in social and political affairs—when something must be done and done quickly—naturally intensifies interest in the hero. No matter what one's political complexion, hope for the resolution of a crisis is always bound up with hope for the appearance of strong or intelligent leadership to cope with difficulties and perils. The more urgent the crisis, the more intense is the longing, whether it be a silent prayer or public exhortation, for the proper man to master it. He may be called "savior," "man on horseback," "prophet," "social engineer," "beloved disciple," "scientific revolutionist," depending upon the vocabulary of the creed or party.[38]

A leader's paradigm will contain more *critical decisions* the more the followers are in a state of critical conflict over basic issues and/or the more the followers are uncertain about the proper course of action in a situation. Thus, in a social system rent by basic conflicts (over general, ultimate decision premises), more ideological, more religious political leaders can be identified.* Rapid social change from traditional to modern society usually causes conflict over critical issues. In such a situation, the leader of a new nation may attempt to create a new paradigm, a new social identity expressed in critical decisions that embrace both traditional elements and modern elements, however defined by the leader. Leaders (especially in modernizing states) may attempt to legitimize their authority by referring to values (critical decision premises) of traditional politics.[39] Nehru, Sukarno, Nkrumah, and Kenyatta appear to have done this. Leaders in new nations who make the character-defining decisions concerning the nature of the political community are men of extraordinary influence, for they can cause great changes in the course of human events. Some of them, such as Castro, Sukarno, and Nkrumah, for a while had great latitude of choice in deciding the character of their political community. (But mistakes can whittle away the latitude of choice and even cause the downfall of the hero himself, as in the cases of Nkrumah and Sukarno.)

ROUTINE LEADERSHIP

It is easier to understand the role of leadership in societies that are rent by basic sociopolitical conflicts than in societies that have limited sociopolitical conflicts and value homogeneity in politics and government. When societies are wandering in the wilderness, when there is fundamental conflict, great dissatisfaction, and demand for change, there is greater leeway for the exercise of influence, the causing of major changes in the flow of political events. On the other hand, if the society is a settled Judea, where there is only limited conflict, general satisfaction, and little demand for basic changes, there is less leeway for the exercise of influence because almost no one desires such basic changes. Ours has been a relatively settled, homogeneous society; accordingly, with the exception of decisions about the racial question, involving the definition of the political community, and the system-maintenance decisions of foreign policy and national defense, we

* Definitions of "ideology" generally presuppose components of generality, critical decision premises, etc., rather than components of specificity, routine decision premises, etc.

cannot expect national political leaders to make critical, value-setting decisions within a short space of time. Most domestic political decisions are "routine," in Selznick's sense, not because they preclude a considerable amount of controversy, but because they involve incremental changes on a previously existing policy base. (However, a number of incremental decisions may add up to a fundamental, critical decision.)[40] In other words, such routine, incremental decisions are specific modifications of previously established general decision premises for governmental policies.[41]

What we have just said should not imply that because politicians (leaders) are often highly influential in unstable situations, they have no influence at all in consensus-settlement situations. This statement—politicians have no influence at all in consensus-settlement situations—appears so extreme that we might think that no observer would even approximate such an assertion. However, if we change the language slightly, we see that some observers *have* approximated this position. I have noted that political influence is political causation, and hence, if one is without influence, one is a dependent variable in a social system. Consequently, to say that politicians have no influence at all in consensus-settlement situations is the same as saying that politicians are dependent variables in consensus-settlement (pluralist) situations.

I think it fair to say that much group theory regards politicians as dependent variables and interest groups and political parties as independent variables. Though this is seldom stated explicitly, the politician as a dependent variable is the dominant image in the group-theory literature. At least we can say that group theorists, with a special interest in groups, quite understandably tend to emphasize the role of groups as independent variables. For example, Latham writes about the relations between groups and legislatures, which are also seen as compounds of "official groups."

The legislature referees the group struggle, ratifies the victories of the successful coalitions, and records the terms of the surrenders, compromises, and conquests in the form of statutes. Every statute tends to represent compromise because the very process of accommodating conflicts of group interest is one of deliberation and consent. The legislative vote on any issue thus tends to represent the composition of strength, i.e., the balance of power among the contending groups at the moment of voting. What may be called public policy is actually the equilibrium reached in the group struggle at any given moment, and it represents a balance which the contending factions of groups constantly strive to weight in their favor.[42]

The role of referee is not supposed to be a powerful one; the baseball umpire calls the balls and strikes, the safes and the outs, but we do not ordinarily expect him to influence significantly the outcome of the game. Accordingly, even though he uses the referee metaphor, Latham is somewhat ambiguous concerning the role of public office holders as independent or dependent variables. But he qualifies the above statement: "In these adjustments of group interest, the legislature does not play the part of inert cash register, ringing up the additions and withdrawals of strength; it is not a mindless balance pointing and marking the weight and distribution of power among the contending groups. Legislatures are groups also and show a sense of identity and consciousness of kind that unofficial groups must regard if they are to represent their members effectively."[43] Thus, although a legislature only makes "adjustments of group interest," i.e., makes only small changes in the formulation of a public policy that is basically a dependent variable of the pattern of group interests, a legislature is, to some extent, an independent variable, partly because it is a status group, with a way of life that must be respected and "a sense of identity and consciousness of kind." However, this is an unsatisfactory formulation, for Latham says only that a legislature will have some force as an independent variable when the norms of the legislative way of life have been violated by outsiders, such as lobbyists. But only a naïve, incompetent lobbyist would commit such gross blunders.[44]

Latham and other group theorists admit that an individual holder of public office can act as an independent variable. However, because of their primary interest in group phenomena, they do not attempt to delineate the role of the individual leader. As Latham writes:

Finally, it may be asked, "Whatever became of the individual?" He
was introduced briefly as the beneficiary of group forms and then
whisked off the page. Are not individuals as well as groups important in the political process? What of a Roosevelt? What of a
Gandhi? *Were these not individuals, and were they not influential
as political actors, and not memorable merely as the passive re-
cipients of the fullness of group life?* To this it may be said that
individuals are, of course, important as political actors, when they
move others to responsive behavior, or represent them, or acquire
their support or tolerance. That is to say, they are significant politically in the group relations they establish and organize, or modify,
or destroy.[45] [Emphasis added.]

However, we want to know, more precisely, how the individual leader acts as an independent variable and exercises influence to cause changes in political events.

As I have noted, the empirical political theory of Robert
Dahl and his students, formulated after group theory, pays
considerable attention to the role of the individual as an independent variable. *Who Governs?*, *Leadership in a Small
Town*, and similar works have managed to treat the leader
as an independent factor, without losing the advantages of
treating interest groups and political parties. Leadership in
such works is defined in terms of influence, i.e., causing
changes in the course of political events by initiating, modifying, or vetoing decisions and political actions.

Dahl's political theory is fruitfully linked to Lindblom's
theory of bargaining, as foreshadowed in the relatively early
joint work by these two authors, *Politics, Economics and Welfare*, and subsequently developed in Wildavsky's *The Politics
of the Budgetary Process*.[46] Dahl's and Lindblom's theories,
as developed up to the present and considered together, provide a good framework for the study of leadership in the environment of general consensus, for this combination focuses
on individuals, defines influence in terms of causality, and
studies specific, routine decisions in an arena of agreement
about the nature of the political community, the governmental regime, and the bases of current governmental policies.
Some might think that Dahl's and Lindblom's theories rele-
gate leadership to a minor role in the value-homogeneous so-

ciety, for politicians are seen as making specific routine decisions within the limiting framework of accepted ongoing governmental policies, social structure, and ideology. In other words, politicians bargain over marginal changes in ongoing governmental policies and make incremental decisions, in Lindblom's terminology. Thus, a description or prescription of incrementalism is a description or prescription of social conservatism or reformism from the standpoint of the radical or the revolutionist. The incrementalist politician does not wish to tamper *suddenly* with the basic social structure or governmental policies of his time. However, we may note the logical possibility that a large number of such conservative, reformist, incremental changes over a period of time could add up to a radical, revolutionary, basic change in sociopolitical structure. Where one draws the line between incremental and basic change, between reform and revolution, is, of course, a matter of definition and personal values.[47] Incremental change is the basic image we have of American and British sociopolitical change in the last century, and certainly many observers would argue that slowly changing governmental policies, over a generation or more, have produced major, radical, revolutionary, and basic changes.*

Consequently, within a restricted time, the pluralist politician, bargaining over incremental changes in governmental policies, may seem to be limited to routine, unimportant decisions. But over a period of time, such decisions may add up to revolutionary change, to new critical decisions and values, setting generalized imperatives concerning the proper scope of governmental activity, as in the U.S. federal government's welfare policies from 1933 to the present. Hence, decisions made by a particular politician may be incremental and routine, but many such decisions made by many such politicians over a length of time may add up to a critical decision. Accordingly, over a length of time, the system compounds a critical decision from numerous routine decisions of individuals. In summary, we may say that politicians, whose leeway

---

* This is implicit in the familiar charge of "creeping socialism," which involves the belief that numerous incremental changes may revolutionize the nature of our political, economic, and social systems.

for independent action is greatly limited by the separations of powers (causality) of social and political pluralism, nevertheless may contribute to critical decisions over a length of time. Hence, for a theory of political power, the analysis of the innovative character of a pluralist politician's decisions, even on routine matters, may be as important as considering the mechanisms of the charisma-paradigm model of the hero of history.

SUMMARY

Leaders are defined as the influential—those who exercise great causal impact on social events. In other words, the leader is one who makes things happen that would not happen otherwise. If the leader causes changes that he intended, he has exercised power; if the leader causes changes that he did not intend or want, he has exercised influence, but not power. Defining leadership as influence is congruent with the usage of Sidney Hook and Robert Dahl.

The analysis of the leadership of entire societies—like policy analysis—can seldom be conducted with a high degree of verifiability, for controlled experiments are not possible, and the data are extremely complex. (As before, I am referring to the restricted sample of top leaders and not to the expanded sample including both top leaders and followers.)[48] The essentials of the judgmental-probabilistic analysis of the independent effects of leadership include the following considerations: (1) We establish the limits on the individual person's action set by general social forces, which structure the particular situation and the responses of the followers. We must always link the analysis of leadership with an analysis of situation and followers. (2) We may consider the structural limits on leadership in the light of a comparative method. Thus, to show the independent effects of individual actions, we may show that in two situations, similar except for the different actions of leaders, the outcomes were different, presumably as a result of varying leadership patterns. (3) An equivalent to this comparative method is mentally eliminating a leader from a situation, and then considering what might have happened if the leader had not existed. Thus, if we compare the probable "if's" of history without the leader with the actual course of historical events, we may assess the magnitude and significance of the influence (causal impact) of the leader. Such consideration of the "if's" of history is a form of hypothesizing, for this is a process of relating different variables (i.e., leaders) to different historical effects. Of course, we may consider the "if's" of the present and future, as well as those of the past.

Much recent writing about leadership can be seen in terms of the charisma-paradigm model. Thus, in times of value strain, a charismatic hero may appear whose psychological processes are paralleled by his public actions perhaps in a widely appealing resolution of a personal identity crisis that provides the critical decisions and values for a new social identity, thereby leading to social change through the establishment of new social structures infused with new ideology. Such a leader provides a new social paradigm, just as great natural scientists, through revolutionary experimental and theoretical discoveries, provide the general framework for most subsequent scientific investigation until another "scientific revolution" occurs.

The prototype of the charisma-paradigm model is the Old Testament story of the Exodus, when Moses provided a new social and personal identity for the Hebrews wandering in the wilderness. The situation for the appearance of the great leader, who was to have extraordinary causal impact on history, is that of a high degree of social and political conflict and/or confusion about basic values. Thus, great leaders may be revolutionary men who appear in revolutionary situations. Accordingly, there should be considerable overlap between a theory of revolutions and a theory of leadership, as both presuppose some theory of social change.

The role of leadership in societies that are rent by basic sociopolitical conflicts seems easier to understand than the role of leadership in settled societies, in which politicians may seem to be limited to routine, unimportant decisions and to bargaining over incremental changes in governmental policies. But over a period of time, such decisions may add up to revolutionary change, to new critical decisions and values, setting generalized imperatives concerning the proper scope of governmental activity. Hence, for a theory of political power, the analysis of the innovative character of politicians' decisions, even on routine matters, may be as important as considering the charisma-paradigm model of the hero of history.

In the next chapter I examine the responses of leaders to limited conflict—that of the pluralist, homogeneous society[49] in which there is almost complete agreement about the fundamental nature of politics and government,[50] and in which most political decisions are routine, specific choices concerning incremental changes in governmental policies.

9. Multilateral Conflict and Leaders' Response

Georg Simmel, Lewis Coser, Ralf Dahrendorf, William Goode, and many other writers have emphasized "the functions of social conflict" until their message has been, I think, widely understood.[1] On the sociological level, conflict theorists show that conflict promotes social solidarity, clarifies social norms, and results in social change as well as disintegrative effects. On the psychological level, conflict may stimulate "search behavior" and creative innovation as well as cause neuroses and psychoses.[2] "Conflict produces consciousness" is a familiar aphorism from Hegel, Marx, and Simmel.

"Conflict between what?" we may ask. First, I should note that conflict is not necessarily dialectical. *Conflict may be multilateral*: it may occur among several different groups, classes, status groups, parties, ideologies, etc. The multilateral nature of conflict must be emphasized because there has been some tendency to perceive only dialectical conflict as natural, perhaps because of the great influence of Hegel and Marx on Western philosophy, social analysis, and social reformation.

THE DUALIST VIEW

Dahrendorf, for example, emphasizes this dualist point of view in his discussion of the contributions of Marx to social analysis. He writes that Marx contributed the emphasis on "the formative force of conflicting social groups or classes," and that this emphasis "is accompanied, in the work of Marx, by two steps of analysis which, although rather formal, are nevertheless worth mentioning and sustaining." The first of these analytic steps is "tracing conflicts that effect change back to patterns of social structure."[3] The second great analytical contribution of Marx is, according to Dahrendorf, the view that conflict is inherently dualist:

Marx properly assumed the dominance of one particular conflict in any given situation. Whatever criticism may be required of the Marxian theory, any theory of conflict has to operate with something like a two-class model. There are but two contending parties —this is implied in the very concept of conflict. There may be coalitions, of course, as there may be conflicts internal to either of the contenders, and there may be groups that are not drawn into a given dispute; but from the point of view of a given clash of interests, there are never more than two positions that struggle for domination. We can follow Marx in this argument (which, for him, is often more implicit that explicit) even further. If social conflicts effect change, and if they are generated by social structure, then it is reasonable to assume that of the two interests involved in any one conflict, one will be pressing for change, the other one for the status quo. This assumption, again, is based on logic as much as on empirical observation. In every conflict, one party attacks and another defends. The defending party wants to retain and secure its position, while the attacking party has to fight it in order to improve its own condition. Once again, it is clear that these statements remain on a high level of formality. They imply no reference to the substance of the origin of conflicting interests. But, again, it will prove useful to have articulated the formal prerequisites of Marx's and, indeed, of any theory of conflict.[4]

I question this model of inherently dualist social conflict. I disagree that "the very concept of conflict" necessarily implies that "there are but two contending parties." Is it correct to say that "there are never more than two positions that struggle for domination"? I doubt it. Think of the internal politics of Vietnam in 1968; think of the internal politics of our country in 1968 on the issue of Vietnam; think of the various positions on the two great domestic issues of civil rights and poverty.

But am I attacking a straw man? Even such a subtle thinker as Maurice Duverger believes that there is "a natural political dualism."[5] Furthermore, he writes that "the idea of a natural political dualism is to be encountered moreover in widely differing sociological conceptions."[6] Duverger regards the basic nature of political conflict as dualist, as may be seen in the following quotations:

None the less the two-party system seems to correspond to the nature of things, that is to say that political choice usually takes the form of a choice between two alternatives. A duality of parties does not always exist, but almost always there is a duality of tendencies. Every policy implies a choice between two kinds of solution: the so-called compromise solutions lean one way or the other. This is equivalent to saying that the centre does not exist in politics: there may well be a Centre party but there is no centre tendency, no centre doctrine. The term "centre" is applied to the geometrical spot at which the moderates of opposed tendencies meet: moderates of the Right and moderates of the Left.

Whenever public opinion is squarely faced with great fundamental problems it tends to crystallize round two opposed poles. The natural movement of societies tends towards the two-party system; obviously it may be countered by tendencies in the opposite direction.[7]

Wildavsky, in criticism, refers to such passages in Duverger as examples of a fallacy of mysticism, which he defines as "the imposition on the data studied of one's personal belief that certain phenomena are 'natural.' This fallacy takes on a more extreme turn when it is joined to the eminently superstitious impression that phenomena occur in pairs. Either everything is forced into one of two major tendencies, or phenomena which do not conform to a particular dualism are treated as aberrations requiring special explanation."[8] I agree with Wildavsky that phenomena do not necessarily occur in pairs. What, then, is the most that we can say about the dualist point of view? First, dualism has the advantages and disadvantages of *simplicity*. Dualism is a simple theory and posits simple analytic systems in the sense of my definition of simplicity-complexity in Chapter 1. Dualism reduces the number of factors in the system to a pair; dualism does not find a large number of relationships between variables, but only one, that of conflict; dualism does not posit extensive changes in relationships between variables with the passage of time. Some readers might object to this last statement, which refers to the third element in my definition of complexity, so let us examine it a bit further. The model of greatest simplicity is the model of a system in a steady state, in which relationships between variables do not change significantly with the passage of time.* Marx's dualist model of social conflict does posit a change in relationships between the variables (the capitalist class, the working class) with time, but this relationship is still quite simple, for the political resources of the proletariat increase with time, and the political resources of the owners decrease with time. (Resources, or "potential influence,"[9] is a relative concept, i.e., relative to the resources of other parties.) We could imagine many relationships that would show greater fluctuation with time—e.g., an increasing but irregularly fluctuating progression, such as the curve representing the American gross national product. When Marx's predictions of revolution were not borne out after two generations, Lenin modified Marx's theory by introducing another variable, by way of his theory of imperialism. In the earlier model, conflict was between factor P and factor C; in the later model, P and C sometimes join (changes in relationships) to exploit O, the outsider colonials. Now we have two systems of dualist conflict and a more complicated model.

Dualist theories of conflict are easier to communicate and hence are more likely to move people to political activism. For example, a left-reformist candidate for a city office in Oakland, California, in his campaign oratory, may dramatize and condense his platform by denouncing the city's "power structure" and describing the city's politics as a dualist conflict between this power structure and the interests of the average citizen. In private, he might complicate his argument by differentiating forces in the "power structure" and noting that some adversaries are worse than others, some elements of the power structure help the poor sometimes, the power structure is often divided within itself, etc. But such complications in campaign speeches would diminish their

---

* I am constantly aware of the relativity of such terms as "important" and "significant." However, it is theoretically possible to define "significant" in terms of definite criteria. Then, if relationships change over time, an observer may say that the change is "significant" *according to specifically stated criteria.*

persuasive impact. Hence, he would still refer to dualist conflict between the power structure and the average citizen. Similar considerations would hold for an activist in the radical right. For instance, a campaigner for Barry Goldwater in the California Republican primary might denounce "the Eastern Republican Establishment" and the Republican "Me-Tooers." In his oratory, he would picture American politics as a dual conflict between the true Americans, led by Goldwater, and the sellouts, led by Kennedy, Johnson, Rockefeller, and Romney. In private conversation, the campaigner might differentiate forces in the "liberal establishment" power structure by noting that there were some differences between Rockefeller Republicans and Kennedy Democrats, but such complications would not appear in campaign speeches. It is clear that dualist theories of conflict are easier to communicate and hence are more persuasive for purposes of political activism. One effect of this is that real-world political activists, unlike my two imaginary figures, may come to believe their dualist theories of conflict (through processes of attaining cognitive balance, psychological closure in respect to contradictory information and differentiation of adversaries, constant reinforcement from political primary groups, and other processes associated with cognitive dogmatism). On the other hand, assertions that "this situation is complicated" can become excuses for complacency and conformist inaction. Thus, a person may assert that one must understand a situation before one can intelligently change it. But he may use his perception of complexity as a blanket excuse for accepting a status quo, since one can argue at any time that men do not fully understand a status quo and consequently that advocating change is premature.

Above I noted that pluralist analysts of American politics repeatedly discover pluralism, decentralization of power, complex systems, and complex causation in every arena of politics. Such pluralist analysts contrast themselves with stratificationists and power-elite analysts, who repeatedly discover power elites, centralization of power, simple systems, and simple causation in every arena of politics. The findings of the pluralists and the stratificationists may be contrasted in terms of the three dimensions of simplicity-complexity: (1) number and diversity of variables; (2) incidence of relational interdependence among the variables; (3) variability of these relationships through time. Here we may see that dualist systems of conflict are more similar to power-elite systems than to pluralist systems of analysis. The dualist system of conflict contains two variables and posits only a few relationships between the two variables, which do not fluctuate greatly through time.* For example, the stratificationist analysis of sociopolitical conflict in American communities links a dualist theory of conflict with power-elite analysis, according to the five-point summary by Nelson Polsby.[10] The first four points of Polsby's summary of stratification analysis state the existence of a power-elite, single-independent-variable, simple system having a concentration of causality (power): the upper class rules in local community life; political and civic leaders are subordinate to the upper class; a single, power elite rules the community; the upper-class power elite rules in its own interests. According to Polsby, the fifth part of the stratificationist model is that "social conflict takes place between the upper and lower classes."[11] Polsby comments: "The reasoning here is that significant social conflicts follow the significant divisions of interest in the community, and these cleavages of interest separate the community's upper from its lower classes rather than divide other groups in the community whose members are recruited on some basis other than class memberships."[12] In this summary, dualist conflict is seen as part of the power-elite model, which contrasts with the pluralist model. We may suspect, then, that complex, mutilateral conflict usually involves a pluralist or complex system of analysis. And, indeed, this is so, almost by definition.

* For example, the Marxist system posits one variable as an independent, power-elite variable, until the revolutionary situation develops when the old power-elite variable disappears and a new independent variable appears, the vanguard of the proletariat. First, the capitalist ruling class acts as the independent variable in the political situation, with the proletarian class acting as the dependent variable. At that time, the capitalists have causal control over politics; the proletarians do not have such causal control. Later the vanguard of the proletariat assumes such causal control, although it is supposed that the mass reaction to the policies of the two ruling elites would be qualitatively different.

MULTILATERAL CONFLICT IN PLURALIST SOCIETIES

Let us presume the following. An equivalent to Polsby's five-point summary of power-elite, stratificationist models is my three-point summary of pluralist models: (1) numerous and diverse variables in the analytical system; (2) a high degree of relational interdependence among the variables; (3) a high degree of variability in these relationships through time as seen in the "pluralist emphasis on the time-bounded nature of coalitions."[13] Further, we may accept Polsby's statement that pluralists usually "see American society as fractured into congeries of hundreds of small special interest groups."[14] Consequently, we may assume that in the pluralist model, group conflict is usually seen as being multilateral, rather than dualist. Thus, the pluralist system posits a multiplicity of significant variables, with shifting relationships among these variables, and one can assume that often *more than two* of these variables will be found *in a complex* conflict relationship. Hence, pluralist systems posit multilateral conflict.

While I assert that pluralist analytic systems posit multilateral conflict, I do *not* mean to imply that pluralist analysis completely precludes dialectical, dualist conflict relationships. In the study of American politics, one type of dialectical analysis concerns organization as a stimulus for counterorganization. As Latham writes:

Organization represents concentrated power, and concentrated power can exercise a dominating influence when it encounters power which is diffuse and not concentrated, and therefore weaker. ... The classic struggle of farmers against business enterprise is a case in point, the latter at first being more efficiently organized, and able (before the farmer became "class conscious") to gain advantages which the farmers found offensive. *But organization begets counterorganization.* The farmer organizes in the American Farm Bureau Federation or the National Grange, and uses his influence with the legislatures to write rules to his advantage. In some states of the Middle West, for example, legislation even prescribes the terms of contracts for the sale of farm equipment. But the organized farmer pays little attention to the tenant and the sharecropper, and they in turn experience an impulse to organize for their own advantage.[15] [Emphasis added.]

David Truman and many other writers have made this point concerning employer-worker conflict in this country. After trade unions rose as a counterorganization to the organized sociopolitical power of the business firm, business counterorganized in response to the organization of labor: "Although it is no doubt incorrect to say that union organization has always preceded association on the other side of the employment relation—employers' groups have tended to form as a result of various circumstances making united action on labor policy desirable—it is nevertheless true that increased strength of workers' groups has been one of the circumstances producing such employers' associations."[16] In *Who Governs?*, we read of the Irishmen's organization of political power as a response to old-stock sociopolitical domination, and the subsequent counterorganization of political power by Italian Republicans as a response to the dominance of Irish Democrats.[17] Similarly, we read of the formation of a pressure group in a working-class neighborhood to counteract a plan to construct a large number of cheap, Quonset-hut dwellings.[18]

Organization begets counterorganization in a dialectical process, but this does not necessarily produce dialectical conflict. Thus, in Latham's example, agricultural pressure groups rose in response to the organized sociopolitical power of the business firm, yet we subsequently had multilateral conflict among agricultural groups themselves, as we see in the history of the Farm Bureau, the Grange, the Farmer's Union, populism, the Minnesota Farmer-Labor party, organizations of sharecroppers and tenant farmers, various producers' associations, production and marketing cooperatives, the Ku Klux Klan of the 1920's, and other groups. The result of rural group organization was not a dialectical conflict with organized business, but multilateral conflict resulting from the existence of numerous groups having a great variety of relationships that changed with time. Similar considerations hold for business-worker conflicts, as may be seen in the conflict among the AFL, the CIO, and the Communist Party in the late 1930's and during the 1940's.

Through a process of analytical simplification, some observers might continue to insist on the existence of dialectical conflict in such situations. By "analytical simplification," I am not taking a pejorative stance; we remember that according to the principle of Ockham's Razor, a simple theory is better than a complex theory, if predictability is equal.* By "simplification," I mean a process whereby all variables, all concrete and/or analytic actors, are collapsed into two variables, together with the dualist insistence that further distinctions are useless. Dahrendorf tends toward such a perspective: "There may be coalitions, of course, as there may be conflicts internal to either of the contenders, and there may be groups that are not drawn into a given dispute; but from the point of view of a given clash of interests, there are never more than two positions that struggle for domination."[19]

In other words, the dualists and the power elitists follow a process of analytical simplification, in the sense of my three-point definition of simplicity-complexity, which is the reverse of the process of analytical complication sometimes practiced by pluralist analysts. In my criticism of such pluralist analysis, I stated that one can find complexity anywhere, if one really wants to, as one could make a "pluralist" analysis of Soviet industrial politics, for example. Similarly, *one can find simplicity anywhere*, if one really wants to. While such analytical simplification is sometimes understandable and forgivable in the case of political activists, who must persuade others as well as maintain their own morale, I have less tolerance for such simplification by social theorists, especially when they do not present considerable evidence for the existence of a simple analytical system and dualist conflict. Clearly, if one states that conflict is somehow inherently, naturally dualist (dialectical), one has assumed before the fact a very important part of one's conclusions.

An example—the Vietnam issue—illustrates how the dual-

* We can see the value of simplicity of scientific theorizing in the following Associated Press release: "Two scientists—an American and an Alsatian-born Frenchman—who have defined some of the basic concepts of the behavior of electrons, atoms, and molecules, were awarded the 1966 Nobel Prizes in chemistry and physics today. . . . 'They made simplicities out of complexities,' fellow scientists said of their work." *San Francisco Chronicle*, Nov. 4, 1966, page 1; my emphasis.

ist model of conflict partially assumes conclusions. If a dualist had a leftist perspective, he would assume that the nature of the Vietnam conflict is American repression of a nationalist social revolution. Analogously, if our dualist had a conservative or pro-Administration perspective, he would describe the conflict as one in which Americans and other freedom fighters were combating Communist aggression. In both cases, the assumption of a dualist model would assume one's conclusions, and ignore distinctions between various parties to the conflict (the N.L.F., Hanoi, Peking, Buddhists, Catholics, etc.), the variety of relationships between the parties, and the change of such relationships with time. (An example of the third point of the simplicity-complexity definition is the possibility of change in the relationships between Buddhists and the N.L.F.)

Clearly, we could multiply such examples. I hope I have illustrated my point that assuming a dualist model of conflict is assuming an important part of one's conclusions. Marx was both a social theorist and a political activist, and accordingly he was not going to address the proletariat with "Reality is very complex and follow me." But such a precedent does not mean that social theory should retain a dualist model of conflict.

Perhaps the most persuasive argument for a dualist model of conflict is that social struggle is inherently between parties attacking or defending the status quo. For example, after maintaining that "any theory of conflict has to operate with something like a two-class model," Dahrendorf argues that "it is reasonable to assume" that social conflict is between forces for and against the status quo.[20] While a dualist model of conflict based on attitudes toward the status quo has much to recommend it, one may often find important drawbacks. For instance, in some conflicts each adversary may be *both for and against* the status quo in some respects. In 1861 the North and South were in conflict over the status quo of slavery, with the North attacking, the South defending. Simultaneously, the North and the South were in conflict over retaining the political status quo, with the South attacking and the North defending. Currently social reformers are attacking dominant urban elites and pressing for changes in the social and political status quo of the poor and of the Negroes. At the same time, dominant urban elites may press for urban renewal projects, automation, metropolitan area reorganization, and additional restrictions on welfare, thereby causing the social reformers to defend the status quo.[21]

On a specific issue, we may be able to say who is attacking and who is defending, but if we aggregate the conflicts between parties, we must presume certain criteria of importance before we can say who is attacking or defending the status quo. For example, we might state that establishing a police review board is a greater change in the status quo than establishing a certain urban renewal project. Accordingly, in terms of these issues, the social reformers might get more "points" in a scale indicating the desire to attack the status quo than dominant urban elites. In other words, establishing a police review board is not somehow a priori a major, "progressive" change or a greater alteration of the status quo than the establishment of an urban renewal project; this is a matter of opinion that can be settled definitively only if observers can agree on criteria rating the significance of changes. In general, we must define the status quo in explicit terms and rate the significance of various changes in explicit terms, before we can say who is attacking or defending the status quo and to what extent. Such calculation may be easy in certain cases, for some policies are clearly revolutionary and others are clearly stand-pat, but in many other cases, such calculations are difficult and relative in terms of values.

Thus we can see that even if we can factor out the problems of defining the status quo, of defining the significance of proposed changes in the status quo, and of dealing with differences in values, the two-party, for-against status quo model may be inadequate. Clearly such a model, involving the number of actors and type of change proposed, can be expanded further. Thus, such an actor-change model may be a two-party model or an *n*-party model. In a two-party conflict, one may be for, one against the status quo; both may be against the status quo in different respects; both may be for the status quo in different respects; both parties may be both for and against the status quo at the same time, as in the American Civil War example. Similar considerations hold for the n-party model when quality of conflict is added.

We notice that the two-party, for-against model assumes only one dimension of conflict. Such a model does not include the "in different respects" mentioned above. In other words, two parties may both be against the status quo, but in different ways, i.e., *on different issues*. Thus, the South was for the status quo on the issue of slavery, the North against; the North was for the status quo on the issue of national political organization, the South against.

Concerning the two-party, for-against model of political conflict, Duverger writes: "If we accept the idea that the two-party system is natural we still have to explain why nature should have flourished so freely in the Anglo-Saxon countries and their imitators and why nature should have been thwarted in the countries on the continent of Europe."[22] But of course one cannot assume that British and American political conflicts are dualist, just because the two-party system flourishes in these conflicts. For example, some critics of Anglo-American politics say that there is *no* significant political conflict in these countries—that the parties are just Tweedledum-Tweedledee twins. A Marxist, for instance, would not say that Anglo-American party conflict is "dialectical." Conversely, we are familiar with the considerable degree of factionalism within both British and American political parties. We know that American political parties are confederations of state and local parties, insofar as we may say that national parties exist at all. Furthermore, Anglo-American party leaders are not commanders of an organizational weapon doing battle with an opposing organizational weapon. At any point, political elites are engaged in n-party, multilateral conflicts among various groups of voters, party activists, and elites, both within a particular political party, within the other party, and outside both parties (e.g., interest group leaders). Such conflicts are "mixed-motive" situations—few, if any, of the actors are in complete opposition; most actors have both compatible and incompatible goals in relation to other actors.[23] In other words, if the goals of individual and group actors were matched in pairs, in almost every situation the goals of each pair would be partially compatible and partially incompatible.

Thus, in most cases, the simple dualist model of two-party, for-against status quo conflict does not apply to pluralist societies, unless one makes a convincing case for the pervasive existence of class struggle, having a two-party, for-against status quo character. Instead, *political conflict is multilateral, multidimensional, and mixed-motive within pluralist societies.*

Politicians in the pluralist setting often must respond to multilateral, multidimensional, mixed-motive conflict. Indeed, the use of the term "pluralist" makes this assertion true by definition. Thus, if one denies that the pluralist politician operates within an arena of multilateral conflict, one must show that the conflicts are illusory or spurious, or must show a system of dualist conflict.

If we accept the model of multilateral conflict, we are concerned with the relationship among pluralist leaders, multilateral conflict, and political innovation within a system of relatively great sociopolitical consensus. In order to understand the relationship between political leaders, multilateral conflict, and sociopolitical innovation, we may examine (following Lewis Coser) the conceptual similarities between the leader (in a situation of conflict) and the marginal man.[24]

THE MARGINAL MAN CONCEPT

The groundbreaking sociologist Robert E. Park, influenced by Georg Simmel, defined a marginal man as "a cultural hybrid, a man living and sharing intimately in the cultural life of two distinct peoples."[25] "In looking at himself from the standpoint of each group he experiences the conflict as a personal problem."[26] Thus, the marginal man *subjectively* and psychologically experiences dualist or multilateral cultural conflict. Simmel's archetype of the marginal man is the Jew in Gentile society; others have referred to immigrants and Negroes in American society as marginal men. However, "this conception has been severely criticized ... as being so lacking in precision as to be scientifically useless."[27] In my opinion, it is necesary to consider the subjective experience of dualist or multilateral conflict if we wish to define a "marginal man." Observers may posit marginality according to objective categories, but such conflict may not be felt by the persons concerned, and consequently may not lead to any sort of distinctive behavior. *The People's Choice, Voting,* and other sociological studies of voting behavior may, according to objective criteria, find sociological cross-pressures acting on people who belong to two or more groups with conflicting political tendencies,[28] but the behavior of such marginal men may differ drastically, depending on whether or not the conflicts among political norms of the various groups are experienced subjectively.

Berelson and Lazarsfeld, as well as David Truman, have related cross-pressures on voting and overlapping group memberships to the maintenance of political moderation and democratic consensus.[29] However, secondary analysis of *The Civic Culture*'s survey data provides no evidence for the overlapping group membership hypothesis, although it does corroborate the reverse hypothesis that reinforcing group memberships are linked to intense preferences and high conflict.[30] Similarly, one can argue that cross-pressures and overlapping group memberships can produce intense activity, search behavior, and innovation, as well as moderation, late decisions, or withdrawal.[31] Thus, we cannot assume that the perception of conflicting norms will somehow a priori produce either moderation or intense activity; this depends on circumstances that will require many years of research for their clear delineation. Hence, we can presently presume that political marginality, cross-pressures, overlapping group memberships, and subjectively experienced conflict in general can produce innovative behavior as well as withdrawal.

Indeed, discussions of marginality are often linked with discussions of creativity and innovation. "For example, as Veblen and Simmel, among others, have pointed out, marginal men are likely to be highly motivated to engage in innovating behavior because they are structurally induced to depart from prevailing social norms."[32] Coser compares marginal roles and leadership roles in respect to social-structural inducement to innovation.[33] Unfortunately, while Coser ties innovative behavior of marginal individuals to the resolution of conflicting norms, he does not clearly deal with the relationship between leadership, conflicting expectations, and innovation. However, Coser's comparison of leadership roles and marginality is relevant to our discussion:

> There are also other positions in a group than those of marginal men that motivate innovating departures from the norms. For example, the status of leader requires the ability to adjust to new circumstances. The rank and file may take the customary for granted, but a break of wont and use may enhance the reputation of the leader. The flexibility required in leadership roles may entail greater or lesser departures from otherwise expected behavior so that a certain amount of license to deviate and to violate norms is built into the very definition of leadership.
>
> Homans, who had argued in an earlier work that "the higher the rank (or status) of a person within a group, the more nearly his activities conform to the norms of the group," stated more recently ... that "we now have experimental evidence that it is not just the members of low status, but members of high status as well, who are prone at times to nonconformity." It will be remembered that in these groups deviant behavior helped the group to adapt to the outside. This suggests that the pressure on the leader to engage in innovating behavior may derive from the structural circumstance that he is the group's representative to the outside. He stands at the point of interchange between in-group and out-group. A leader may be considered a special case of the marginal man: having the task to relate his group to the demands of the environment, he is oriented, at the same time as he is the group's representative, toward extra-group values.[34]

There is a considerable literature on the leader as marginal man in Coser's sense. The conflict between the representative role and "extra-group values" is the familiar Burkean dilemma of conflict between constituency values and the representative's personal values, or conflicts between constituency demands and party demands, Presidential demands, and the demands of the national interest, however it is perceived.[35] Other such conflicts include those between party activists and the general public of voters or between party activists and their representatives in legislatures.[36] There is much literature on these topics in political science. However, perhaps the relationship between leaders, conflicting expectations for leaders' behavior, and sociopolitical innovation has not received sufficient emphasis. Thus, while it is interesting to categorize legislators into "trustee," "delegate," and "politico" roles, such analysis is rather static.[37] Perhaps in the future a more dynamic analysis of the role of legislators (as one type of political leader) may be devised by relating the resolution of conflicting expectations to innovation and other forms of behavior. Thus, we would be interested not only in categorizing the types of conflict situations of political leaders, but also in analyzing *the leaders' responses to political conflict*.

MANNHEIM'S MULTIPERSPECTIVE APPROACH

In *Ideology and Utopia*, Karl Mannheim develops interesting insights into a person's response to multilateral conflict, whether political conflict or intellectual conflict. Accordingly, Mannheim has something to contribute to the study of the relationships between leadership, conflict, and innovation.[38]

Mannheim's concern with the sociological determination of intellectual output led him to consider how an intellectual may escape being the mouthpiece for some class or group. His answer is that the intellectual should be open to the sociologically determined perspectives of the various classes and groups. Thus, being able to identify and understand the viewpoints of everyone, the intellectual would be committed to no particular group or class. Consequently, if the intellectual could avoid premature closure on some particular perspective, he could attempt to synthesize all viewpoints in a spirit of relative detachment, being committed to no particular perspective.* Thus, the intellectual might achieve a synthesis

* Personally, I think the best check on the sociological determination of intellectual output is the formation of autonomous intellectual professional groups, whose procedural norms and collective intellectual judgment can act as a check against the conscious or unconscious production of propaganda in scholarly guise. Similarly, intellectual professionalism can act as a check on conscious or unconscious scholarly opportunism—producing intellectual works designed to increase one's own power and prestige by pleasing others without a particular concern for veracity. However, the resort to professionalism only limits the problems of unconscious or conscious propaganda and opportunism. Thus, scholars may become motivated to increase their economic welfare, power, and prestige by producing work consciously or unconsciously designed to please professional leaders without particular regard for veracity.

from a comprehensive point of view, through a process of "dynamic intellectual mediation."[39]

Within some intellectual professions, such as political science, we find restrained, multilateral conflict between various groups, differentiated by adherence to somewhat different "ways of life," such as varying attitudes toward verification, travel, classical knowledge, humanistic concerns, other disciplines, the importance of speaking foreign languages, political activism and reform, knowledge of current events, giving advice to national and local governments, giving advice to business concerns, and developing a liberally educated personality. Perhaps the most important criterion of differentiation among professional intellectual subgroups is attitude toward the value of various types of research. In this situation of restrained, multilateral conflict, we should seriously consider Mannheim's prescription of avoiding premature closure, attempting to understand the distinctive way of life and varying perspectives of all the groups, and attempting to synthesize the varying perspectives into a comprehensive point of view through a process of intellectual mediation from a detached perspective.

It is significant that Mannheim derived his image of many perspectives from his observations of the twentieth-century political process in the industrialized nations. The German sociologist's prescriptions for intellectual activity are derived from his observations concerning the "path that every clear-sighted political person lives and thinks, even though he may not always be aware of it."[40] Thus:

Political life, involving, as it always does, thinking which proceeds from opposite poles, is modified in the course of its own development by toning down the exaggeration due to one point of view by what is revealed through another. In every situation, it is, therefore, indispensable to have a total perspective which embraces all points of view. . . .

Summing up the main difference between . . . [the] contemplative, intellectualistic point of view and the living standpoint which is accepted in the realm of practice, we might say that the scientist always approaches his subject matter with an ordering and schematizing tendency, whereas the practical man—in our case the political person—seeks orientation with reference to action. It is one thing to aim at a schematically ordered bird's eye view; it is quite another thing to seek a concrete orientation for action. The desire for concrete orientation leads us to view things only in the context of the life-situations in which they occur. . . .

There are three possible approaches to modern political theories. . . . The first mode of exposition represents that of the collector, the second that of the philosophical systematizer. What happens in both cases is that the forms of experience of contemplative types of men are arbitrarily imposed upon political reality. . . . As over against these two extremes, there is a third possibility which consists in selecting the middle road between abstract schematization on the one hand and historical immediacy on the other. It is precisely in this third path that every clear-sighted political person lives and thinks, even though he may not always be aware of it. This third course proceeds by attempting to comprehend the theories and their mutations in close relation to the collective groups and typical total situations out of which they arose and whose exponents they are. The inner connections between thought and social existence must in this case be reconstructed.[41]

Instead of politicians learning from intellectuals, intellectuals can learn from politicians, according to Mannheim. For example, the politician must be a specialist in dealing with multilateral conflict and understanding the interests, perspectives, and total situations of the various groups and individuals making demands on the leadership. Similarly, the social analyst must do the same things to detach his analysis from social forces leading to the production of propaganda or works exclusively motivated by either conscious or unconscious desire for economic gain, power, and prestige.

Further, just as the more admirable politician devotes some thought to the national interest and to the welfare of society as a whole and thus attempts to develop "a total perspective which embraces all points of view," so the intellectual caught in the arena of multilateral conflict among classes, groups, or professional subgroups might do well to develop "a total perspective which embraces all points of view." Although one might try to criticize Mannheim's total-perspective theory from Lindblom's standpoint, we should realize that Mannheim's comprehensive process does not involve static, utilitarian, rational calculation,[42] but rather a dynamic, existential process of learning by placing oneself in real situations and by going through cycles of identification and detachment toward the perspectives of others. Accordingly, Mannheim's comprehensiveness has more in common with the incrementalist, partisan-mutual-adjustment model than with the rational-comprehensive, synoptic model, for the comprehensiveness of Mannheim's theory of intellectual and political activity is the comprehensiveness of the results of a process over time —in this case the learning of the individual intellectual or politician. Hence, it is not subject to Lindblom's critique of synoptic rationality, the static process of relating means and ends at one point of time.[43]

It is interesting to note that Mannheim advises both the politician and the intellectual to avoid the extremes of descriptive specificity (or, for the politician, extremely atheoretical pragmatism) and grand theory tenuously related to data (or the extremes of political ideology). Mannheim's prescriptions for the intellectual and politician are similar to the picture that Arthur Schlesinger, Jr., constructs of the politician-intellectual John F. Kennedy. First, Schlesinger sees Kennedy as autonomous, as standing outside of his class and group background, perhaps because this background was too complex to produce any clear type of sociologically determined personality and thought.

It was autonomy which this humane and self-sufficient man seemed to embody. Kennedy simply could not be reduced to the usual complex of sociological generalizations. He was Irish, Catholic, New England, Harvard, Navy, Palm Beach, Democrat and so on; but no classification contained him. He had wrought an individuality which carried him beyond the definitions of class and race, region and religion. He was a free man, not just in the sense of the cold-war cliché, but in the sense that he was, as much as man can be, self-determined and not the servant of forces outside him.[44]

Moreover, Kennedy had an unusual interest in the dilemmas and conflicts of political life. He was deeply aware of the leader's situation of dealing with multilateral conflict. He saw political life as filled with moral dilemmas; such interests led him to write *Profiles in Courage*, the applicability of which to such analytic topics as role conflict was recognized by Robert Merton before Kennedy became President.[45] Schlesinger writes:

His sickness provided an unaccustomed chance to reflect on such questions [the tension between means and ends]; and *Profiles in Courage* represented his most sustained attempt to penetrate the moral dilemmas of the political life. "Politics is a jungle," he wrote in his notes, "—torn between doing right thing & staying in office—between the local interest & the national interest—between the private good of the politician & the general good." In addition, "we have always insisted academically on an unusually high—even unattainable—standard in our political life. We consider it graft to make sure a park or road, etc., be placed near property of friends —but what do we think of admitting friends to the favored list for securities about to be offered to the less favored at a higher price? ... Private enterprise system ... makes OK private action which would be considered dishonest if public action."[46]

In addition to being relatively autonomous from his sociological background and viewing the world in terms of complex, conflicting imperatives, Kennedy had some sense of detachment from the political game (e.g., writing *Profiles in Courage*) and was capable of understanding and openness to various shades of political position and opposing argument.

These were his years of concentration on politics and he soon showed the toughness, adroitness and intuition of a master. Yet while he considered politics—in another phrase he cherished from *Pilgrim's Way*—"the greatest and most honorable adventure," took pride in his political skills, delighted in political maneuver and combat, and never forgot political effects for a single second, he stood apart, in some fundamental sense, from the political game. When David Ormsby Gore visited him in the hospital, Kennedy remarked that he was not sure he was cut out to be a politician; he saw the strength of opposing arguments too well; it would be easier if he had divine certitude that he was right. In his preliminary notes for *Profiles in Courage*, he wrote of Robert A. Taft, "He was partisan in the sense that Harry Truman was—they both had the happy gift of seeing things in bright shades. It is the politicians who see things in similar shades that have a depressing and worrisome time of it."[47]

And, as in Mannheim's model, Kennedy had understood, partially identified with, and participated in various groups that have distinctive ways of life, but was detached from each and attempted to develop a more comprehensive viewpoint, in terms of the public welfare, that deviated from the stock liberalism of his time.

His detachment from traditional American Catholicism was part of the set of detachments—detachment from middle-class parochialism, detachment from the business ethos, detachment from ritualistic liberalism—which gave his perceptions their peculiar coolness, freshness and freedom, and which also led those expecting commitments of a more familiar sort to condemn him as uncommitted. In fact, he was intensely committed to a vision of America and the world, and committed with equal intensity to the use of reason and power to achieve that vision. This became apparent after he was President: and this accounts in part for the sudden realization that, far from being just a young man in a hurry, a hustler for personal authority, a Processed Politician, he was, as politicians go, an intellectual and one so peculiarly modern that it took orthodox intellectuals a little time before they began to understand him.[48]

Thus, because of his relative autonomy from sociological predetermination, his understanding and identification with various differing points of view, his detachment from any single point of view, his concern with multilateral conflict, and his interest in designing a comprehensive perspective through a synthesis of various partial perspectives, Kennedy exemplified Mannheim's model of the politician and the intellectual.

Moreover, according to Michael Davie of the London *Observer*, Lyndon Johnson has many of these same characteristics. For instance, according to this description (written in 1965), Johnson is sensitive to possible conflicts; the image of the political jungle, used by Kennedy in his notes, recurs: " 'Some of his [Johnson's] worries are of his own making,' one man remarked. 'He sees troubles where none exists. He's liable to wake up in the morning and think everything's got loose during the night.' Another explained: 'He sees life as a jungle. No matter how long a rein you think you're on, he's always got the reins in his own hands.'" Besides being sensitive to conflict and possible conflict, Johnson attempts to understand varying points of view, according to this description. "'One of the keys to Lyndon Johnson is that he is a perfectionist—a perfectionist in the most imperfect art in the world: politics,' remarks an old associate. 'He has a passion for detail and a mastery of detail. Decision-making, he gets all the information, wants to know every point of view, leaves the decision as long as possible, and then decides—strong, firm and to the jugular.'"[49] Delaying decision making can be dangerous, but it also has the advantage of avoiding premature closure before sufficient information is in. Furthermore, it is one of Mannheim's prescriptions/descriptions of the politician and intellectual:

The very quintessence of political knowledge seems to us to lie in the fact that increased knowledge does not eliminate decisions but only forces them farther and farther back. But what we gain through this retreat from decisions is an expansion of our horizon and a greater intellectual mastery of our world. Consequently, we may expect, from the advances in sociological research into ideology, that interrelations of social position, motives, and points of view, which have hitherto been only partially known, will now become more and more transparent. This will enable us, as we have already indicated, to calculate more precisely collective interests and their corresponding modes of thought and to predict approximately the ideological reactions of the different social strata.[50]

Clearly, this could be a political strategy, as well as an intellectual strategy. Obviously, if this strategy works, and if it does enable one to "calculate more precisely collective interests and their corresponding modes of thought and to predict approximately the ideological reactions of the different social strata," then it would be valuable to the political success of one such as Johnson.

In addition to an awareness of political conflicts, and the interest and ability to understand others' perspectives on a situation, Johnson developed a certain detachment from his surroundings, related to his inability and/or disinterest in presenting a sophisticated image to the Washingtonian and general public. According to Davie's description, Johnson felt himself to be an outsider in Washington, or in different terms, he felt marginal to his surroundings. (Here we see the difficulty of using such terms as "marginality" and "alienation" with much precision.) By a loose definition, Johnson as President was marginal, he felt like an outsider in Washington, a Jew in the land of Gentiles. According to one of the uses of the term "alienated," Lyndon Johnson was alienated: that is to say, he felt like "an outsider looking in," like a stranger in a strange land.

The most extraordinary feature of [the President's] character is that he feels an outsider in Washington. "He doesn't feel, even now [1965], that he belongs here," explained one of the aides who knows him best. "From the beginning of his career he was *an outsider looking in*—a country boy without education and without money. He's always felt that people from his part of the country have had a raw deal, and he always felt he was being looked down on. He still feels it. He's got to be President and yet he feels he hasn't made it. This is the cause of most of his frustrations and erraticisms."[51] [Emphasis added.]

One may infer that Johnson was open to the point of view of political and economic elites, but he felt detached from the circles of the elites. Consequently, he might have conceived a more comprehensive personal identification and perspective —identifying with the common people, envisioned in terms of the country folk in the Texas of his youth. This is mostly supposition on my part, although there is some evidence for this pattern. As Davie writes: "The President attributes the Capital's rejection of himself to regional prejudice. He thinks they don't approve of him because he comes from Texas. In return he feels about Washington, and the East Coast three-button-suit crowd generally, that they are a bunch of snobs who look down their noses at you while they are stealing your wallet. The people the President likes are the people."[52] The image presented by Mannheim of the comprehensive synthesis after partial self-identification with many different perspectives, and the image presented by Schlesinger of Kennedy's detachment from any single perspective and his interest in deriving comprehensive ideas concerning the welfare of the entire nation, are both intellectual in content—the comprehensive synthesis is one of abstract ideas. However, it seems to me that one could derive a useful comprehensive perspective, one that would help a president derive specific policy preferences, by picturing the world of people one has known, analyzing this world for problems and insufficiencies, and then picturing another improved world, in which the social, economic, political, and personal problems of specific people have been remedied. Evidently, Johnson has not had a comprehensive synthesis concerning the public good in the abstract, intellectual sense of Mannheim and Kennedy, but he may have had a synthesized picture in the personal, pragmatic sense I have just outlined.

Mannheim's image of decision making, intended both for the politician and the intellectual, is similar to Neustadt's theory of presidential staffing.[53] Just as the intellectual can be "captured" by his particular sociological background, so a president can be captured into making decisions by over-identification and over-reliance on a particular bureaucratic status group (a group having its distinctive way of life and its distinctive goals). President Kennedy, to his great regret, was captured thus by the CIA and the military in planning the Bay of Pigs operation.[54] Franklin Delano Roosevelt's staffing (as analyzed by Neustadt) and Mannheim's image of decision making are both designed to prevent errors resulting from the acceptance of one, inevitably biased perspective on reality. Neustadt's theory contains the central elements of Mannheim's theory: (1) recognition of conflict; (2) partial identification and understanding of many perspectives; (3) the retention of a stance of detachment; (4) the attempt to derive a synthetic comprehensive perspective, through the process of "dynamic mediation" among the various partial perspectives. Neustadt in one example describes Roosevelt's pattern of ordering different people to work on the same task as a means of discovering various perspectives on a problem. Roosevelt would then listen to several conflicting viewpoints with sympathy, adopting one or the other, or some combination of them, as his policy. In other words, Roosevelt utilized conflict as an aid to policy making.

In *Who Governs?*, Robert Dahl viewed the professional

politician in a way similar to Mannheim's multiperspectivism. Dahl notes that it "is impossible to say with confidence why some citizens find participation in public life so highly rewarding that they are impelled along the path toward professionalism" in politics.[55] But as Mannheim stressed the importance of forming numerous relationships with various groups and persons in order for the politician to gain detached objectivity, so Dahl notes that "perhaps the most obvious requirement that one must have [to be a professional politician] is an unusual toleration for creating and maintaining a great number and variety of personal relationships." Such a multiplication of personal relationships may result in the politician's developing "a cool detachment that many citizens would find it impossibly wearisome to sustain,"[56] as we find in Mannheim's model and in Schlesinger's description of Kennedy. Thus, Dahl writes that this unusual toleration for creating and maintaining a great number and variety of personal relationships

does not mean that the professional [politician] actually likes other people to any unusual degree or even that he has an unusual need to be liked by others. Indeed, a study by Rufus Browning indicates that among businessmen the "need for affiliation"—the desire to have the liking and approval of others—is lower among those who are active in politics than those who are inactive, and it is lower among leaders than among subleaders. Browning's findings suggest the tantalizing hypothesis that the distinguishing characteristic of the professional is an inordinate capacity for multiplying human relationships without ever becoming deeply involved emotionally. Despite his appearance of friendliness and warmth, the professional may in fact carry a cool detachment that many citizens would find it impossibly wearisome to sustain.[57]

In summary, Mannheim's theory of political and intellectual innovation and leadership is an interesting model of response to conflict, which we can use to relate leaders, followers, conflict, and innovation. Mannheim focuses on the ability of the person: (1) to partially identify himself with many individuals, groups, and classes and understand their different perspectives on reality; (2) to be open to the conflicts between these perspectives; (3) to retain a stance of detachment; (4) to attempt to derive a synthetic comprehensive perspective through the process of "dynamic mediation" among the various partial perspectives, which necessitates the avoidance of premature closure. Mannheim's model of decision making does not prescribe comprehensive synoptic rationality in the sense described by Lindblom, but instead prescribes a comprehensiveness as the synthetic product of an existential learning process. Thus, Mannheim's theory of leadership, conflict, and innovation is not subject to Lindblom's critique of synoptic rationality.

THEORIES OF ROLE CONFLICT

A fruitful method for studying leaders' response to conflict and sociopolitical innovation is the examination of models of role conflict. Unfortunately, although the concept "role" is central in the social sciences, "role," like "power" and "culture," has been used in many somewhat different ways.[58] However, as I stated earlier, "role" implies (1) who expects (2) whom (3) to do what (4) in which situation. Rewards for conformity and punishments for deviance might play a part in such a description.[59] Yinger describes the concept similarly: "We can say that a role is the list of what most members of a social group believe a position occupant should and should not, may and may not, do. It is *not* a list of what most occupants of a position *in fact do*."[60] (Emphasis added.) Here we see a disagreement in the definition of "role"—the definition may stress expectations (norms) or it may stress behavior. Though one can aptly stress behavior, I prefer to focus on expectations. Only research can show which is the better usage; however, anyone using the term should state precisely which way he is using it. Gross, Mason, and McEachern, in their brilliant *Explorations in Role Analysis*, conclude their survey of definitions of "role" with this observation: "Although their formulations have some fundamental differences, most of the authors whose definitions have been presented are concerned with the same phenomena. Three basic ideas which appear in most of the conceptualizations considered, if not in the definitions of role themselves, are that individuals: (1) in *social locations* (2) *behave* (3) with reference to *expectations.*"[61] In this section, I am interested in how *leaders* (individuals in a social location or position) *behave with reference to conflicting expectations.* Hence, I am interested in the theory of role conflict.

First, however, let us note one ambiguity in the theory of role conflict. A person's social location is variously termed "position," "role," or "status," depending on the author. (Moreover, authors may use each of the three terms to mean something other than social location.) For example, the social locations of occupation or family (e.g., father) are called positions, roles, or statuses by various authors (e.g., the role of professor, the status of professor, the position of professor). Following Yinger, I use the term "position" (instead of "status" or "role") to denote social location.[62] For a position, there are counterpositions, which taken together form a self-other combination. Counterpositions for the position of professor include student in course A, student in course B, department chairman, dean of the college, etc. We can call the set of position-counterpositions a "position-set." (Merton calls it a "role-set.")[63] Hence we see that there are two different types of role conflict: conflicting expectations among the others *within* a position-set and conflicting expectations *among* position-sets. An example of the latter is the professor's conflict between professional expectations and family expectations, such as in the allocation of his time. When I consider conflicting expectations involving pluralist politicians, I am most interested in conflicting expectations among the others within the position-set of his political role, e.g., as legislator. At times, however, we may be interested in conflicting expectations among the politician's position-sets, such as the conflict between political activity and attention to family.[64] This sort of conflict must have a lot to do with the entry and exit of persons into politics. Certain personality types may tend to be screened in or out of leadership positions, a process that may have some impact on the character of the political process and policy outcomes.[65]

What happens when there are conflicting expectations among others about the person's behavior in a position? What are the types of response to such multilateral conflict? Robert

Merton outlines six such responses of the position holder and the others in the position-set, which he terms a "role-set."[66] Two of these "social mechanisms articulating role-sets" are among the basic stuff of politics: "differences of power of those in the role-set"; "insulation of role-activities from observability by members of the role-set."[67] Obviously, when faced with conflicting demands, the politician may respond to the demands of the most powerful, or he may carry out both demands but attempt to hide the fact. (Such deception is difficult in a polity with organized interest groups that disseminate information to their members.)

The other four of Merton's "social mechanisms articulating role-sets" are also important to the student of leadership: "observability of conflicting demands by members of a role-set"; "mutual support among status-occupants"; "relative importance of various statuses"; "abridging the role-set."[68] In the first, the members of a position-set may become conscious of their own conflicting expectations and subsequently resolve them, attaining such agreement either through a power struggle or through compromise. In such cases, the constituents (i.e., those in the counterposition), not the politician, resolve their conflicting expectations. Perhaps insufficient attention has been paid by scholars to such resolution of conflicts. This mechanism may be found in administrative organization; Eisenhower, for example, preferred to force others to resolve their conflicting expectations, but evidently went too far. Roosevelt and Kennedy, on the other hand, preferred to let others bring their conflicting expectations to the President, thereby providing the leader with more information and more policy alternatives.[69]

"Mutual support among status-occupants" is a familiar theme in the literature of legislatures. Partly because of the conflicting demands thrust on the legislator, holders of this position often have a considerable degree of feeling for fellow legislators, and thereby form a self-conscious status group, valuing a distinctive way of life. Such solidarity has mitigated conflict over redistricting at the state level; loyalty to the legislative status group may override loyalty to party platform, leading to the protection of seats of minority-party incumbents in the event of redistricting.[70] The socially stipulated relative importance of various positions (statuses) limits the conflicting expectations of others. I shall deal with the political relevance of such phenomena in my subsequent discussion of hierarchies of role obligations. Likewise, I shall treat the sixth of Merton's categories, abridging the role-set, in my subsequent discussion of "escape" and "repudiation."

In general we can see that, by reducing conflicting expectations, Merton's six "social mechanisms articulating role-sets" refer to political phenomena. There is, then, some relevance of the literature on role conflict to the understanding of the relationships between leadership, conflict, and sociopolitical innovation.

Although less known than Merton's article on the theory of role-sets, Jackson Toby's article "Some Variables in Role Conflict Analysis"[71] provides a useful framework for the study of leadership, conflict, and innovation. In his introduction, Toby aligns himself with those who point to the relationship between social conflict and social change: "It is obvious that an individual in a role conflict situation is uncomfortable. For him, the cross-fire of competing claims is an obnoxious problem to be solved as quickly as possible. From society's point of view, however, role conflicts may be useful; they often give a social system flexibility by providing an entering wedge for social change."[72] This observation can be applied to our interest in politics and politicians. We may say that the politician, having conflicting constituent expectations, is uncomfortable if these conflicting demands are subjectively experienced by him. "For him, the cross-fire of competing claims is an obnoxious problem to be solved as quickly as possible," although a solution might be the strategy of detachment from the conflict situation and subsequent waiting until a clear preponderance of forces emerges.

Toby notes that to deal with contradictory demands of others on the self, social mores provide hierarchies of role obligations, which can be applied to some situations. Consequently, we can observe such socially approved strategies of noncompliance as the excuse, the accident, systems of etiquette, and tact.[73] All of these are relevant to political situations characterized by conflicting demands. In specific situations, they may be linked to policy innovations.

Toby notes that "the 'excuse' is a highly important sociological category. It is an approved technique for avoiding sanctions by asserting that an equally high or higher claim prevented the individual from fulfilling his obligations."[74] For example, when California's Governor Brown was challenged by the Delano grape strikers to meet them on the Easter Sunday conclusion of their 250-mile march to Sacramento, the Governor stated that he had promised to spend the day with his family, and that he could not break this promise. While this excuse infuriated the strikers, it provided a persuasive "out" for the Governor, who probably wished to avoid being put on the spot in a widely publicized, dramatic confrontation.

Another such socially justified solution is the strategy of commitment to conscience. For example, Senator Wayne Morse was in 1965 the most outspoken Senatorial critic of the American position in Vietnam, even though the majority of his Oregon constituents did not support his position; nevertheless, Morse's political popularity did not immediately drop in Oregon, evidently because he was able to convince a large number of his constituents that he is a political conscientious objector. In other words, many Oregon voters, disagreeing with Morse's stand on Vietnam, excused his actions because he was seen as a man who must act according to the dictates of his conscience.[75] Such political conscientious objectors within a democracy provide opportunities for sociopolitical changes. Such leaders operate beyond the normal limits imposed by social controls (in this case the sanctions of voting), and thus have greater leeway for imposing their personal preferences on policy making; i.e., they exercise more power, defined in terms of causality.*

The second of Toby's socially legitimated solutions to conflicting demands is the "accident," which is similar to Thomas Schelling's concept of "commitment."[76] "Another kind of le-

---

* However, we must note that the activities of such conscientious objectors may be highly controversial, as in the case of Morse's stand on Vietnam, although his electoral defeat in November 1968 evidently did not result primarily from the Vietnam issue.

gitimate non-compliance, a cousin of the 'excuse,' is the claim of the actor that his failure to fulfill his obligations is involuntary. No higher claims are invoked, but the actor escapes sanctions by demonstrating that circumstances beyond his control prevented him from carrying out his good intentions."[77] For example, Franklin Roosevelt argued that economic events beyond his control prevented him from reducing the federal budget, as he had promised in his 1932 campaign. Supporters of Lyndon Johnson have argued that he, indeed, was a peace candidate in the 1964 election, but that circumstances beyond his control prevented him from carrying out his good intentions in Vietnam.

Toby's third category of role-conflict resolution is etiquette, which he describes as "rituals for reducing social friction." He notes that "Emily Post is sometimes ridiculed by people who pride themselves on being rational. They naively suppose that etiquette consists of meaningless ceremonials, for they do not realize the importance of prescribed rituals in solving the dilemmas [conflicts] of daily life."[78] This conclusion is familiar to those students of international diplomacy who have perceived the conflict-reducing and stabilizing functions of diplomatic etiquette.[79] The etiquette of systems of political bargaining among top leaders of a nation's politics is also worth noting. For example, Brazilian political leaders, even though they use threats of force in national crises, have had an etiquette of retreat, when it is clear to one person that he is weaker than his opponent. Such systems of etiquette among the political leaders of a country are an important part of an "elite political ethos," the aggregate of elite political culture (attitudes) and their overt behavior, which differentiates the political style of various nations.*

Etiquette, defined as prescribed rituals for mitigating the severity of conflict, is an important phenomenon in legisla-

---

* The study of elite political etiquette within particular countries will provide a way to link the study of international relations, bargaining, and diplomacy and the study of comparative politics. Application of symbolic-interaction sociology, as represented by the work of Herbert Blumer and Erving Goffman, may provide a common conceptual framework for the study of *intra*national elite ethos and *inter*national diplomacy. See works by Blumer, Goffman, and Jervis cited in the Bibliography, pp. 253–65.

tures of democratic systems. The American Senate and the British Parliament are especially noted in this respect. Thus, it is not surprising that the next lines of Toby's discussion of etiquette are also an important conclusion of students of legislative behavior:

Consider the chaos of competing demands for social recognition which would ensue if etiquette did not exist. Etiquette formalizes the rank order of claims for deference, thus avoiding in most cases the problem of deciding between one individual's right to attention and another's. The very arbitrariness of the ritual takes the problem out of the realm of idiosyncratic judgment; precedence is automatically evaluated according to the institutionalized criteria. Less specific than etiquette but analogous in function are rules of social intercourse like "first come, first served."[80]

We have, for example, an etiquette of seniority in our national Congress; seniority is the institutionalization of the everyday first-come-first-served rule, and hence "formalizes the rank order of claims for deference." Matthews and Huitt, among others, have delineated the Senatorial etiquette involved in "one individual's right to attention and another's" on the Senate floor by observing the informal folkways restricting the junior Senator's speechmaking.[81] Fenno, Manley, and others have observed similar patterns in some House committees, and even in House subcommittees. They have concluded that such systems of etiquette (e.g., seniority, committee norms of minimal partisanship) are "rituals for reducing social friction" in Toby's terms. Nevertheless, integrative norms, which hold the group together by reducing conflict, can contradict the social function of goal attainment, however it is partisanly defined. Thus we may wish to restrict legislative minuets for the sake of achieving our policy preferences, even at the expense of increasing conflict within the legislature. For example, an observer such as the liberal Congressman Richard Bolling, while accepting the ritualized first-come-first-served rule of seniority, will also ask: "All right; it's first-come, first-served, but how much should the first-comer get?"[82]

Thus, we see that political etiquette is an institutionalized mechanism for reducing social friction. As such, it is a sociopolitical innovation of leaders responding to conflict. However, we must distinguish a system of etiquette itself, such as the congressional seniority system, from its policy consequences, which often are not innovative, if we use the latter term in any kind of useful sense. Thus, in recent years, congressional political etiquette has usually helped stand-pat conservatives. Yet, as Wolfinger has pointed out, liberals in the Congress are increasingly profiting from the seniority system, which therefore may become a conflict-reducing mechanism that aids the cause of sociopolitical innovation.[83]

Toby's fourth social mechanism for legitimating conflict resolution is tact, or legitimate deception: "This solicitude for the feelings of others is the circumstance that makes the white lie socially 'right.' The ordinary lie is unreservedly disapproved because it lacks precisely this quality. It is a selfish attempt to manipulate other people by controlling their access to information. Tact, on the other hand, is institutionalized deception for the primary purpose of sparing the feelings of others."[84] Actually, we may view such legitimate deception in terms of a continuum from the white lie (an actual untruth) through various forms of tact (not telling the whole truth, partial lying). A cynical or sardonic attitude toward the statements of political leaders is a part of folk wisdom throughout the world. However, I think that scholars have paid insufficient attention to analyzing political lying and political tact. For instance, few American politicians are outright liars, but, on the other hand, few will tell the whole truth. Most politicians must be tactful and avoid the whole truth, for "this solicitude for the feelings of others" gains votes. Tact, like lying, can help you get ahead.

Because tact gains votes, avoiding the whole truth is an inherent part of democratic elections. But we should note that, in Toby's words, tact "is institutionalized deception for the primary purpose of sparing the feelings of others." To realize the function of tact in democratic campaigning, imagine an electoral campaign in which two politicians tell the whole truth as they see it. Candidate Conservative viciously attacks the squalor and crime of Negro slums, and states that while some of the finest men he knows are Negroes, in general colored people are inferior to other Americans. Candidate Con-

servative states that he believes that Negro squalor and crime
are the fault of the Negroes themselves, because in our individualistic society, all men have an equal chance to get ahead
and it is the person's own fault if he lives in a slum, as the
Chinese and Japanese have proven. Candidate Liberal, on the
other hand, states that although some of the finest men he
knows are real-estate salesmen, morticians, and loan-company
executives, in general men in these trades are bloodsucking
leeches on society. Thus, such telling of the truth, the whole
truth, and nothing but the truth (as seen by each person)
in political oratory could increase viciousness and hatred
throughout society. One man's meat is another man's poison.
Thus, we see the importance of tact, or sugarcoated deception, as a response to conflict.

Toby writes: "Institutionalized techniques exist for pre-
venting role conflicts from arising. These are not perfect, however, and role conflicts arise. But there are only a limited number of possible solutions to these dilemmas. The problem for
research is the conditions under which one solution is chosen
over another."[85] Toby lists seven alternatives open to persons
who "find themselves in situations where two or more groups
make incompatible demands upon them," a statement that
applies to political behavior. These seven alternatives are: repudiation of one group, playing off one group against the
other, stalling until the pressures subside, redefinition of the
role, leading a double life, escaping from the field, and illness.
All these behavior patterns are important for understanding
political leaders. Some of them are equivalent to Merton's
categories of "social mechanisms articulating role-sets." Thus,
"playing off one group against the other" (Toby) is seen by
Merton as one instance of relying on differences of power of
those in the role-set. "Leading a double life" is subsumed under Merton's "observability of conflicting demands by members of a role-set." "Repudiation of one group" and "escaping
from the field" are equivalent to Merton's "abridging the role-
set."[86]

Repudiation of one group making an incompatible demand
is certainly a common course of action. However, the competi-
tive, economic-model electoral system, with its competing

elites pursuing public office,[87] restricts such repudiation as a mechanism for reducing conflict. For example, Barry Goldwater's beliefs about the nature of the federal system and the United States Constitution forced him to vote against the Civil Rights Bill of 1964, a de facto repudiation of the Negro vote, which was cast 28 percent for Nixon in 1960, but only 6 percent for Goldwater in 1964. If Goldwater had voted for the Civil Rights Bill, thereby avoiding the repudiation of the Negro vote, he not only would have faced incompatible demands from Negroes, Southern segregationists, and ultra-conservative Goldwater activists, but also would have complicated his own conservative conscience. On the other hand, Lyndon Johnson, the master politician, repudiated nobody but Communists and Klansmen, and accordingly suffered the complexities of finding himself "in situations where two or more groups make incompatible demands" upon him. Parenthetically, it is interesting to note that by March 1966 Johnson was reportedly on reasonably civil terms with Wayne Morse, whereas he was reacting almost savagely to the milder, sporadic, and more institutionally expressed criticism of Senator Vance Hartke of Indiana, whom Johnson regarded as a double-crossing protégé.[88] We see that if a politician repudiates a group or a person whose demands contradict those of another group or person, the politician's life becomes simpler, except that he loses political support. If the politician repudiates nobody, his life is full of complicated situations, yet he may retain massive political support.

(We have all known at least one attractive girl who has followed this political pattern: for one reason or another, our subject will not choose one male admirer and repudiate the rest. If she were to do this, her life would become simpler, yet her band of admirers would become smaller. However, our femme fatale cannot repudiate any man she likes, and thus she has a large band of admirers/supporters but finds herself constantly in complicated situations, when two or more admirers make incompatible demands on her. Our lovable female might be an egoist, or she might be very kind. More likely, she is a very kind egoist, like Abraham Lincoln and Franklin Delano Roosevelt.)

Illness and resigning from politics are leaders' responses to

conflict that deserve more attention by scholars. However, political conflicts may or may not produce extreme psychological and physical stress in the leader who is subjectively aware
of incompatible demands. My impression is that Theodore
Roosevelt, Franklin Roosevelt, Truman, Kennedy, and Johnson often regarded political conflicts, even those involving incompatible demands, as psychologically and physically invig-
orating up to a certain point. On the other hand, Taft, Wilson,
Harding, Coolidge, Hoover, and Eisenhower seem to have
had a lower tolerance for conflict; they found incompatible
demands psychologically and physically depressing. Taft was
a first-class judge and administrator but a poor manager of
political conflict; Wilson had great political talent yet he pro-
pelled himself into tragically needless dilemmas, rendered in-
solvable by his own peculiar combination of principled moral-
ism and stubbornness.[89]

The failure of Wilson in the Versailles Treaty controversy,
and the tragic promotion of Warren Harding to a post beyond
his abilities and thus to his early death, bring to mind one of
Chester Barnard's observations about "the executive function." Barnard states that "the higher the grade [of executive
responsibility] the more complex the *moralities* involved, and
the more necessary higher abilities to discharge the responsi-
bilities, that is, to resolve the moral conflicts implicit in the
positions."[90] The situations of role conflict, or "situations
where two or more groups make incompatible demands" on
the politician, are situations of complex moral conflict. Thus,
Barnard is concerned with the same questions that I am dealing with here, using the role-conflict model. Barnard continues: "It is apparent that executives frequently fail. This failure may be ascribed in most cases, I believe, to inadequate
abilities as a first cause, usually resulting in the destruction of
responsibility. But in many cases it may be inferred that the
conditions impose a moral complexity and a moral conflict
presumably not soluble. Some actions which may within reason appear to be dictated by the good of the organization as
a whole will obviously be counter to nearly all other codes,
personal or official."[91] Woodrow Wilson, for example, was a
man of tremendous abilities, but among the least of these was

a reliable capacity to deal with "moral complexity." He was
morally incapable of compromising his principles, as embodied in the League of Nations Covenant, to meet the demands
of Senator Lodge and his supporters. Wilson's conduct and
subsequent collapse were instrumental in the complete defeat of the Versailles Treaty in the Senate. Wilson seems to
have had a significant impact on history by his sagacious management of America's entry into World War I and his personal
influence on the peace settlement and on the League Covenant. But Wilson's personal influence was also an important
factor in the American nonparticipation in the League. In this
case, too, if Wilson had acted differently, the course of human
events (at least in the short run) would have been significantly different. Wilson's inability to deal with moral complexity was the cause of his defeat in the League controversy,
but it is interesting to note that he handled the extraordinarily
complex morality of American diplomacy in the August 1914–
March 1917 period with impressive judiciousness. As Alexander and Juliette George note in their biography and psychological interpretation of Wilson, this unusual man seems to
have asked for trouble by assuming needlessly moralistic positions at certain times, although he was quite capable of en-
gaging in adroit maneuvering of a complex moral nature at
other times.[92] Thus, Wilson seemed capable of dealing with
situations of great moral complexity, but at times he just re-
fused to do so. Harding, on the other hand, was promoted to
a position beyond his abilities. In particular, he was destroyed
by the moral complexity of having to punish his corrupt, boor-
ish friends of the Ohio gang. (More specifically, perhaps
Harding was unable to deal with the moral complexity of
refusing prestigious jobs to friends who were technically and
morally incapable of filling them.)

Coolidge escaped from conflict and complexity by sleeping
twelve hours a day.[93] Hoover, on the other hand, was a most
energetic man but an ideologue. We could term Hoover a
"Christian technocratic individualist" (individualism in the
sense of Adam Smith and laissez-faire liberalism). He was
not a politician—someone who specialized in authoritatively
allocating scarce values and hence dealing with political con-

flict. Nor was he ideologically flexible or pragmatic; thus he was a magnificent organizer of resources toward agreed ends, but he was unable to deal with situations or people that contradicted his belief in laissez-faire liberalism, Smithian economics, the preeminence of business, and the subordination of government. He too was a man of tremendous ability who could not deal with certain situations of moral complexity—i.e., when economic events contradicted his personal ideology. Lenin could institute a New Economic Policy, but not Hoover! Hoover had much in common with Wilson, as Hoover himself perhaps realized.* Hoover could not deal with certain situations because of his personal ideology, which was no doubt inextricably linked with his personality structure. Similarly, Wilson, with his Calvinist psychological structure, sometimes could not deal with complex situations, in which it became necessary to compromise the specific content of particular policies.

Neustadt writes: "Everything suggests that with his motivations as with methods, Eisenhower has been a sort of [Franklin] Roosevelt in reverse,"[94] for, whereas Roosevelt delighted in sorting out conflicting information and policy alternatives presented by conflicting personalities in his administrative organization, Eisenhower evidently was annoyed by disagreement, especially intense disagreement, about "the one best way" of achieving a goal. Hence, Franklin Roosevelt had an informally organized ad hoc staffing system; Eisenhower established a formally organized system under the guidance of the assistant president, Sherman Adams. According to Neustadt, Eisenhower thought of himself as a great conciliator.

He [Eisenhower] genuinely thought himself the hero others thought him. . . . And he genuinely thought the Presidency was, or ought to be, the source of unifying, moderating influence above the struggle, on the model of George Washington—the Washington, that is to say, of legend, not of life. . . . What drew him to the Presidency and held him there, it seems, was a conception of the good man above politics, emulating the Father of his Country. . . . With this to guide him he could not dispute the arguments of all his friends that his "place in the world was unique," that he had "a

---

* Hoover certainly admired Wilson and even wrote a book about him—*The Ordeal of Woodrow Wilson*—in which the preface is especially interesting.

God-given ability for reconciling differences among . . . nations," and for "healing divisions among the American people." . . . But the reverse side of the coin was a diminished confidence when he dealt with the hard, divisive issues forced upon a President by dates and by events.[95]

On illness and death as a response to complex conflict, this quotation from Neustadt is very intriguing: "Robert Donovan supplies us Eisenhower's answer when it was suggested to him a few weeks before his heart attack that Congress might be called back for a special session in the fall of 1955: 'He slowly twisted his head around to [Arthur] Burns and told him painfully that the cost of a special session might be the sanity and possibly the life of one Dwight D. Eisenhower.' Such comments simply strengthen the suggestion . . . that this man neither liked the game he was engaged in nor had gained much understanding of its rules."[96] Thus, in the solution of role conflicts, escape from the field and illness are important responses of politicians to "situations where two or more groups make incompatible demands."

The sixth of Toby's seven behavioral patterns aimed at reducing conflict "in situations where two or more groups make incompatible demands" is "stalling until the pressures subside." Toby describes this pattern as follows: "If the cross-pressures are of a temporary nature, it may be possible for the individual to postpone making a decision until one or both of the groups relax their demands. Stalling is, however, not passive waiting; it is an art. It involves placating and promising while the competing obligations are not being fulfilled."[97] Stalling alleviates political conflict while the leader waits until the conflicting interests subside or the conflicting groups resolve their differences. Stalling thus is linked to the strategies of relying on differences of power among the others in the position-set (role-set) and playing off one group against the other. On the other hand, stalling is another word for *immobilisme*—inaction—the term descriptive of a serious weakness of some representative governments. During the Fourth Republic, the French National Assembly followed a policy of stalling on the major issues of the Algerian War, for example.

Stalling, and observing the balance of forces in the group

environment, is the central political strategy pursued by Chicago politicians, as observed by Banfield in the six case studies described in his *Political Influence*. Banfield writes:

The political heads are slow to take up an issue presented to them by the "civic leaders." *They know from experience that what one organization wants is almost certain to be opposed by others.* Chicago is much too big a city, and the interests in it far too diverse, to allow of quick and easy agreement on anything. By approaching an issue slowly, the political head gives opposing interests time to emerge, to formulate their positions, and to present their arguments. Before he commits himself he wants to see what the alignment on each side is likely to be and what is at stake politically. The longer the evil hour of decision can be postponed, the better he likes it; he has nothing to lose as long as the argument continues, and *any settlement he imposes will make him enemies.* What the public housing leader said of Mayor Kennelly—that his idea of a beautiful world was to sit around a table and have the opposing parties come to an agreement for which he would then take the credit without ever having opened his mouth—can be said of the other politicians as well.[98] [Emphasis added.]

The political strategy of stalling maintains the politician's popularity, since in most situations those annoyed at the leader's indecision have more diffused emotions than the (probably) smaller group that would be intensely angry, no matter which decision the leader makes. The political behavior of stalling until a clear balance of forces emerges is a response of leadership to conflict, but it is seldom an innovative response, for the political leader merely rubber-stamps a coalescence of group influence. In such a case, group forces are the *independent* variable, while the politician is the *dependent* variable.

The last of Toby's seven behavior patterns for reconciling conflicting demands is "redefinition of the role or roles." He defines this pattern as follows: "The individual reacts upon the situation and changes it so that the role expectations are no longer incompatible."[99] In other words, the person (leader), in redefining the situation, acts as an independent variable, exercises causal impact on events, or exerts power, as he changes the situation to mitigate the conflicting demands and thus realizes his will. Furthermore, in redefining the situation, he exercises creativity—i.e., he innovates—a new situation. In situations of extreme value heterogeneity and confusion, such a redefinition of the situation denotes extraordinary leadership, defined as influence, of the great man of history, described by the charisma-paradigm model. In situations of value homogeneity, general agreement, and conflict over only limited changes in political policy, the redefinition of the situation is an important case of pluralist leaders' changing the course of events in a significant way (albeit less significant than that of a hero of history or revolution). By redefining a conflict situation in order to resolve incompatible demands, the politician acts as an independent force, exercises influence, and introduces sociopolitical innovation. Hence, the concept of redefinition of the situation, as a means of reducing role conflict, helps the analyst link leadership, political conflict, and sociopolitical innovation.

Ernst Haas' concept of "upgrading the common interest" is a type of redefinition of the situation by leaders responding to multilateral conflict, which leads to sociopolitical innovation (in this case international integration). Haas categorizes the outcomes of international bargaining among leaders into three types: (1) "accommodation on the basis of the minimum common denominator"; (2) "accommodation by 'splitting the difference'"; (3) "accommodation on the basis of deliberately or inadvertently upgrading the common interests of the parties."[100] Haas comments that upgrading the common interests may mean

that the parties succeeded in redefining their conflict so as to work out a solution at a higher level, which almost invariably implies the expansion of the initial mandate or task. In terms of results, this mode of accommodation maximizes what I have elsewhere called the "spill-over" effect of international decisions: policies made in carrying out an initial task and grant of power can be made real only if the task itself is expanded, as reflected in the compromises among the states interested in the task. In terms of method, the upgrading of the parties' common interests relies heavily on the services of an *institutionalized mediator,* whether a single person or a board of experts, *with an autonomous range of powers.*[101] [Emphasis added.]

In a pluralist society, the "institutionalized mediator" "with an autonomous range of power" can be a certain type of politician who is sensitive to multilateral conflict and accordingly redefines particular, limited situations to resolve conflict, satisfy the majority of conflicting interests involved, and enhance his own popularity. A case of such redefinition of a multilateral conflict situation, involving the upgrading of common interests of Democratic senators, is described in Huitt's analysis of Lyndon Johnson's leadership in the Senate.[102] In 1954, Democratic senators were split into a pro-labor Northern group and an anti-labor predominantly Southern group over the nomination of a certain Albert Beeson to the National Labor Relations Board. Pro-labor senators wanted to reject Beeson's nomination because he retained connections with a California corporation; anti-labor senators saw no reason why an NLRB appointee should be friendly to unions. As minority leader, Johnson unified the Democrats on this issue by redefining the situation in terms of the honor of the Senate itself. Johnson, finding that Beeson had contradicted himself in testimony between hearings, succeeded in persuading Senator Walter George that Beeson should be rejected for flouting the dignity of the Senate. George, highly influential with conservative Southern Democrats, convinced them to accept Johnson's new definition of the situation, and consequently the Democratic minority (of 1954) "stood solidly together on the kind of issue which usually divided them."[103] Accordingly, Lyndon Johnson, serving as a mediating leader, redefined a situation by deliberately "upgrading the common interests of the parties" involved.

Another case, more directly involving task expansion and political innovation, is that of the outstanding urban renewal program of New Haven's Mayor Richard Lee. Dahl reports that Lee's unusual political success has been based to a great extent on his creation of an urban renewal program that unified otherwise conflicting interests. Lee's response to multilateral political conflict led to a partial redefinition of the political situation, an upgrading of the common interest, dynamic political mediation satisfying the majority of otherwise contending interests, and an increase in the popularity of a political leader. The person's innovative response resulted in the exercise of power—the Mayor caused substantial changes in others' behavior according to his intentions (support for urban renewal, getting reelected).[104]

Haas' concept of upgrading common interests evidently has much in common with Mannheim's concept of dynamic intellectual (or political) mediation. Thus Mannheim shows that an awareness of conflicting perspectives (goals, interests) is crucial for redefining a situation in terms of dynamic political mediation. In many cases, a pluralist political system, having multilateral conflict, may force its political leadership to gain such an awareness of conflicting perspectives. Such leaders may exhibit an innovative response—a creative, if limited, redefinition of the situation in terms of upgrading common interests.

In this chapter I have furthered my discussion of leadership within a pluralist political system, a system in which leaders' actions are interdependent with the actions of numerous others. Accordingly, I view pluralist leadership in terms of individual response to multilateral conflict. The concept of the marginal man, Mannheim's theory of multiperspective comprehension, and theories of role conflict aid in understanding such elite responses to conflict. Both Mannheimian and role-conflict models converge around the concepts of redefining conflict situations and upgrading common interests. Further study of such dynamic mediation should be important for understanding the leader's role within the pluralist political system.

10. Summary

Although the concept "power" is used in a confusing variety of ways, we find considerable agreement among empirical political theorists that power is a type of causation, and therefore that a system of power is a system of causation. Viewing power as social causation excludes the other views of power as freedom, as coercion, as a nonrelational attribute, and as referring to the world of nature. However, we may question the usefulness of "power" defined as social causation, for this definition of power refers to all social science. Further, we may wish to distinguish power from influence by restricting our denotation of power to mean the exercise of intended social causation against resistance, and using influence to refer to social causation in general. Nevertheless, since power is often used by social scientists to mean social causation, it has been useful to examine the implications of viewing power in this more general way.

In the second chapter, I suggest that four concepts—hypothesis, system, causal system, and as a subset of these three, power structure—can be related in certain circumstances. In turn, these four concepts can be characterized by the dimensions of simplicity-complexity, which I define as follows:

The COMPLEXITY *of a system varies directly, but non-additively, with (1) the number and variety of its components; (2) the amount and incidence of relational interdependence among the components; (3) the variability of the components and their relationships through time. The* SIMPLICITY *of a system varies inversely with these factors.*

I maintain that a pluralist political system is a complex political system, having complex causation, a complex power structure, and requiring complex hypotheses for its explanation. In other words, power is usually seen as dispersed among a large number of diverse actors (variables), who form numerous differing coalitions (relational interdependence), while both the actors and their relationships change constantly. An elitist system, on the other hand, is a simple political system, having simple causation. Accordingly, demonstrating pluralism is the same as demonstrating systemic complexity. Thus, within almost every substantive area of the descriptive study of American politics, there is a polarization between those who assert systemic complexity and those who assert systemic simplicity. The complex systemic viewpoint of most political scientists studying American politics is represented by the works of such leading political scientists as Robert Dahl, Charles Lindblom, Arthur Bentley, and David Truman.

I maintain that the value of pluralist findings depends on the "significance" of elitist conclusions, and that such value judgments may vary with the observer. My own opinion is that pluralist findings in the study of American politics are quite valuable because of the continuing appeal of various types of elitist theories of power structure. Nevertheless, we may wish to further differentiate systems of power and "bargaining," a term describing the activities of a pluralist power structure over time. Such an extension of the theory of power structure can profit from further attention to sociological theory, whose generality contrasts with the individualistic approach of Dahl and many other political scientists. Moreover, the student of power structure must deal with the question "power over what?" in a theoretically systematic way, which implies an examination of general social theory, administrative theory, and normative political philosophy.

In stating the existence of pluralism and complexity, the political scientist must realize that one can find complexity almost anywhere from one perspective or another. Thus, if we compare the distribution of power within the U.S. Forest Service to that within Soviet industrial administration, we find a spurious pluralism, a bogus complexity within both systems. At first glance, the Forest Service seems to be an extraordinarily decentralized system of power relations, but experienced analysts state that such decentralization is only superficial, for the Service is bound together by a professional-ideological consensus, which limits the issue scope of possible initiatives. Similarly, the literature on Soviet industrial administration gives us a picture of bargaining, with the low-level industrial manager often "realizing his will against opposition" through a combination of persuasion and deception. Yet we would not say that this political-managerial system is highly decentralized, for the actors are bargaining over increments within the limitations set by shared goals. Similar considerations arise in the field of community-power studies; Dahl and Polsby, for example, find a decentralized power structure in the city of New Haven, but their critics maintain that such decentralization is bounded by social-structural and ideological limitations on the formation of issues.

The examples above suggest that analyzing the distinction between politics and administration may be fruitful for deriving theory concerning systems of power. For instance, we might say that the finding of decentralization within the Forest Service and Soviet industrial administration is spurious, because the actors are controlling only "routine" decisions, not "critical" decisions. This comment is equivalent to recent criticism of the pluralist community-power studies. But then how do we distinguish critical decisions, especially if we do not rely on the criteria of the actors' perceptions? Borrowing from Selznick, Waldo, Simon, and others, I see the difference between critical and routine decisions as one of generality, conceptualized in terms of the behavior tree and the relative inclusiveness of activity sets. Viewing power and critical decisions in terms of a hierarchy of sets helps delineate some important theoretical problems, especially the observation that an infinity of decision-making alternatives may be distinguished in numerous situations, simply by the process of subdividing previous stated alternatives. Here the discussion of critical decisions meshes with the logical theory of finitude and the normative theory of freedom, subjects that are beyond the scope of this work.

The use of Apter's structure-behavior distinction is helpful for understanding the gap between comparative political sociology and the pluralist study of American politics. Apter describes this distinction as follows: "The structure may be defined as the relationships in a social situation which limit the choice process to a particular range of alternatives. The behavioral may be defined as the selection process in choice, i.e., deciding between alternatives." I develop this structure-behavior distinction by examining these differing approaches toward the same subject matter. Disagreements occur between those following the two approaches, because of the pluralist-behaviorist's greater emphasis on strict canons of verification and the tendency (usually implicit) of the structuralist to dismiss behavioral studies as of secondary significance. In this context, I view the recent interest in political culture as an attempt to formulate a structural category, going beyond the relative specificity of the Bentley-Truman group-process approach and analytic categories.

One of my concerns in the second part of this book is to note, particularly to those who focus on behavioral considerations (such as decision making, political process, political attitudes), that structural factors must be considered in formulating a theory of power and democracy, even though such factors might seem diffuse and of doubtful verifiability. I do not mean to imply that structural theory is somehow more basic or more important. Structural analysis often explains the origin and development of critical social and political decisions; accordingly, we often must use structural analysis to discuss problems of power and democracy, if we remember the fundamental importance of the inquiry—power over what?

The last section of the book concerns leadership, since this concept naturally combines the two preceding central concepts of power and critical decisions (issue salience). If a leader is defined as a person who exercises considerable power, then the theory of leadership is a theory of power, causation, and issue salience. I focus on political leadership and its relation to the development of values, conceived as "a generalized imperative concerning scope of activity." By considering leadership and innovation, I am paralleling the sort of analysis made by Philip Selznick in *Leadership in Adminis-*

tration. I view the charismatic hero and the pluralist politician in relation to the generation of political values and to policy innovation. Such an analysis, concerned with the relations among past value commitments and present choices, or with present choices and future commitments, links structural and behavioral theory.

I define leaders as the influential—those exercising the greatest causal impact on social events. In other words, the leader is one who makes things happen that would not happen otherwise. This definition is congruent with the usage of Sidney Hook and Robert Dahl. When we study leaders' behavior, we attempt to establish the limits on individual action set by general social forces, which structure the alternatives available to the leader and the responses of his followers. We must always analyze leadership in conjunction with an analysis of situation and followers. We may consider the structural limits on leadership in the light of comparative method, or through its less convincing equivalent, the mental experiment. In general, the study of leadership must consider both the structural and the behavioral aspects of a situation.

The analysis of leadership is related to the study of critical decisions in the charisma-paradigm model, which might be termed the "Mosaic" model of individual influence on social events. Thus, in times of value strain, a charismatic hero may appear whose psychological processes are paralleled by his public actions, perhaps through a widely appealing resolution of a personal identity crisis that provides the critical decisions and values for a new social identity, thereby leading to social change through the establishment of new social structures infused with new ideology. The prototype of the charisma-paradigm model of leadership is the Old Testament tale of the Exodus.

The Mosaic leader may be a revolutionary man who appears in a revolutionary time—his task is to lead his followers out of the wilderness of fundamental sociopolitical conflict and confusions. However, the Mosaic model does not apply to the analysis of leaders' behavior in the situation of sociopolitical agreement and limited conflict. Thus, pluralist analysis, a theory of power, has greater applicability to homogeneous societies, characterized by pluralism, fundamental sociopolitical agreement, limited conflict, and consensus about the fundamental nature of politics and government, and in which most political decisions are routine, specific choices concerning incremental changes in governmental policies. In this situation of multilateral conflict bounded by fundamental sociopolitical agreement, the individual leader's response to subjectively experienced conflict may be described by role-theory models and by Mannheim's theory of multiperspective comprehension. Occasionally, this subjective conflict produces the response of redefining the situation, which is one mode of independent action and influence exercised by leaders ordinarily restricted by the dispersal of power in the pluralist society. The systemic aggregation of such leaders' innovations, the scope of which is limited by the decentralization of influence and causation in the pluralist society, may produce new critical decisions with the passage of time.

Perhaps the most important substantive conclusion of this book is that one must deal with the question "power over what?" before one can show the existence of democracy defined as a high amount of control over leaders by followers. Democracy increases with a "true" increase in the dispersal of power, seen as followers causing intended changes in leaders' behavior. But somehow the salience of varying types of issues and decisions must be evaluated. Thus we must show that the people control many *important* decisions, and we must somehow derive criteria of importance. Demonstrating widespread dispersal of power, pluralist systems, and complexity cannot ipso facto show democracy, unless we answer "power over what?" Consequently, to discriminate theoretically among important and unimportant political events is central to any theory of political democracy.

Notes

Notes

Complete authors' names, titles, and publication data are given in the Bibliography, pp. 253–65.

INTRODUCTION

1. Easton, *Framework for Political Analysis*, pp. vii–viii.
2. See Polsby, *Community Power and Political Theory*, Ch. 6. Other uses of the term "pluralism" have referred to normative political philosophy (e.g., Laski, "The Pluralistic State," in *The Foundations of Sovereignty and Other Essays*; Hsiao, *Political Pluralism: A Study in Contemporary Political Theory*); social theory stressing the importance of group mediation between politics and the individual (e.g., Kornhauser, *The Politics of Mass Society*); and empirical political theory stressing the importance of "the group basis of politics" (e.g., Bentley, *The Process of Government*; Truman, *The Governmental Process*; and Latham, "The Group Basis of Politics: Notes for a Theory"). Power-structure pluralism and group-theory pluralism share certain important characteristics.

CHAPTER 1

1. An excellent statement of the relationship between power and causation may be found in Dahl, "Power." See also Dahl, "Concept of Power," pp. 201–3; Dahl, "Cause and Effect"; Simon, *Models of Man*, pp. 4–9, 72–78; March, "Theory and Measurement of Influence," esp. pp. 434–37; Cartwright, "Influence, Leadership, Control," pp. 3–4; Riker, esp. pp. 346–49; Walter, pp. 350–51.
2. The value of causation as a concept has been challenged by philosophers and natural scientists. Nevertheless, after verbally denying the existence of causation, many proceed to think in such terms anyway, when they refer to independent variables (causes) and dependent variables (effects). I agree with this statement of Herbert Simon: "The impact of Hume, together with the kinds of mathematical methods that are used by the natural sciences, have led to wide acceptance of the slogan: 'There is no causation, only functional interdependence.' Of course, deep down in our hearts we have never believed this (and a

few brave souls, e.g. MacIver, have said so). Even though we accept the critique of Hume, we find it hard to think that there is no difference between a 'spurious' and a 'genuine' correlation." (Here Simon cites his own work, later published in *Models of Man*. Quoted from Simon, "Research in Comparative Politics," p. 665.) Thus, I am aware that insofar as my analysis is based on the concept of causation, it is subject to the pitfalls of that idea. For example, certain ambiguities in defining power are related to ambiguities in defining causation. Thus, Nagel, in a stimulating essay, questions whether *C* must act in order to exercise power over *R* and whether there must be a connection between *C* and *R* as a necessary condition of the power relation. See Nagel; Dahl, "Concept of Power"; Dahl, "Cause and Effect." The well-known book by Blalock, *Causal Inferences in Nonexperimental Research,* may be read as a work on power and influence.

3. By "social causation," I am referring to causation in which both the causal agent and the affected object are human beings.

4. See Dahl, "Concept of Power," p. 203; Dahl, "Power."

5. Emerson, p. 32.

6. Wolfinger, "Reputation and Reality." While reputation for power should not be confused with the actual exercise of power, it may be considered a resource base for exercising power: Neustadt, *Presidential Power*, Ch. 4, "Professional Reputation"; Wildavsky, *Leadership in a Small Town*, p. 318; Gamson.

7. Dahl, *Modern Political Analysis*, pp. 48–49. The recognition of the difference between potential power (resources) and the actual exercise of power is apparent in the following. At a cocktail party in July 1966 "[a] former Naval person speaks up: 'We are the most powerful country in the world, so we have to use our power. What good is it otherwise? Crush 'em! We will impose a *pax Americana* on the world'" (Herb Caen, *San Francisco Chronicle*, Sunday, July 17, 1966).

8. Dahl, *Modern Political Analysis*, pp. 47–48. See also Dahl, *Who Governs?*, Ch. 21; Schulze, pp. 3–9.

9. Emerson, pp. 31–32; Friedrich, pp. 22–24.

10. Simon, *Models of Man*, pp. 63–64.

11. *Ibid.*, p. 64.

12. *Ibid.*

13. Wolfinger, "Reputation and Reality," p. 644; Dahl, *Modern Political Analysis*, p. 54; Polsby, "Sociology of Community Power," p. 232; Rossi, pp. 366–69; Wildavsky, *Leadership in a Small Town*, pp. 316–17; Polsby, *Community Power*, pp. 115–18.

14. Hospers, Chs. 2–5.

15. See Cartwright, "Influence, Leadership, Control," pp. 4–5. Cartwright cites Barnard's distinction between "authority of position" and "authority of leadership" in Barnard, *The Functions of the Executive*. An authority role might also regularize the production of *unintended* effects on subordinates. Later in this book, I treat the issue of intentionality and the definition of power.

16. See note 13 above.
17. Neustadt, *Presidential Power*; Gamson.
18. Three researchers found that the reputational method uncovers about one-half of the leaders found by a decision-making study. See Wildavsky, *Leadership in a Small Town*, pp. 303–19; Presthus, pp. 109–24, 147–55; Jennings, pp. 155–61 *passim*. The most successful usage of reputation as an indicator for the actual successful exercise of power is, I think, Gamson.
19. Cartwright, "Influence, Leadership, Control," pp. 7–11.
20. Dahl, *Who Governs?*, Ch. 14.
21. Russell, *Power*, p. 35.
22. *Ibid.*
23. The dimension of intentionality in some definitions of power suggests a theoretical confluence with Merton's well-known concepts of manifest and latent functions. See Merton, *Social Theory*, Ch. 1.
24. This usage of "influence" is, I think, common parlance among political scientists. Unfortunately, influence also commonly denotes a specific mode of exercising power (or "influence"!): the use of *persuasion* to realize one's will, as opposed to the use of force or remuneration.
25. Simon, *Models of Man*, p. 66.
26. March, "Theory and Measurement of Influence," p. 437. See Dahl, "Concept of Power," p. 201, footnote 1.
27. March, "Theory and Measurement of Influence," pp. 434–35.
28. Dahl, "Concept of Power," pp. 202–3.
29. Cartwright notes that "in the definition given by Dahl (1957, p. 202) the notion of intention is only implicit" (Cartwright, "Influence, Leadership, Control," p. 10). Thus *C* could *get R* to do something that *R* would not otherwise do, which was the *opposite* of *C*'s intention, as in Dahl's discussion of negative power" (Dahl, "Concept of Power," p. 205).
30. The issue of intentionality in the definition of power has contributed to the confusion surrounding the term. As an example of a definition of power including intentionality, we might modify Dahl's statement slightly: *C* has power over *R* to the extent that he can get *R* to do something *that C wants* which *R* would not otherwise do. Some theorists, such as Russell, include the actor's intentions within a definition of power, but other theorists, such as Simon, do not include intentions. See Cartwright, "Influence, Leadership, Control," pp. 10–11; Oppenheim, pp. 92–94, 106.
31. Dahl, *Modern Political Analysis*, p. 40.
32. Dahl, "Concept of Power," p. 202.
33. *Ibid.*, p. 203.
34. *Ibid.*
35. See Dahl, "Power." Paradoxes concerning the concept of causation may be linked to paradoxes concerning the concept of power. Also see Nagel.

36. Dahl, "Concept of Power," p. 204.
37. *Ibid.* Nagel has questioned this.
38. *Ibid.*, pp. 204–5.
39. Again we see an equivalence between the languages of power, causation, and functionalist theory.
40. Dahl, "Concept of Power," pp. 204–14.
41. *Ibid.*
42. For example, Cartwright, "Conception of Power," pp. 183–220. For another treatment of Cartwright's, Karlsson's, and Shapley and Shubik's definitions of power, see Riker.
43. For example, Karlsson, pp. 193–202.
44. For example, Shapley and Shubik, pp. 787–92.
45. Wildavsky, "Intelligent Citizen's Guide," p. 831.
46. Dahl, "Concept of Power," p. 202.
47. March, "Power of Power."
48. Riker, p. 348.
49. Easton, *Political System*, p. 143.
50. "If C acts and then R changes . . . did C want R to change in this way? If not, we might mistakenly attribute power to a blundering oaf whose efforts bring down disaster on his head" (Barber, *Power in Committees*, pp. 127, 128).
51. Easton, *Political System*, pp. 143–44.
52. Weber, p. 152.
53. Barber, *Power in Committees*, p. 128: "Does R resist C's attempt to change him? If not, we might be calling a man powerful who can make another do something about which the latter is fundamentally indifferent, as in the solicitation of votes for corresponding secretary of a lodge."
54. Private correspondence with the author. See also *ibid.*, pp. 127–58.
55. March, "Theory and Measurement of Influence," p. 437.

CHAPTER 2

1. Easton, *Framework for Political Analysis*, p. 30.
2. Tiryakian, p. 73.
3. See the chapter "The Philosophy of Logical Atomism" in Russell, *Logic and Knowledge*, esp. pp. 190–202.
4. Other definitions of simplicity-complexity include an implicit statement by Stafford Beer, p. 13, and pp. 12–19 *passim*; an explicit definition by Berlyne, pp. 38–40; and an implicit definition in Huntington's article. I discuss Beer's definition in the text of Ch. 2. Berlyne's definition of complexity is: "Other things being equal, complexity increases with the number of distinguishable elements. . . . If the number of elements is held constant, complexity increases with dissimilarity between elements. . . . Complexity varies inversely with the degree to which several elements are responded to as a unit" (pp. 38–39, original

italics omitted). Huntington states that organizational "complexity may involve both multiplication of organizational subunits (i.e., multiplication of systemic components) . . . and differentiation of separate types of organizational subunits (i.e., systemic components)" (p. 399). In other words, Huntington defines complexity as increasing with the number and diversity of a system's components, which are Berlyne's first two dimensions of complexity. In this book, I treat number and variety of systemic components as one dimension, although I recognize that they can be separated, thus yielding four dimensions of complexity. I prefer to do this in order to avoid classification controversies. Thus, reference to variety in a system's components implies the discrimination of particular categories as being qualitatively different from one another. Consequently, disagreement may arise as to whether the categories "are really different from one another" or whether the variety is superficial, degenerating after analysis into large numbers of the same thing.

5. See Ashby, *Design for a Brain*, pp. 206–7 and *passim*, for an interesting example of complex systemic analysis, which probably applies to pluralist political systems. My description of this dimension is adequate at a gross level of analysis, but I recognize that a more explicit formulation, probably emanating from statistical and cybernetic theory, will be necessary for work requiring great analytic precision. In *An Introduction to Cybernetics*, p. 5, Ashby wrote: "Science stands today on something of a divide. For two centuries it has been exploring systems that are either intrinsically simple or that are capable of being analysed into simple components. The fact that such a dogma as 'vary the factors one at a time' could be accepted for a century, shows that scientists were largely concerned in investigating such systems as *allowed* this method; for this method is often fundamentally impossible in the complex systems. Not until Sir Ronald Fisher's work in the '20's, with experiments conducted on agricultural soils, did it become clearly recognised that there are complex systems that just do not allow the varying of only one factor at a time—they are so dynamic and interconnected that the alteration of one factor immediately acts as cause to evoke alterations in others, perhaps in a great many others. Until recently, science tended to evade the study of such systems, focusing its attention on those that were simple. . . . But science today is also taking the first steps towards studying 'complexity' as a subject in its own right. Prominent among the methods for dealing with complexity is cybernetics."

6. Stafford Beer, p. 13.

7. See Wiener; Deutsch, *Nerves of Government*.

8. Polsby, *Community Power*, p. 118.

9. *Ibid.*, p. 115.

10. Legality, a form of legitimacy, is a highly important resource base for the exercise of power within a political system such as ours. Criticism of formalistic legal studies should not be carried to the extreme of overlooking or denigrating the role of legality in power relations. See Dahl, *Who Governs?*, pp. 246–48.

11. See Polsby, *Community Power*, pp. 115–18; and his *Congress*, p. 9; Wildavsky, *Dixon-Yates*, pp. 311–25.

12. Simon, *Models of Man*, p. 5.

13. Compare March, "Theory and Measurement of Influence," p. 437; and Goldhamer and Shils, p. 175.

14. See Selznick, *Leadership*, pp. 29–64; Bachrach and Baratz, "Two Faces of Power"; Polsby, *Community Power*, pp. 95–97; Dahl, "Concept of Power," pp. 205–9, and his *Modern Political Analysis*, p. 46.

15. Such a condition is impossible in the real world. Absolute totalitarian government is as utopian as absolute democracy. Conceptually, this is demonstrated by Goldhamer and Shils, p. 177, and by Dahl and Lindblom, p. 324.

16. See Wildavsky, *Politics of the Budgetary Process, passim*.

17. Of course formulators of simple hypotheses are not ipso facto simpleminded. Indeed, the reverse is often the case. Thus, the derivation of the simplest possible hypothesis to explain a given body of phenomena is a long-established principle of scientific inquiry, known as "Ockham's razor."

18. In Apter's terms, power-elite behavior, described with simple systems and simple hypotheses, might be limited by a complex structure, a complex system described with complex hypotheses. See Apter, "Comparative Politics"; Apter, *Politics of Modernization*, pp. 16–22. A perspective similar to Apter's may be found in Blumer, "Society as Symbolic Interaction."

19. See, for example, Committee on Political Parties; Bailey; Schattschneider, *Party Government*; Woodrow Wilson; Burns, *Congress on Trial*; Burns, *Deadlock of Democracy*.

20. See, for example, Polsby and Wildavsky, *Presidential Elections*, pp. 143–88. See also Herring, *Politics of Democracy*; Ranney and Kendall; Truman; Stedman and Sonthoff; Turner; Goodman, "Party Centralization"; Ranney, *Responsible Party Government* (all cited in Polsby and Wildavsky, *Presidential Elections*, pp. 185–86).

21. For example, see Dahl, *Who Governs?*, pp. 311–15; Wildavsky, *Leadership in a Small Town*, pp. 320–51; Polsby, *Community Power*, pp. 112–38. Polsby cites in support of his position: Truman; Tocqueville, esp. I: 181–205, 281–342; II: 114–35; Dahl, *Preface to Democratic Theory*; Wildavsky, *Dixon-Yates*.

22. For example, see Mills, *Power Elite*; Mills, "Structure of Power"; Hunter; Goldwater. Goldwater, like Mills, maintains that the national government is controlled by a power elite. Goldwater (p. 20) refers to the federal government as "a Leviathan, a vast national authority out of touch with the people, and out of their control. This monolith of power is bounded only by the will of those who sit in high places."

23. For a criticism of such theories, see Dahl, "Critique." Also see Bell.

24. White; Polsby, *Congress*, pp. 32–41; Huitt, "Outsider in the Senate."

25. Matthews, "Folkways"; Matthews, *U.S. Senators*, pp. 92–117; Huitt, "Outsider in the Senate"; Polsby, *Congress.*

26. Neustadt, *Presidential Power*; Rossiter, *American Presidency.* Aaron Wildavsky demonstrates, however, that Presidents exercise more power over military and foreign policy than over domestic policy: "Two Presidencies." Mills, "Structure of Power," p. 36.

27. Neustadt, *Presidential Power*, Ch. 8 and *passim.*

28. Rossiter, *American Presidency*, Ch. 5.

29. For example, see Truman, pp. 395–478; Long, "Power and Administration"; Simon *et al.*; Neustadt, *Presidential Power*; Wildavsky, *Dixon-Yates*, esp. pp. 295–325; Wildavsky, *Politics of the Budgetary Process*; Polsby, *Congress*, Chs. 2, 6; McConnell, esp. pp. 161–65.

30. Mills, *Power Elite*; Mills, "Structure of Power."

31. Key, "Lack of a Budgetary Theory"; Lewis; Smithies, pp. 163–74 and *passim.* Wildavsky criticizes such views in *Politics of the Budgetary Process*, pp. 127–80; see also his "Political Economy of Efficiency."

32. Lindblom, *Intelligence of Democracy*, pp. 165–290; also see Deutsch, "Cracks in the Monolith."

33. Wildavsky, "Radical Incrementalism."

34. For example, see Godfrey.

35. See notes 19 and 20, above.

36. For a summary of such arguments, see Polsby and Wildavsky, *Presidential Elections*, pp. 144–48, 172–77; and Ranney and Kendall, pp. 525–32.

37. The theories of Charles E. Lindblom seem especially promising in this respect. See "Muddling Through"; Braybrooke and Lindblom, pp. 3–143; Lindblom, *Intelligence of Democracy.* For a very original and significant analysis of decentralized power in America, see McConnell, esp. Ch. 10. McConnell's American political system—co-opted by the haves at the expense of the have-nots, yet remaining somewhat responsive to appeals for equality—is a wealthier version of the postrevolutionary Mexican political system. Cf. Padgett; Navarro.

38. Checks on the Court's power include the following: First, the Court operates within a normative system comparable to a restricting ideological framework. The sociology of the legal profession is comparable to the sociology of other professional groups in which independent, precipitous actions are restrained by the inculcation of professional norms. The Court is operating within the framework of one of the world's oldest and most influential normative systems, the tradition of Anglo-Saxon law, whose restraining power is similar to that of a religion. Besides being constrained by a normative system, the Court is checked by more specific rules embodied in the case law of constitutional interpretation. Second, the Court is dependent on normative compliance (legitimacy) for the enforcement of its decisions. Thus federal troops must be sent to Little Rock to enforce school integration. Hence the Court must retain its legitimacy with the executive branch, with Congress (needed for supplementary laws for enforcement), and with

the predominating tendencies of public opinion. Much evidence points to the rule of anticipated reactions as a powerful constraint on the Court. Third, a large number of institutional checks exist, which serve principally as institutionalized threats: the President's power of appointment, Senatorial ratification, the possibility of impeachment, Congressional power to regulate the Court's appellate jurisdiction, the possibility of expanding the number of justices on the Court, Congressional revision of statutes to avoid Court declarations of unconstitutionality, the possibility of Constitutional amendments. Also the Court remains in touch with the political process through the President's power of appointment and through interest-group utilization of the judicial process as a political strategy (e.g., the N.A.A.C.P., checked in other arenas, systematically pursued its goals in the Court system). Hence, through the President and through the actions of interest groups, the Court remains somewhat responsive to current political and social trends. (Note that "responsive" indicates a reaction to other variables, other causal agents.)

39. McCloskey, pp. 227–31.

40. Bentley; Odegard; Herring, *Group Representation*; Schattschneider, *Politics, Pressures and Tariff*; see Truman, biblio., pp. 537–44, for the earlier works in this field.

41. Schattschneider, *Party Government*; McConnell, esp. Ch. 10.

42. The preference for a powerful interest-group system is seldom explicitly stated. However, I think this is a valid inference from leading analyses of the functions of political decentralization, e.g., the works of Lindblom, Truman, Ranney, and Wildavsky.

43. See Schattschneider, *Party Government*, pp. 187–205.

44. Truman, pp. 159–87, 299–301, 501–35; Lazarsfeld *et al.*; Berelson *et al.*; Lipset, *Political Man*, pp. 86–90. Much criticism is now appearing concerning the value of unalloyed cross-pressures hypotheses as explanations for group political moderation and for individual political apathy. See Verba; Lijphart; Eckstein, *Division and Cohesion*, pp. 71–75. In the realm of individual behavior, Berlyne states many hypotheses contrary to the cross-pressures argument; see also Sperlich.

45. Banfield, "Politics of Metropolitan Area Organization"; Long, *Polity*, pp. 139–64.

46. See, for example, Polsby, *Community Power*; Dahl, *Who Governs?*; Wildavsky, *Leadership in a Small Town*; Long, "The Local Community as an Ecology of Games," pp. 139–55, in *Polity*.

47. Polsby, *Community Power*, pp. 7–13.

48. *Ibid.*

CHAPTER 3

1. Dahl, *Who Governs?*; Polsby, *Community Power*; Wildavsky, *Leadership in a Small Town*.

2. Dahl, "Critique," pp. 463–69.

3. Polsby, *Community Power.*
4. Wildavsky, *Leadership in a Small Town*, pp. 320–31.
5. Dahl, "Critique," p. 466.
6. For example, see Truman, pp. 395–478; Long, "Power and Administration," pp. 257–64; Simon *et al.*; Neustadt, *Presidential Power*; Wildavsky, *Dixon-Yates*, esp. pp. 295–325; Wildavsky, *Politics of the Budgetary Process*; Polsby, *Congress*, Chs. 2, 6; McConnell, esp. pp. 161–65. For an interesting case study, excellently illustrating the limitations of presidential power over the executive branch, see Maass.
7. Huitt, "Outsider in the Senate"; Polsby, *Congress*, pp. 32–41.
8. See, for example, Key, *Politics, Parties and Pressure Groups*; Bone; Goodman, *Two-Party System*; Polsby and Wildavsky, *Presidential Elections*, pp. 20–28.
9. Bauer *et al.*, pp. 265–76 and *passim*; Dahl, *Who Governs?*; Polsby, *Community Power*; Wildavsky, *Leadership in a Small Town*, and *Dixon-Yates*; Jennings.
10. Morton Grodzins' "sharing of powers" thesis is now predominant. See Grodzins, pp. 265–82.
11. Truman, *passim*; Bauer *et al.*, *passim.*
12. Wildavsky, "Two Presidencies."
13. See the works on community power by Dahl, Polsby, Wildavsky, and Jennings, cited above.
14. Dahl, *Who Governs?*, pp. 330–40.
15. *Ibid., passim.*
16. Bentley, Part 1.
17. *Ibid.*, p. 207.
18. Polsby, *Community Power*, p. 118. Polsby cites in support of his position: Truman; Tocqueville, esp. I: 181–205, 281–342, II: 114–35; Dahl, *Preface to Democratic Theory*; Wildavsky, *Dixon-Yates.*
19. Truman, pp. 14–44.
20. Newcomb *et al.*, p. 40.
21. See, for example, Newcomb, *Acquaintance Process.*

22. Truman, p. 55.	23. *Ibid.*, p. 44.
24. *Ibid.*, p. 53.	25. *Ibid.*, p. 391.
26. *Ibid.*	27. *Ibid.*
28. *Ibid.*, p. 392.	29. *Ibid.*, p. 437.
30. *Ibid.*	31. Latham.

32. *Ibid.*, p. 396.
33. *Ibid.*, p. 397. In this connection, refer to the writings concerning anomy and politics, e.g., Fromm; McClosky and Schaar; for the existentialist perception of Bentley's group-process world, see Jacobson.
34. For example, see Dahl, *Who Governs?*, pp. 190–205; Polsby, *Community Power*, pp. 115–21 and his *Congress*, p. 9; Wildavsky, *Dixon-Yates*, p. 311.
35. Truman, p. 391.
36. The work of Lindblom is particularly promising in this respect. Lindblom, "Muddling Through," and other published articles; Bray-

brooke and Lindblom, pp. 3–143; Lindblom, *Intelligence of Democracy*; Wildavsky, *Politics of the Budgetary Process*; Davis *et al.*; Hilsman.

37. Dahl, *Who Governs?*, p. 184. See also Sayre and Polsby, pp. 134–35.

38. *Ibid.*, pp. 330–40, esp. p. 333.

39. See Chs. 4–6 below; Selznick, *Leadership*, pp. 29–64; Bachrach and Baratz, "Two Faces of Power"; Polsby, *Community Power*, pp. 95–97; Dahl, "Concept of Power," pp. 205–9, and his *Modern Political Analysis*, p. 46.

40. Implicit in Dahl, *Who Governs?*, pp. 223–25; also implicit in Polsby and Wildavsky, *Presidential Elections*.

41. Dahl and Lindblom, p. 324.

42. *Ibid.*, pp. 324, 328.

43. *Ibid.*, p. 302 (original emphasis omitted).

44. *Ibid.*, p. 306.   45. *Ibid.*, pp. 324, 326.

46. *Ibid.*, p. 328.   47. *Ibid.*, p. 324.

48. For a provocative discussion of the social theory of the political economists and other classical liberals, see Wolin, pp. 286–351.

49. For example, Dahl and Lindblom. See also the various writings of Lindblom, such as "Muddling Through"; Braybrooke and Lindblom; Lindblom, *Intelligence of Democracy*. Also see Wildavsky, "Private Markets," pp. 33–37; *Politics of the Budgetary Process*; "Political Economy of Efficiency"; and other works on the budgetary process.

50. Lipset, *Political Man*, and other works; Mills, *Power Elite*, and other works. Clearly, one can be class conscious in one's studies without being radical. One might also compare the individualism of Polsby's *Community Power* with the class consciousness of the authors he attacks.

51. Dahl and Lindblom, p. 324.

52. Berliner.

53. Kaufman; Gulick; Schiff; Fesler, esp. pp. 555–57.

54. Dahl has stated: "If one tries to establish a useful definition of personal power, one must elaborate the formal definition of power. For example, the notion of power implies the question: power in respect to what? We cannot simply say that A has more power than B. It is always enjoined on us to say that A with respect to C; that A has power over B with respect to the action of C" (Dahl, "Cause and Effect," p. 92). However, Dahl has developed this consideration along different lines (the concept of issue area) than I do in this work.

55. Berliner, pp. 182–206.

56. Polsby, *Community Power*, p. 55.

57. Dahl, Polsby, and Wildavsky are aware of this consideration. Thus, the criteria for Dahl's selection of three issue areas seem quite reasonable: political nominations are central in the political process of New Haven; education involves a larger expenditure than other sectors of local government and involves the crucial activity of socializing the young; urban renewal is important because of the nationally known

quality of New Haven's program, which was critical in Mayor Lee's formation of a bipartisan coalition (*Who Governs?*, pp. 89–165). In *Community Power*, pp. 95–97, Polsby states criteria for selection of issues; see also pp. 114–15. Wildavsky studied all the issues in Oberlin over a four-year period: see *Leadership in a Small Town*, p. 8.

58. Selznick, *Leadership*, pp. 29–64.

59. Easton, *Political System*, p. 143.

60. Merton, *Social Theory*, pp. 197–200.

61. Presthus. Also see Bendix.

62. See the works of Lindblom; Cyert and March, *passim*; March and Simon; Simon, *Administrative Behavior*; Wildavsky, *Politics of the Budgetary Process*; Davis *et al.* See also Polsby and Wildavsky, "Uncertainty and Decision-Making"; Wildavsky, "What Can I Do?"

63. Wildavsky, "Goldwater Phenomenon"; James Q. Wilson; Gross *et al.*, pp. 222–43 and *passim*; Dahl, *Modern Political Analysis*, pp. 87–92 (in this connection, Dahl cites Richard Hofstadter's interesting study of Wendell Phillips as an uncompromising, principled agitator: "Wendell Phillips: The Patrician as Agitator," in *The American Political Tradition*, pp. 135–61); Gerth and Mills, pp. 110–28.

64. See Maslow.

CHAPTER 4

1. Fesler.

2. Berliner.

3. Easton, *Political System*, p. 129.

4. Berliner, p. 224.

5. *Ibid.*, p. 18.

6. *Ibid.*, p. 327.

7. Lindblom, "Muddling Through," and other published articles; Braybrooke and Lindblom, pp. 3–143; Lindblom, *Intelligence of Democracy*; Wildavsky, *Politics of the Budgetary Process*; Davis *et al.*; Fenno; Hilsman.

8. Berliner, pp. 327–28.

9. Braybrooke and Lindblom; and Lindblom, "Muddling Through."

10. Braybrooke and Lindblom, pp. 99–104; Berliner, p. 328.

11. Wildavsky, *Politics of the Budgetary Process*; Davis *et al.*; Fenno. Jowitt has reached similar conclusions in his comparison of Soviet and American administrative behavior.

12. Wildavsky, *Politics of the Budgetary Process*, pp. 1–2.

13. Berliner, pp. 224–25; Jowitt.

14. Wildavsky, *Politics of the Budgetary Process*, pp. 74–84; Jowitt.

15. Fainsod, *How Russia Is Ruled*, pp. 417–18, cited by Jowitt.

16. *Ibid.*   17. Berliner, *passim*.

18. See, for example, Arnow.   19. Berliner, pp. 259–63.

20. Fainsod has also noted the existence of family circles. See Fainsod, *Smolensk*, pp. 270–73 and *passim*, and *How Russia Is Ruled*, pp.

235–37, 388–89, and *passim;* Jowitt has analyzed other similar observations by David Granick, *Management of the Industrial Firm in the U.S.S.R.* (New York: Columbia Univ. Press, 1959) and *The Red Executive* (Garden City, N.Y.: Doubleday Anchor paperback, 1961).

21. Jowitt.

22. See Kautilya, pp. 62–65, 66, 69, 70; cited by Jowitt.

23. Berliner, pp. 182–206. *Blat* refers to illegitimate personal influence or "pull."

24. Wildavsky, *Leadership in a Small Town,* pp. 5–8.

25. Fainsod, *How Russia Is Ruled,* p. 235. Called to my attention by Kenneth Jowitt.

26. Of course this is not the main emphasis of Fainsod's description of the party's power structure; cf. *ibid.,* pp. 210–13.

27. Kaufman; Fesler, esp. pp. 555–57; Gulick; Schiff.

28. Kaufman, p. 40.	29. *Ibid.,* pp. 43, 45.
30. *Ibid.,* p. 47.	31. Fesler, p. 556.
32. *Ibid.*	33. *Ibid.*
34. Gulick, pp. 150–51.	35. *Ibid.,* p. 74.
36. *Ibid.*	37. Kaufman, p. 95.
38. *Ibid.,* pp. 95–96.	39. Gulick, p. 74.
40. Schiff, p. 170.	41. *Ibid.*
42. Gulick, p. 151.	43. Kaufman, p. 230.

44. Dahl, *Who Governs?, passim.* Of course I do not imply that Dahl himself (or Polsby, Wildavsky, Wolfinger, myself, etc.) would find pluralism in the Soviet Union after conducting an empirical decision-making study. Thus Dahl and Lindblom (p. 324) wrote in 1953: "Bargaining exists in all societies. In general, the extent to which it takes place is inversely related to the amount of hierarchy and the extent of initial agreement. Even in modern totalitarian societies, however, some bargaining takes place." I noted in Ch. 3 above that "bargaining" refers to the activities of a pluralist political system over time.

45. Gulick, p. 74.

46. *Ibid.,* p. 150.

47. Kaufman, p. 65.

CHAPTER 5

1. Fesler, p. 556.	2. *Ibid.*
3. *Ibid.*	4. *Ibid.,* pp. 556–57.

5. *Ibid.,* p. 557.

6. Bachrach and Baratz, "Two Faces of Power."

7. *Ibid.,* p. 951.

8. Fesler, p. 556.

9. *Ibid.,* p. 557.

10. Bachrach and Baratz, "Two Faces of Power," p. 947.

11. *Ibid.,* p. 950.

12. *Ibid.,* p. 948.

13. I regard Bachrach and Baratz's contribution as a critical rather than a positive theoretical advance. Thus, considerable analysis is necessary if we are to gain coherent, operationally useful advances from "Two Faces of Power." Unfortunately, the writers' subsequent article, "Decisions and Nondecisions," has little to offer. Thus, as far as these authors are concerned, we are left with the task of analyzing and criticizing "Two Faces of Power," which, nevertheless, remains an outstanding theoretical contribution.

14. Bachrach and Baratz, "Two Faces of Power," p. 952. Regarding the third point, Bachrach and Baratz cite Wallace S. Sayre and Herbert Kaufman, *Governing New York City* (New York: Russell Sage Foundation, 1960), p. 640.

15. Schattschneider, *Semisovereign People*, p. 71; cited in Bachrach and Baratz, "Two Faces of Power," p. 949.

16. For an interesting example showing the effects of Protestant ideology on Mexican rural culture, see McClelland, pp. 406–11. See also Blalock; Webb *et al.*; Campbell and Stanley.

17. Cf. Morris, pp. 60–64. Jack Nagel called this work to my attention.

18. Bachrach and Baratz, "Two Faces of Power," p. 948.

19. *Ibid.*, p. 948, note 11. Pluralists Dahl and Wildavsky, and political scientists in general, usually pay considerable attention to the value (i.e., reward) redistributive effects of changing the rules of political procedure. For example, see *Who Governs?*, pp. 264–67; and *Leadership in a Small Town*, pp. 44–51.

20. Bachrach and Baratz, "Two Faces of Power," p. 949.

21. *Ibid.*, p. 952.

22. *Ibid.*, p. 949.

23. Wildavsky, *Leadership in a Small Town*, p. 11.

24. See Polsby, *Community Power*, p. 96.

25. Dahl, *Who Governs?*, pp. 103, 115–16, 142–43, and 104–62 *passim*.

26. Polsby, *Community Power*, pp. 95–96.

27. See Feierabend and Feierabend; Tanter; Rummel; and the bibliographies of these articles.

28. Bachrach and Baratz, "Two Faces of Power," p. 950.

29. Wildavsky examines such questions, but not directly in terms of issue scope: *Leadership in a Small Town*, pp. 100–126.

30. Bachrach and Baratz, "Two Faces of Power," p. 952.

31. Fesler, p. 555.

32. Selznick, *Leadership*, pp. 29–64.

33. Fesler cites Fainsod, *How Russia Is Ruled*, pp. 381–83.

34. Fesler again cites Fainsod, *How Russia Is Ruled*, pp. 403–18.

35. Apter, "Comparative Politics"; Apter, *Politics of Modernization*, pp. 16–22. For a similar perspective, see Blumer, "Society as Symbolic Interaction."

CHAPTER 6

1. Contrasting critical and routine decisions is the center of Philip Selznick's theory of leadership and administration. See Selznick, *Leadership*, pp. 29–64.
2. Waldo, *Public Administration*, p. 42.
3. Albert Lepawsky pointed this out to me.
4. Simon, *Administrative Behavior*, p. xxvii.
5. *Ibid.*, p. xxix.
6. *Ibid.*, p. xxix, note 10.
7. Von Neumann and Morgenstern, pp. 60–66.
8. Rapoport, *Fights, Games, and Debates*, pp. 140f, 241, © by The University of Michigan, 1960. Material in Figs. 1 and 2 is reprinted by permission of the publisher.
9. Cyert and March, *A Behavioral Theory of the Firm*, pp. 141, 145, © 1963. Material in Figs. 3 and 4 is reprinted by permission of Prentice-Hall, Inc., Englewood Cliffs, N.J.
10. Von Neumann and Morgenstern, *Theory of Games and Economic Behavior*, pp. 64–66, © by Princeton University Press, 1953. Material in Fig. 5 is reprinted by permission of the publisher.
11. See, for example, Russell, "On the Relations of Universals and Particulars," "The Philosophy of Logical Atomism," and "Logical Atomism," in *Logic and Knowledge*.
12. Simon, *Administrative Behavior*, pp. 62–66.
13. Waldo, *Administrative State*, pp. 204–5.
14. *Ibid.*, p. 204.   15. *Ibid.*
16. *Ibid.*, pp. 204–5.   17. *Ibid.*, p. 205.
18. *Ibid.*
19. *Ibid.*, pp. 123–25, where Waldo discusses Luther Gulick's "Politics, Administration, and the New Deal," *Annals*, 169 (Sept. 1933), pp. 55–66.
20. Braybrooke and Lindblom, pp. 35–57.
21. See Schelling, esp. pp. 53–80.
22. Cyert and March, pp. 118–20, 295–97, and *passim*.
23. Selznick, *Leadership*, pp. 29–64; Wolin, Ch. 10.
24. Selznick, *Leadership*, pp. 40–41.
25. *Ibid.*, pp. 28–42.
26. *Ibid.*, p. 33. Selznick quotes Fromm, p. 15.
27. *Ibid.*, pp. 37–38. Selznick quotes E. P. Learned, D. N. Ulrich, and D. R. Booz, *Executive Action* (Boston: Harvard University Graduate School of Business Administration, 1951), p. 57.
28. *Ibid.*, pp. 55f, 60, 62.
29. Simon, *Administrative Behavior*, p. 63.
30. *Ibid.*
31. *Ibid.*
32. *Ibid.*, p. 64.

33. "Mobilization state" is a term used by Apter. See his *Politics of Modernization*, p. 25 and *passim*.

34. Simon, "Birth of an Organization," pp. 227–36.

35. For Lindblom's point of view on this matter, see Braybrooke and Lindblom, pp. 106–10. For an exchange on this topic, see Dror, pp. 153–57, and a rejoinder by Lindblom, in *Public Administration Review*, 24 (Spring 1964), 157–58. See also Dahl, *Pluralist Democracy*, pp. 263–68.

36. See Bertrand Russell, "Mathematical Logic as Based on the Theory of Types," and "The Philosophy of Logical Atomism," esp. pp. 254–69, in *Logic and Knowledge*. Also see Kohl, pp. 41–50.

37. Since World War II, U.S. national fiscal policy has often been viewed as a more critical, general, important policy area than national defense policy. See Warner R. Schilling, "The Politics of National Defense: Fiscal 1950," and Glenn H. Snyder, "The 'New Look' of 1953," in Schilling *et al.*

38. Lindblom, "Muddling Through"; Braybrooke and Lindblom, pp. 93–98.

39. Simon, *Administrative Behavior*, p. xxix.

CHAPTER 7

1. Apter, "Comparative Politics," p. 732.

2. Cf. *ibid.*, pp. 729–38.

3. Levy; comments by Hoffmann, pp. 174–84.

4. Snyder, Bruck, and Sapin, "Decision-Making as an Approach to the Study of International Politics," and other monographs in Snyder *et al.*, pp. 14–185. See also Simon, *Administrative Behavior*, *Models of Man*, and other works.

5. Hartz, *Liberal Tradition in America*, and *Founding of New Societies*, pp. 3–122.

6. Chalmers Johnson, pp. 22–26 and *passim*.

7. Blumer, "Society as Symbolic Interaction." Thomas Bruneau called this article to my attention.

8. Cited by Apter, "Comparative Politics," p. 732.

9. Cited in *ibid.*

10. Cited in *ibid.*

11. Dahl, *Who Governs?*, pp. 11–62.

12. Lasswell; Fromm; Lane, *Political Ideology*; Greenstein.

13. Selznick, *Leadership*, pp. 29–64.

14. Polsby, *Community Power*, pp. 45–68 and *passim*.

15. Presthus, pp. 116–21 and *passim*, for his usage of the concept "leg-men."

16. Dahl, *Who Governs?*, pp. 63–84, 228, 271–75, and *passim*; Dahl, *Modern Political Analysis*, pp. 48–49; Polsby, *Community Power*.

17. Of course many sociologists do not equate power (or "influence") with resources. For example, Weber's definition of power (*Macht*) is

relational: " 'Power' [*Macht*] is the probability that one actor within a social relationship will be in a position to carry out his own will despite resistance" (Weber, p. 152). Robert Merton follows a Weberian usage of power: "By power . . . is meant nothing more than the observed and predictable capacity for imposing one's own will in a social action, even against the resistance of others taking part in that action" (Merton, *Social Theory*, p. 372).

18. Dahl, *Who Governs?*; Polsby, *Community Power*; Wildavsky, *Leadership in a Small Town*, esp. "Why American Cities Are Pluralist," pp. 332–51.

19. Simon, *Administrative Behavior*; March and Simon.

20. See note 16 above.

21. Gross *et al.*, pp. 11–20.

22. See, for example, Parsons, p. 230: "A structure is a set of relatively stable patterned relationships of units. Since the unit of the social system is the actor, social structure is a patterned system of the social relationships of actors. It is a distinctive feature of the structure of systems of social action, however, that in most relationships the actor does not participate as a total entity, but only by virtue of a given differentiated 'sector' of his total action. Such a sector, which is the unit of a system of social relationships, has come predominantly to be called a 'role.' Hence, the previous statement must be revised to say that social structure is a system of patterned relationships of actors in their capacity as playing roles relative to one another. Role is the concept which links the subsystem of the actor as a 'psychological' behaving entity to the distinctively *social* structure."

According to Newcomb *et al.*, pp. 350–51, 356: "A group *is* what its role relationships are, our descriptions and explanations of any group as a whole must be stated in terms of its entire network of role relationships. The most effective way of doing this is to regard a total set of roles as a *system*. This term refers to any set of things that continue to interact with each other in such ways that the total set, viewed as a single entity, maintains relatively constant properties. . . . Any particular role, describing an individual's actual or prescribed contributions to a behavioral relationship with one or more other persons, is necessarily interdependent with the roles of others with whom that individual interacts. One role cannot exist apart from one or more other roles, and a change in any one of them is likely to induce change in one or more of the others. Such interdependence is characteristic of systems, and interaction groups may thus be viewed as systems of roles."

23. Von Neumann and Morgenstern, p. 67.

24. Hartz, *Liberal Tradition*, and his *Founding of New Societies*, pp. 3–122.

25. Hartz, *Liberal Tradition*, Part 4, "The Feudal Dream of the South."

26. Rothman.   27. *Ibid.*, p. 28.

28. *Ibid.*, p. 15.   29. *Ibid.*, pp. 28–29.

30. Apter, *Politics of Modernization*, p. 24.
31. Rothman, p. 29.   32. *Ibid.*
33. *Ibid.*   34. *Ibid.*, p. 30.
35. Beer and Ulam, p. 32.   36. Rothman, p. 32.
37. Beer and Ulam, pp. 32–63.   38. Macridis, pp. 23–24.
39. *Ibid.*, p. 23.
40. Almond, "A Functional Approach to Comparative Politics," in Almond and Coleman, esp. pp. 26–58.
41. Pye and Verba, p. 513.
42. *Ibid.*, p. 518.

CHAPTER 8

1. For a different view, see Pool, p. 37.
2. Apter, *Politics of Modernization*, p. 24.
3. See Merton, *Social Theory*, Ch. 1.
4. Hook, p. xiv.
5. *Ibid.*, p. 153.
6. *Ibid.*, p. 229.
7. Dahl, *Who Governs?*, pp. 330–40.
8. *Ibid.*, pp. 104–89, 330–40; Wildavsky, *Leadership in a Small Town*, pp. 253–81.
9. Hook, p. 28.
10. *Ibid.*, pp. 184–228. For an interesting case study of an event-making man who changed a Papuan society, see Pospisil.
11. Hook, p. 184.   12. *Ibid.*
13. *Ibid.*, p. 185.   14. *Ibid.*, p. 113.
15. *Ibid.*   16. See Plekhanov.
17. Hook, p. 114.   18. *Ibid.*
19. *Ibid.*, p. 134.   20. Harry M. Johnson, p. 75.
21. *Ibid.*, pp. 75–77.   22. *Ibid.*, p. 76.
23. *Ibid.*, p. 77.
24. For an exposition of cybernetic models for social systems, see Deutsch, *Nerves of Government*, pp. 75–97 and *passim*.
25. *Newsweek*, March 28, 1966, p. 28.
26. See Silverman.
27. For examples of such models, see Richardson, "Generalized Foreign Policy," and his "War Moods," pp. 147–74, 197–232.
28. See Smelser, esp. pp. 62–64, 313–81; Gerth and Mills, pp. 245–52; Hook, pp. 151–83 and *passim*; Lasswell; Erickson; Pye, "Personal Identity"; Pye, *Politics, Personality and Nation Building*; Selznick, *Leadership*, pp. 29–64; Selznick, *Organizational Weapon*, and his *TVA and the Grass Roots*.
29. Kuhn, p. 10 and *passim*.
30. Deutsch, *Nationalism and Social Communication*.
31. Haas, *Beyond the Nation-State*, pp. 464–75, esp. p. 468.
32. Lipset, *First New Nation*.

33. Cf. Freud.
34. See, for example, Gibb, esp. p. 915; Bavelas, pp. 491–98.
35. Weber, pp. 324–423.
36. Hoffer, p. 109.
37. *Ibid.*, p. 110.
38. Hook, p. 12.
39. Apter, *Ghana*, pp. 303–8 and *passim*.
40. Incremental decisions within the realm of our government's domestic policy making may add up to a fundamental, critical decision, as in the establishment of the mixed economy and the welfare state within the last generation. See Dahl, *Pluralist Democracy*, pp. 263–68.
41. See the works of Lindblom on the theory of incremental decision making and those of Wildavsky on the national budgetary process.
42. Latham, p. 390.
43. *Ibid.*, p. 391.
44. See, for example, Matthews, *U.S. Senators*, Ch. 8; Dexter, pp. 17–19.
45. Latham, p. 397.
46. For a reformulation of such work in terms of predictive statistical theory, see Davis *et al.*, pp. 529–47.
47. See Braybrooke and Lindblom, pp. 106–10; Dror, pp. 153–57, and a rejoinder by Lindblom, in *Public Administration Review*, 24 (Spring 1964), 157–58.
48. In the latter category, we have several excellent, well-verified surveys, such as Stouffer; Prothro and Grigg; McClosky *et al.*; McClosky, "Consensus."
49. See Almond, "Comparative Political Systems."
50. In the terminology of Easton, *Systems Analysis*, pp. 171–219.

CHAPTER 9

1. See Simmel, *Conflict*, and other works; Coser, *Functions of Social Conflict*, and other works; Dahrendorf; Goode.
2. For a summary and interpretation of this psychological literature, see Berlyne.

3. Dahrendorf, p. 125.   4. *Ibid.*, p. 126.
5. Duverger, p. 215.   6. *Ibid.*
7. *Ibid.*, pp. 215–16.
8. Wildavsky, "Methodological Critique," p. 305.
9. Dahl, *Who Governs?*, pp. 270–75.
10. Polsby, *Community Power*, pp. 8–10.
11. *Ibid.*, p. 10.   12. *Ibid.*, pp. 10–11.
13. *Ibid.*, p. 117.   14. *Ibid.*, p. 118.
15. Latham, pp. 387–88.   16. Truman, p. 82.
17. Dahl, *Who Governs?*, Ch. 4.   18. *Ibid.*, pp. 192–99.
19. Dahrendorf, p. 126.   20. *Ibid.*
21. See Banfield, "Politics of Metropolitan Area Organization."
22. Duverger, p. 216.

23. Schelling, pp. 89, 102–3, 158–60.
24. See Coser, "Functions of Deviant Behavior."
25. Park, p. 892.
26. Stonequist, p. 6.
27. Wardwell, p. 339. He cites Arnold W. Green, "A Re-examination of the Marginal Man Concept," *Social Forces,* 26 (Dec. 1947), 167–71.
28. Lazarsfeld *et al.*; Berelson *et al.*
29. Truman, Ch. 16; Berelson *et al.*, pp. 318–20.
30. See Verba.
31. Berlyne. See also Sperlich.
32. Coser, "Functions of Deviant Behavior," p. 179.
33. *Ibid.*, pp. 179–81.
34. *Ibid.*, p. 180. Coser cites George Homans, *The Human Group* (New York: Harcourt, Brace, 1950), p. 141, and Homan, *Social Behavior; Its Elementary Forms* (New York: Harcourt, Brace, 1961), p. 346.
35. See, for example, Miller and Stokes; Dexter; Bauer *et al.*, Part V; Jones and the literature cited therein; Eulau *et al.*; Pitkin.
36. A classic treatment of the tension between party activists and their legislators is Michels' treatment of *embourgeoisement* of socialist parliamentarians: Michels, pp. 357–63 and *passim*. A classic treatment of the tension between party activists and the average party identifier in the United States is McClosky *et al.*
37. Eulau *et al.*
38. Unfortunately, Mannheim's diffuse organization obscures his central ideas. At some future time, perhaps someone will systematize Mannheim's ideas regarding conflict and individual intellectual creativity or sociopolitical innovation.
39. Mannheim, p. 189.
40. *Ibid.*, p. 175.
41. *Ibid.*, pp. 172–75 *passim*.
42. Braybrooke and Lindblom, pp. 3–57.
43. Lindblom, "Muddling Through"; Braybrooke and Lindblom, pp. 3–143.
44. Schlesinger, *A Thousand Days,* p. 114.
45. Merton, *Social Theory,* pp. 367–68, in a footnote.
46. Schlesinger, *A Thousand Days,* p. 101.
47. *Ibid.*, p. 100.   48. *Ibid.*, pp. 108–9.
49. Davie, pp. 24–25, 26–27.   50. Mannheim, p. 189.
51. Davie, pp. 39–40.   52. *Ibid.*, p. 43.
53. Neustadt, *Presidential Power,* pp. 152–61, and his "Staffing the Presidency."
54. Schlesinger, *A Thousand Days,* pp. 233–97.
55. Dahl, *Who Governs?*, p. 298.
56. *Ibid.*
57. *Ibid.* Dahl cites Rufus Browning, "Businessmen in Politics" (Doctoral dissertation, Yale University, 1960).
58. Gross *et al.*, pp. 11–20; Yinger, Ch. 6.
59. My description of "role" is nearly equivalent to Harry M. Johnson's description of "norm," p. 9.
60. Yinger, p. 100.

61. Gross *et al.*, p. 17.
62. Yinger, p. 99.
63. Merton, "The Role-Set," and *Social Theory*, pp. 368–84.
64. Clapp, pp. 444–93.
65. See Barber, *Lawmakers*.
66. Merton, "The Role-Set," pp. 113–17.
67. *Ibid.*, pp. 113f.
68. *Ibid.*, pp. 113, 116f.
69. Neustadt, *Presidential Power*.
70. Jewell, pp. 13, 26–28; Matthews, *U.S. Senators*, pp. 68–117; Polsby, "Two Strategies."
71. Toby, pp. 323–27.
72. *Ibid.*, p. 324.
73. *Ibid.*, pp. 324–26.
74. *Ibid.*, p. 324. Original emphasis omitted.
75. A. Robert Smith, pp. 19–21 and *passim*; *Newsweek*, "Oregon: The Morse Code," March 21, 1966, p. 29: "A recent state poll (in Oregon) revealed public sentiment running about 4 to 1 in support of the Administration's handling of the war. At the same time, political observers report no important loss of popularity by Wayne Morse as a result of his persistent attack on Administration policy."
76. Schelling, pp. 24–28, 121–23, 184–86.
77. Toby, p. 325.
78. *Ibid.*
79. See Jervis.
80. Toby, p. 325.
81. See, for example, Matthews, *U.S. Senators*, pp. 92–94; Huitt, "Outsider in the Senate."
82. Bolling, pp. 237–44.
83. See Wolfinger and Heifetz.
84. Toby, p. 325.
85. *Ibid.*, p. 327.
86. Merton, "The Role-Set," pp. 113–17; Toby, pp. 326–27.
87. Downs; Schumpeter, pp. 269–302; Schattschneider, *Semisovereign People*, pp. 129–42; Wildavsky, "The Goldwater Phenomenon."
88. *Newsweek*, "Congress: One-Way Street," March 28, 1966, pp. 34–36.
89. See George and George.
90. Barnard, p. 276.
91. *Ibid.*, pp. 277–78.
92. For an example of Wilson's adroit political maneuvering, see George and George, pp. 47–74.
93. Schlesinger, *Crisis of the Old Order*, p. 57.
94. Neustadt, *Presidential Power*, p. 163.
95. *Ibid.*, pp. 165, 166.
96. *Ibid.*, p. 165. Neustadt cites Robert J. Donovan, *Eisenhower: The Inside Story* (New York: Harper, 1956), p. 357.
97. Toby, p. 327.
98. Banfield, *Political Influence*, p. 270.
99. Toby, p. 327.
100. Haas, *Beyond the Nation-State*, p. 111. See also his "Interna-

tional Integration." In this connection, see also Metcalf and Urwick, pp. 30–49 and *passim*.

101. Haas, *Beyond the Nation-State*, p. 111.
102. Huitt, "Democratic Party Leadership," pp. 339–40.
103. *Ibid.*, p. 340.
104. Dahl, *Who Governs?*, pp. 115–40.

Bibliography

Bibliography

The following abbreviations are used in the Bibliography:

AJS   American Journal of Sociology
APSR   American Political Science Review
ASR   American Sociological Review

Almond, Gabriel. "Comparative Political Systems," *Journal of Politics*, 18 (Aug. 1956), 391–409.
———, and James S. Coleman, eds. The Politics of Developing Areas. Princeton, N.J.: Princeton Univ. Press, 1960.
———, and G. Bingham Powell, Jr. Comparative Politics: A Developmental Approach. Boston: Little, Brown, 1966.
———, and Sidney Verba. The Civic Culture: Political Attitudes and Democracy in Five Nations. Princeton, N.J.: Princeton Univ. Press, 1963.
Apter, David E. "Comparative Politics and Political Thought: Past Influences and Future Development," in Eckstein and Apter, pp. 725–40.
———. Ghana in Transition. New York: Atheneum, 1963, paperback rev. ed.
———. The Politics of Modernization. Chicago: Univ. of Chicago Press, 1965.
Arnow, Kathryn Smul. The Department of Commerce Field Service. University, Ala.: Univ. of Alabama Press, 1954. The Inter-University Case Program, ICP Case Series, No. 21, Feb. 1954.
Ashby, W. Ross. Design for a Brain. New York: Wiley, 1960, 2d ed. rev.
———. An Introduction to Cybernetics. London: Chapman & Hall, 1958.
Bachrach, Peter, and Morton Baratz. "Decisions and Nondecisions: An Analytical Framework," APSR, 57 (Sept. 1963), 632–42.
———, and Morton Baratz. "Two Faces of Power," APSR, 56 (Dec. 1962), 947–52.
Bailey, Stephen K. The Condition of Our National Political Parties. New York: Fund for the Republic, 1959.

Banfield, Edward C. Political Influence. New York: The Free Press, 1961.
————. "The Politics of Metropolitan Area Organization," *Midwest Journal of Political Science*, 1 (May 1957), 77–91. Reprinted in Polsby, Dentler, and Smith, pp. 802–9.
Barber, James David. The Lawmakers. New Haven, Conn.: Yale Univ. Press, 1965.
————. Power in Committees. Chicago: Rand McNally, 1966.
Barnard, C. I. The Functions of the Executive. Cambridge, Mass.: Harvard Univ. Press, 1938.
Bauer, Raymond A., Ithiel de Sola Pool, and Lewis Anthony Dexter. American Business and Public Policy. New York: Atherton Press, 1963.
Bavelas, Alex. "Leadership: Man and Function," *Administrative Science Quarterly*, 4 (March 1960), 491–98.
Beer, Samuel H., and Adam B. Ulam, eds. Patterns of Government. New York: Random House, 1962, 2d ed. rev.
Beer, Stafford. Cybernetics and Management. New York: Wiley, 1959.
Bell, Daniel. "Is There a Ruling Class in America?" in Bell, ed., The End of Ideology (New York: Collier, 1962, paperback rev. ed.), 47–74.
Bendix, Reinhard. "Concepts and Generalizations in Comparative Sociological Studies," *ASR*, 28 (Aug. 1963), 532–39.
Bentley, Arthur F. The Process of Government. Evanston, Ill.: Principia Press, 1935 (orig. publ. 1908).
Berelson, Bernard R., Paul Lazarsfeld, and William N. McPhee. Voting. Chicago: Univ. of Chicago Press, 1963, rev. ed.
Berliner, Joseph S. Factory and Manager in the U.S.S.R. Cambridge, Mass.: Harvard Univ. Press, 1957.
Berlyne, D. E. Conflict, Arousal, and Curiosity. New York: McGraw-Hill, 1960.
Blalock, Hubert M., Jr. Causal Inferences in Nonexperimental Research. Chapel Hill: Univ. of North Carolina Press, 1964.
Blau, Peter M., and W. Richard Scott. Formal Organizations: A Comparative Approach. San Francisco: Chandlers, 1962.
Blumer, Herbert. "Society as Symbolic Interaction," in Arnold M. Rose, ed., Human Behavior and Social Processes (Boston: Houghton Mifflin, 1962), 179–92.
————. "Sociological Analysis and the Variable," *ASR*, 21 (Dec. 1956), 683–90.
Bolling, Richard. House Out of Order. New York: Dutton, 1965.
Bone, Hugh A. American Politics and the Party System. New York: McGraw-Hill, 1955.
Braybrooke, David, and Charles E. Lindblom. A Strategy of Decision. New York: The Free Press, 1963.
Burns, James M. Congress on Trial. New York: Harper, 1949.
————. The Deadlock of Democracy. Englewood Cliffs, N.J.: Prentice-Hall, 1963.

Campbell, Angus, Phillip E. Converse, Warren E. Miller, and Donald E. Stokes. The American Voter. New York: Wiley, 1960.
Campbell, Donald T., and Julian Stanley. Experimental and Quasi-Experimental Designs for Research. Chicago: Rand McNally, 1966.
Cartwright, Dorwin. "A Field Theoretical Conception of Power," in Cartwright, ed., Studies in Social Power (Ann Arbor: Univ. of Michigan, Inst. for Soc. Res., 1959).
————. "Influence, Leadership, Control," in James G. March, ed., Handbook of Organizations (Chicago: Rand McNally, 1965), 1–47.
Clapp, Charles L. The Congressman: His Work as He Sees It. Garden City, N.Y.: Anchor Books, 1964.
Committee on Political Parties, American Political Science Association. Toward a More Responsible Two-Party System. New York: Rinehart, 1950.
Coser, Lewis A. The Functions of Social Conflict. Glencoe, Ill.: The Free Press, 1956.
————. "Some Functions of Deviant Behavior and Normative Flexibility," AJS, 68 (Sept. 1962), 172–81.
Cyert, Richard M., and James G. March, with contributions by G. P. E. Clarkson and others. A Behavioral Theory of the Firm. Englewood Cliffs, N.J.: Prentice-Hall, 1963.
Dahl, Robert A. "Cause and Effect in the Study of Politics," in Daniel Lerner, ed., Cause and Effect (New York: The Free Press, 1965), 75–98.
————. "The Concept of Power," Behavioral Science, 2 (June 1957), 201–15.
————. "A Critique of the Ruling Elite Model," APSR, 52 (June 1958), 463–69.
————. Modern Political Analysis. Englewood Cliffs, N.J.: Prentice-Hall, 1963, paperback ed.
————. Pluralist Democracy in the United States. Chicago: Rand McNally, 1967.
————. "Power," in International Encyclopedia of the Social Sciences (New York: Macmillan and Free Press, 1968), vol. 12, 405–15.
————. Preface to Democratic Theory. Chicago: Univ. of Chicago Press, 1956.
————. Who Governs? New Haven, Conn.: Yale Univ. Press, 1961.
————, and Charles E. Lindblom. Politics, Economics, and Welfare. New York: Harper, 1953, paperback ed.
Dahrendorf, Ralf. Class and Class Conflict in Industrial Society. Stanford, Calif.: Stanford Univ. Press, 1959.
Davie, Michael. LBJ: A Foreign Observer's Viewpoint. New York: Ballantine, 1967, paperback.
Davis, Otto A., M. A. H. Dempster, and Aaron Wildavsky. "A Theory of the Budgetary Process," APSR, 60 (Sept. 1966), 529–47.
Deutsch, Karl W. "Cracks in the Monolith: Possibilities and Patterns of Disintegration in Totalitarian Systems," in Charles J. Friedrich, ed., Totalitarianism: Proceedings of a Conference Held at the

American Academy of Arts and Sciences (Cambridge, Mass.: Harvard Univ. Press, 1954), 308–333. Repr. in Eckstein and Apter, pp. 497–508.

———. Nationalism and Social Communication. New York: Wiley, 1953.

———. The Nerves of Government. New York: The Free Press, 1963.

Dexter, Lewis Anthony. "The Representative and His District," in Robert L. Peabody and Nelson W. Polsby, eds., New Perspectives on the House of Representatives (Chicago: Rand McNally, 1963).

Downs, Anthony. An Economic Theory of Democracy. New York: Harper, 1957.

Dror, Yehezkel. "Muddling Through—Science or Inertia? *Public Administration Review*, 24 (Spring 1964), 153–57.

Duverger, Maurice. Political Parties. Barbara and Robert North, trans. New York: Wiley, 1959.

Easton, David. A Framework for Political Analysis. Englewood Cliffs, N.J.: Prentice-Hall, 1965.

———. The Political System. New York: Knopf, 1953.

———. A Systems Analysis of Political Life. New York: Wiley, 1965.

Eckstein, Harry. Division and Cohesion in Democracy: A Study of Norway. Princeton, N.J.: Princeton Univ. Press, 1966.

———, and David E. Apter. Comparative Politics. New York: The Free Press, 1963.

Emerson, Richard M. "Power-Dependence Relations," *ASR*, 27 (Feb. 1962), 31–41.

Erikson, Erik H. Young Man Luther: A Study in Psychoanalysis and History. New York: Norton, 1958.

Etzioni, Amitai. Modern Organizations. Englewood Cliffs, N.J.: Prentice-Hall, 1964.

Eulau, Heinz, et al. "The Role of the Representative: Some Empirical Observations on the Theory of Edmund Burke," *APSR*, 53 (Sept. 1959), 742–56.

Fainsod, Merle. How Russia Is Ruled. Cambridge, Mass.: Harvard Univ. Press, 1963.

———. Smolensk Under Soviet Rule. Cambridge, Mass.: Harvard Univ. Press, 1958.

Feierabend, Ivo K. and Rosalind L. "Aggressive Behaviors Within Politics, 1948–1962: A Cross-National Study," *Journal of Conflict Resolution*, 10 (Sept. 1966), 249–71.

Fenno, Richard F., Jr. "The House Appropriations Committee as a Political System: The Problem of Integration," *APSR*, 56 (June 1962), 310–24.

Fesler, James W. "Approaches to the Understanding of Decentralization," *Journal of Politics*, 27 (Aug. 1965), 536–66.

Freud, Sigmund. Moses and Monotheism. Katherine Jones, trans. New York: Vintage, 1959.

Friedrich, Carl J. Constitutional Government and Democracy. Boston: Ginn, 1950, rev. ed.

Fromm, Erich. Escape From Freedom. New York: Holt, Rinehart & Winston, 1963.

Gamson, William A. "Reputation and Resources in Community Politics," *AJS*, 72 (Sept. 1966), 121–31.

George, Alexander L. and Juliette L. Woodrow Wilson and Colonel House: A Personality Study. New York: John Day, 1956.

Gerth, H. H., and C. Wright Mills, trans. From Max Weber. New York: Oxford Univ. Press, 1958, Galaxy Book ed.

Gibb, Cecil A. "Leadership," in Gardner Lindzey, ed., Handbook of Social Psychology (Cambridge, Mass.: Addison-Wesley, 1954), II, 877–920.

Godfrey, E. Drexel, Jr. "The Transfer of the Children's Bureau," in Harold Stein, ed., Public Administration and Policy Development (New York: Harcourt, Brace, 1952), 17–29.

Goffman, Erving. Asylums. Chicago: Aldine, 1962.

———. Behavior in Public Places. New York: The Free Press, 1963.

———. Encounters. Indianapolis, Ind.: Bobbs-Merrill, 1961.

———. The Presentation of Self in Everyday Life. Garden City, N.Y.: Doubleday, 1959.

———. Stigma. Englewood Cliffs, N.J.: Prentice-Hall, 1963.

Goldhamer, Herbert, and Edward A. Shils. "Types of Power and Status," *AJS*, 45 (Sept. 1939), 171–82.

Goldwater, Barry M. The Conscience of a Conservative. New York: Hillman, 1961, paperback ed.

Goode, William J. "A Theory of Role Strain," *ASR*, 25 (Aug. 1960), 483–96.

Goodman, William. "How Much Political Party Centralization Do We Want?" *Journal of Politics*, 13 (Nov. 1951), 536–61.

———. The Two-Party System in the United States. New York: Van Nostrand, 1956.

Gouldner, A. W. Patterns of Industrial Bureaucracy. Glencoe, Ill.: The Free Press, 1954.

Granick, David. The Red Executive. Garden City, N.Y.: Doubleday, 1961, Anchor paperback edition.

Greenstein, Fred I. Children and Politics. New Haven, Conn.: Yale Univ. Press, 1965.

Grodzins, Morton. "The Federal System," in Goals for Americans, The President's Commission on National Goals (Englewood Cliffs, N.J.: Prentice-Hall, 1960), paperback ed.

Gross, Neal, Ward S. Mason, and Alexander W. McEachern. Explorations in Role Analysis. New York: Wiley, 1958.

Gulick, Luther Halsey. American Forest Policy. New York: Duell, Sloan & Pearce, 1951.

Haas, Ernst B. Beyond the Nation-State. Stanford, Calif.: Stanford Univ. Press, 1964.

———. "International Integration," *International Organization*, 15 (Summer 1961), 367–92.

Hartz, Louis. The Founding of New Societies. New York: Harcourt, Brace, 1964.
————. The Liberal Tradition in America. New York: Harcourt, Brace, 1955.
Herring, E. Pendleton. Group Representation Before Congress. Baltimore, Md.: The Johns Hopkins Press, 1929.
————. The Politics of Democracy. New York: Rinehart, 1940.
Hilsman, Roger. "The Policy Consensus: An Interim Research Report," *Journal of Conflict Resolution*, 3 (Dec. 1959), 361–82.
Hoffer, Eric. The True Believer. New York: Harper, 1951.
Hoffmann, Stanley, ed. Contemporary Theory in International Relations. Englewood Cliffs, N.J.: Prentice-Hall, 1960.
Hofstadter, Richard. The American Political Tradition. New York: Knopf, 1948.
Hook, Sidney. The Hero in History: A Study in Limitation and Possibility. New York: The Humanities Press, 1943.
Hoover, Herbert. The Ordeal of Woodrow Wilson. New York: McGraw-Hill, 1958.
Hospers, John. An Introduction to Philosophical Analysis. New York: Prentice-Hall, 1953.
Hsiao, Kung Chuan. Political Pluralism: A Study of Contemporary Theory. New York: Harcourt, Brace, 1927.
Huitt, Ralph K. "Democratic Party Leadership in the Senate," *APSR*, 55 (June 1961), 333–44.
————. "The Outsider in the Senate: An Alternative Role," *APSR*, 55 (Sept. 1961), 566–75.
Hunter, Floyd. Community Power Structure. Chapel Hill: Univ. of North Carolina Press, 1953.
Huntington, Samuel P. "Political Development and Political Decay," *World Politics*, 17 (April 1965), 386–430.
Jacobson, Norman. "Causality and Time in Political Process: A Speculation," *APSR*, 58 (March 1964), 15–22.
Jennings, M. Kent. Community Influentials. New York: The Free Press, 1964.
Jervis, Robert. "Hypotheses on Misperception," *World Politics*, 20 (April 1968), 454–79.
Jewell, Malcolm E. The Politics of Reapportionment. New York: Atherton, 1962.
Johnson, Chalmers. Revolution and the Social System. Stanford, Calif.: Hoover Institution Studies No. 3, 1964.
Johnson, Harry M. Sociology: A Systematic Introduction. New York: Harcourt, Brace, 1960.
Jones, Charles O. "Representation in Congress: The Case of the House Agriculture Committee," *APSR*, 55 (June 1961), 358–67.
Jowitt, Kenneth. "A Study of Soviet Administrative Behavior," unpublished manuscript. Dept. of Political Science, Univ. of Calif., Berkeley.

Kahn, Herman. On Thermonuclear War. Princeton, N.J.: Princeton Univ. Press, 1961.

Karlsson, Georg. "Some Aspects of Power in Small Groups," in Joan H. Criswell, Herbert Solomon, and Patrick Suppes, eds., Mathematical Methods in Small Group Processes. Stanford, Calif.: Stanford Univ. Press, 1962.

Kaufman, Herbert. The Forest Ranger. Baltimore, Md.: The Johns Hopkins Press, 1960.

Kautilya. Kautilya's Arthasastra. R. Shamasastry, trans. Mysore: Wesleyan Mission Press, 1929. 3d ed.

Key, V. O., Jr. "The Lack of a Budgetary Theory," APSR, 34 (Dec. 1940), 1137–44.

––––––. Politics, Parties, and Pressure Groups. New York: Crowell, 1964, 5th ed.

––––––. "A Theory of Critical Elections," Journal of Politics, 17 (Feb. 1955), 3–18.

Kohl, Herbert. The Age of Complexity. New York: New American, 1965, paperback ed.

Kornhauser, William. The Politics of Mass Society. New York: The Free Press, 1959.

Kuhn, Thomas S. The Structure of Scientific Revolutions. Chicago: The Univ. of Chicago Press, 1962.

Lane, Robert E. Political Ideology. New York: The Free Press, 1962.

––––––. Political Life. New York: The Free Press, 1959.

Laski, Harold J. The Foundations of Sovereignty and Other Essays. New York: Harcourt, Brace, 1921.

Lasswell, Harold D. Psychopathology and Politics. Chicago: Univ. of Chicago Press, 1930.

Latham, Earl. "The Group Basis of Politics: Notes for a Theory," APSR, 46 (June 1952), 376–97.

Lazarsfeld, Paul, Bernard R. Berelson, and Helen Gaudet. The People's Choice. New York: Columbia Univ. Press, 1960, 2d ed.

Lerner, Daniel, ed. Cause and Effect. New York: The Free Press, 1965.

Levy, Marion J. The Structure of Society. Princeton, N.J.: Princeton Univ. Press, 1952.

Lewis, Verne B. "Toward a Theory of Budgeting," Public Administration Review, 12 (Winter 1952), 42–54.

Lijphart, Arend. The Politics of Accommodation: Pluralism and Democracy in the Netherlands. Berkeley: Univ. of Calif. Press, 1968.

Lindblom, Charles E. The Intelligence of Democracy. New York: Macmillan, 1965.

––––––. "The Science of 'Muddling Through,'" Public Administration Review, 19 (Spring 1959), 79–88.

Lipset, Seymour Martin. The First New Nation: The United States in Historical and Comparative Perspective. New York: Basic Books, 1963.

––––––. Political Man. Garden City, N.Y.: Doubleday, 1960.

Long, Norton E. The Polity. Chicago: Rand McNally, 1962.
————. "Power and Administration," *Public Administration Review*, 9 (Autumn 1949), 257–64.
Maass, Arthur A. "The Kings River Project," in Harold Stein, ed., Public Administration and Policy Development (New York: Harcourt, Brace, 1952), 533–72.
Macridis, Roy C. The Study of Comparative Government. New York: Random House, 1955.
Manley, John F. "The House Committee on Ways and Means: Conflict Management in a Congressional Committee," *APSR*, 59 (Dec. 1965), 927–39.
Mannheim, Karl. Ideology and Utopia: An Introduction to the Sociology of Knowledge. New York: Harvest Books, n.d. (1st U.S. ed. publ. 1936.)
March, James G. "An Introduction to the Theory and Measurement of Influence," *APSR*, 49 (June 1955), 431–51.
————. "The Power of Power," in David Easton, ed., Varieties of Political Theory (Englewood Cliffs, N.J.: Prentice-Hall, 1966), 39–70.
————, and Herbert Simon. Organizations. New York: Wiley, 1958.
Maslow, A. H. Motivation and Personality. New York: Harper, 1954.
Matthews, Donald. "The Folkways of the U.S. Senate," *APSR*, 53 (Dec. 1959), 1064–89.
————. U.S. Senators and Their World. Chapel Hill: Univ. of North Carolina Press, 1960.
McClelland, David. The Achieving Society. Princeton, N.J.: Van Nostrand, 1961.
McCloskey, Robert G. The American Supreme Court. Chicago: Univ. of Chicago Press, 1960.
McClosky, Herbert. "Consensus and Ideology in American Politics," *APSR*, 58 (June 1964), 361–82.
————, Paul J. Hoffman, and Rosemary O'Hara. "Issue Conflict and Consensus Among Party Leaders and Followers," *APSR*, 54 (June 1960), 406–27.
————, and John H. Schaar. "Psychological Dimensions of Anomy," *ASR*, 30 (Feb. 1965), 14–40.
McConnell, Grant. Private Power and American Democracy. New York: Knopf, 1966.
McKenzie, Robert T. British Political Parties. New York: St. Martin's Press, 1963.
Merton, Robert K. "The Role-Set: Problems in Sociological Theory," *British Journal of Sociology*, 8 (June 1957), 106–20.
————. Social Theory and Social Structure. New York: The Free Press, 1957, rev. ed.
Metcalf, Henry C., and L. Urwick, eds. Dynamic Administration: The Collected Papers of Mary Parker Follett. London: Pitman, 1941.
Michels, Robert. Political Parties. Eden and Cedar Paul, trans. New York: Collier, 1962.

Miller, Warren E., and Donald E. Stokes. "Constituency Influence in Congress," *APSR*, 57 (March 1963), 45–56.
Mills, C. Wright. The Power Elite. New York: Oxford Univ. Press, 1956.
——. "The Structure of Power in American Society," *The British Journal of Sociology*, 9 (March 1958), 29–41.
Morris, Charles. Signs, Language, and Behavior. New York: Braziller, 1955.
Nagel, Jack Henry. "Some Questions About the Concept of Power," *Behavioral Science*, 13 (March 1968), 129–37.
Navarro, Moises Gonzales. "Mexico: The Lop-Sided Revolution," in Claudio Velez, ed., Obstacles to Change in Latin America (New York: Oxford Univ. Press, 1965), 206–30.
Neustadt, Richard E. "Approaches to Staffing the Presidency: Notes on FDR and JFK," *APSR*, 57 (Dec. 1963), 855–63.
——. Presidential Power. New York: Wiley, 1960.
Newcomb, Theodore M. The Acquaintance Process. New York: Holt, Rinehart & Winston, 1961.
——, Ralph H. Turner, and Phillip E. Converse. Social Psychology. New York: Holt, Rinehart & Winston, 1965.
Odegard, Peter H. Pressure Politics: The Story of the Anti-Saloon League. New York: Columbia Univ. Press, 1928.
Oppenheim, Felix E. Dimensions of Freedom. New York: St. Martin's Press, 1961.
Padgett, L. Vincent. The Mexican Political System. Boston: Houghton Mifflin, 1966.
Park, Robert E. "Human Migration and the Marginal Man," *AJS*, 33 (May 1928), 881–93.
Parsons, Talcott. Essays in Sociological Theory. Glencoe, Ill.: The Free Press, 1954, rev. ed.
Pitkin, Hanna F. The Concept of Representation. Berkeley: Univ. of Calif. Press, 1967.
Plekhanov, George. The Role of the Individual in History. New York: International Publishers, 1940 (orig. publ. 1898).
Polsby, Nelson W. Community Power and Political Theory. New Haven, Conn.: Yale Univ. Press, 1963.
——. Congress and the Presidency. Englewood Cliffs, N.J.: Prentice-Hall, 1964, paperback ed.
——. "The Sociology of Community Power: A Reassessment," *Social Forces*, 37 (March 1959), 232–36.
——. "Two Strategies of Influence: Choosing a Majority Leader, 1962," in Robert L. Peabody and Nelson W. Polsby, eds., New Perspectives on the House of Representatives (Chicago: Rand McNally, 1963), 237–70.
——, Robert A. Dentler, and Paul A. Smith, eds. Politics and Social Life. Boston: Houghton Mifflin, 1963.
——, and Aaron B. Wildavsky. Presidential Elections. New York: Scribner's, 1964.

————, and Aaron B. Wildavsky, "Uncertainty and Decision Making at the National Conventions," in Polsby, Dentler, and Smith, pp. 370–89.

Pool, Ithiel de Sola. "The Public and the Polity," in Pool, ed., Contemporary Political Science: Toward Empirical Theory. New York: McGraw-Hill, 1967.

Pospisil, Leopold. "Social Change and Primitive Law: Consequences of a Papuan Legal Case," *American Anthropologist*, 60 (Oct. 1958), 832–36.

Presthus, Robert. Men at the Top. New York: Oxford Univ. Press, 1964.

Prothro, James W., and C. W. Grigg. "Fundamental Principles of Democracy: Bases of Agreement and Disagreement," *Journal of Politics*, 22 (Spring 1960), 276–94.

Pye, Lucian W. Guerrilla Communism in Malaya. Princeton, N.J.: Princeton Univ. Press, 1956.

————. "Personal Identity and Political Ideology," in Dwaine Marvick, ed., Political Decision Makers (Glencoe, Ill.: The Free Press, 1961), 290–313.

————. Politics, Personality and Nation Building. New Haven, Conn.: Yale Univ. Press, 1963.

————, and Sidney Verba, eds. Political Culture and Political Development. Princeton, N.J.: Princeton Univ. Press, 1965.

Ranney, Austin. The Doctrine of Responsible Party Government. Urbana: Univ. of Illinois Press, 1954.

————, and Willmoore Kendall. Democracy and the American Party System. New York: Harcourt, Brace, 1956.

Rapoport, Anatol. Fights, Games and Debates. Ann Arbor: Univ. of Michigan Press, 1960.

Richardson, Lewis F. "Generalized Foreign Politics," *British Journal of Psychology Monographs Supplements*, 23 (1939).

————. "War Moods," *Psychometrika*, 13 (Sept. 1948), 147–74; (Dec. 1948), 197–232.

Riker, William H. "Some Ambiguities in the Notion of Power," *APSR*, 58 (June 1964), 341–49.

Rossi, Peter H. "Community Decision Making," in Roland Young, ed., Approaches to the Study of Politics. Evanston, Ill.: Northwestern Univ. Press, 1958.

Rossiter, Clinton. The American Presidency. New York: Harcourt, Brace, 1960, paperback rev. ed.

————. Parties and Politics in America. Ithaca, N.Y.: Cornell Univ. Press, 1960.

Rothman, Stanley. "Systematic Political Theory: Observations on the Group Approach," *APSR*, 54 (March 1960), 15–33.

Rummel, R. J. "Dimensions of Conflict Between Nations," *Journal of Conflict Resolution*, 10 (March 1966), 65–73.

Russell, Bertrand. Logic and Knowledge. London: Allen & Unwin, 1956.

————. Power. London: Allen & Unwin, 1938.
Sayre, Wallace S., and Herbert Kaufman. Governing New York City. New York: Russell Sage Foundation, 1960.
————, and Nelson Polsby. "American Political Science and the Study of Urbanization," in Philip M. Hauser and Leo F. Schnore, The Study of Urbanization (New York: John Wiley, 1965), pp. 115–56.
Schattschneider, E. E. Party Government. New York: Holt, Rinehart & Winston, 1942, paperback ed.
————. Politics, Pressures, and the Tariff. New York: Prentice-Hall, 1935.
————. The Semisovereign People. New York: Holt, Rinehart & Winston, 1960.
Schelling, Thomas C. The Strategy of Conflict. Cambridge, Mass.: Harvard Univ. Press, 1960.
Schiff, Ashley L. Fire and Water: Scientific Heresy in the Forest Service. Cambridge, Mass.: Harvard Univ. Press, 1962.
Schilling, Warner R., Paul Y. Hammond, and Glenn H. Snyder. Strategy, Politics, and Defense Budgets. New York: Columbia Univ. Press, 1962.
Schlesinger, Arthur M., Jr. The Crisis of the Old Order. Boston: Houghton Mifflin, 1964, paperback ed.
————. A Thousand Days. Boston: Houghton Mifflin, 1965.
Schulze, Robert O. "The Role of Economic Dominants in Community Power," ASR, 23 (Feb. 1958), 3–9.
Schumpeter, Joseph A. Capitalism, Socialism, and Democracy. New York: Harper, 1950, 3d ed.
Selznick, Philip. Leadership in Administration. New York: Harper & Row, 1957.
————. The Organizational Weapon. New York: The Free Press, 1960.
————. TVA and the Grass Roots. Berkeley: Univ. of Calif. Press, 1953.
Shapley, L. S., and Martin Shubik. "A Method for Evaluating the Distribution of Power in a Committee System," APSR, 48 (Sept. 1954), 787–92.
Silverman, Corinne. "The Little Rock Story," in Edwin A. Bock and Alan K. Campbell, eds., Case Studies in American Government (Englewood Cliffs, N.J.: Prentice-Hall, 1962), 1–46.
Simmel, Georg. Conflict. Kurt H. Wolff, trans. Glencoe, Ill.: The Free Press, 1955.
Simon, Herbert A. Administrative Behavior. New York: Macmillan, 1957, 2d ed.
————. "Birth of an Organization: The European Cooperation Administration," Public Administration Review, 13 (Autumn 1953), 227–36.
————. Models of Man. New York: Wiley, 1957.
————. "Research in Comparative Politics: Report of the Inter-University Summer Seminar on Comparative Politics, Social Science Research Council, Comments . . ." APSR, 47 (Sept. 1953), 664–66.

————, Donald W. Smithburg, and Victor A. Thompson. Public Administration. New York: Knopf, 1950.
Smelser, Neil J. Theory of Collective Behavior. New York: The Free Press, 1963.
Smith, A. Robert. The Tiger in the Senate: The Biography of Wayne Morse. Garden City, N.Y.: Doubleday, 1962.
Smith, M. Brewster, Jerome S. Bruner, and Robert W. White. Opinions and Personality. New York: Wiley, 1956.
Smithies, Arthur. The Budgetary Process in the United States. New York: McGraw-Hill, 1955.
Snyder, Richard C., H. W. Bruck, and Burton Sapin, eds. Foreign Policy Decision-Making: An Approach to the Study of International Politics. New York: The Free Press, 1962.
Sperlich, Peter W. Voters in Conflict. Chicago: Rand McNally, forthcoming.
Stedman, Murray, and Herbert Sonthoff. "Party Responsibility: A Critical Inquiry," *Western Political Quarterly*, 4 (Sept. 1951), 454–86.
Stonequist, Everett V. "The Problem of the Marginal Man," *AJS*, 41 (July 1935), 1–12.
Stouffer, Samuel A. Communism, Conformity, and Civil Liberties. Gloucester, Mass.: Peter Smith, 1962.
Tanter, Raymond. "Dimensions of Conflict Behavior Within and Between Nations, 1958–1960," *Journal of Conflict Resolution*, 10 (March 1966), 41–64.
Tiryakian, Edward A. Sociologism and Existentialism. Englewood Cliffs, N.J.: Prentice-Hall, 1962, paperback ed.
Toby, Jackson W. "Some Variables in Role Conflict Analysis," *Social Forces*, 30 (March 1952), 323–27.
Tocqueville, Alexis de. Democracy in America. New York: Vintage, 1952.
Truman, David B. The Governmental Process. New York: Knopf, 1953.
Turner, Julius. "Responsible Parties: A Dissent from the Floor," *APSR* 45 (March 1951), 143–52.
Verba, Sidney. "Organizational Membership and Democratic Consensus," *Journal of Politics*, 27 (Aug. 1965), 467–97.
Von Neumann, John, and Oskar Morgenstern. Theory of Games and Economic Behavior. Princeton, N.J.: Princeton Univ. Press, 1953, 3d ed.
Waldo, Dwight. The Administrative State. New York: Ronald Press, 1948.
————. The Study of Public Administration. New York: Random House, 1955.
Walter, E. V. "Power and Violence," *APSR*, 58 (June 1964), 350–60.
Walton, John. "Discipline, Method, and Community Power: A Note on the Sociology of Knowledge," *ASR*, 31 (Oct. 1966), 684–89.
Wardwell, Walter I. "A Marginal Professional Role: The Chiropractor," *Social Forces*, 30 (March 1952), 339–48.
Webb, Eugene J., Donald T. Campbell, Richard D. Schwartz, and Lee

Sechrest. Unobtrusive Measures: Nonreactive Research in the Social Sciences. Chicago: Rand McNally, 1966.
Weber, Max. The Theory of Social and Economic Organization. A. M. Henderson and Talcott Parsons, trans. New York: Oxford Univ. Press, 1947.
White, William S. Citadel: The Story of the U.S. Senate. New York: Harper, 1957.
Wiener, Norbert. The Human Use of Human Beings: Cybernetics and Society. Garden City, N.Y.: Doubleday, 1954.
Wildavsky, Aaron B. Dixon-Yates: A Study in Power Politics. New Haven, Conn.: Yale Univ. Press, 1962.
————. "The Goldwater Phenomenon: Purists, Politicians, and the Two-Party System," *The Review of Politics*, 27 (July 1965), 386–413.
————. "The Intelligent Citizen's Guide to the Abuses of Statistics: The Kennedy Document and the Catholic Vote," in Polsby, Dentler, and Smith.
————. Leadership in a Small Town. Totowa, N.J.: The Bedminster Press, 1964.
————. "A Methodological Critique of Duverger's *Political Parties*," *Journal of Politics*, 21 (May 1959), 303–18.
————. "The Political Economy of Efficiency: Cost-Benefit Analysis, Systems Analysis, and Program Budgeting," *Public Administration Review*, 26 (Dec. 1966), 292–310.
————. The Politics of the Budgetary Process. Boston: Little, Brown, 1964.
————. "Private Markets and Public Arenas," *American Behavioral Scientist*, 9 (Sept. 1965), 33–37.
————. "Toward a Radical Incrementalism: A Proposal to Aid Congress in Reform of the Budgetary Process," in Congress: First Branch of Government (Washington, D.C.: American Enterprise Institute for Public Policy Research, 1966), 115–65.
————. "The Two Presidencies," *Trans-Action*, 4 (Dec. 1966), 7–14.
————. "What Can I Do?: Ohio Delegates View the Democratic Convention," in Paul Tillett, ed., Inside Politics: The National Convention, 1960 (Dobbs Ferry, N.Y.: Oceana Publications, 1962), 112–30.
Wilson, James Q. The Amateur Democrat. Chicago: Univ. of Chicago Press, 1962.
Wilson, Woodrow. Congressional Government. Boston: Houghton Mifflin, 1889.
Wolfinger, Raymond E. "Reputation and Reality in the Study of 'Community Power,'" *ASR*, 25 (Oct. 1960), 636–44.
————, and Joan Heifetz. "Safe Seats, Seniority, and Power in Congress," *APSR*, 59 (June 1965), 337–49.
Wolin, Sheldon S. Politics and Vision. Boston: Little, Brown, 1960.
Yinger, J. Milton. Towards a Field Theory of Behavior. New York: McGraw-Hill, 1965.

Index

Index

Administration: in executive branch, 36; and politics, 93–94, 97; and behavior tree, 94–97; routine decisions, 105–6
—Soviet: in industry, 53–55 *passim*; comparison with American, 54–57; and pluralism, 58–63; reciprocal interaction in, 60; decentralization in, 88–89
Almond, Gabriel: on political functions, 148; concept of political culture, 149
Anticipated reactions, 75–76, 79–80
Apter, David: on structure of values, 90; structural and behavioral analysis, 126–28; behavioral theory, 147
Ashby, W. Ross: on systemic complexity, 17
Autonomy: in systems, 41

Bachrach, Peter: on issue selection, 70; on values and issue scope, 72–73, 79; on nondecision making, 87
Banfield, Edward, 29, 216
Baratz, Morton: on issue selection, 70; on values and issue scope, 72–73; on nondecision making, 87
Bargaining: definition of, 40–41; conditions for, 41–42; and pluralism, 42; in politics, 55
Bay-fill issue, 129–32
Beer, Stafford, 17, 148
Behavior tree: and administration, 94–97; and set theory, 97; and

leadership, 110–11; paradox of transfinity, 120; and structural sociology, 139
Behavioral analysis: definition of, 126–28; and socialization, 134; and pluralist theory, 135–38; and leadership, 154, 160
Bentham, Jeremy, 43
Bentley, A. F., 28, 33–34
Berliner, Joseph, 44, 53, 89
Boundary decisions: identification of, 85–86; and issue selection, 85; significance of, 87–88; in U.S. Forest Service, 90; and power, 91; in structural-behavioral analysis, 129
Brown, Edmund G., 206

Castro, Fidel, 169
Causality: and influence, 7; and power, 8–9. *See also* Power
Change: basic and incremental, 173
Charisma-paradigm: model of leadership, 164–65, 167
Civil Rights Bill of 1964, 211
Class: in structural analysis, 130, 136; economic, 137; definition of, 139–40; as set, 139
Community power: pluralist and elitist findings, 29–32 *passim. See also* Elite theory; Pluralism
Comparative method, 47f, 76–77, 126
Complexity, in systems: definition of, 16; as related to pluralism, 18–19, 30; spurious, 53. *See also* Systems
Conflict: multilateral, 177, 192; dia-